SPRING
AND THE LABOUR STORY

This is the dramatic story of forty-five years of the Labour Party,
and of the Spring political dynasty – Dan Spring TD and
his son Dick Spring, Tánaiste and Minister for
Foreign Affairs in the current Government.

**Based on interviews with Dick Spring,
his family and political colleagues.**

It tells the inside story of the Spring background and the
establishment of the family political machine; the growth and
difficulties of the Labour Party through the fifties to the eighties
under Norton, Corish, Cluskey and O'Leary; its brief rise to
prominence in the seventies; leadership conflicts and the
taking of control by Dick Spring; election failure and success;
vicious in-fighting and the ousting of the left;
the Mary Robinson election triumph; the final defeat of
Charles Haughey; the inside story of the
formation of today's Government.

**The first substantial account of Dick Spring's
intriguing background and rise to fame.**

For my parents

SPRING
and the
Labour Story

STEPHEN COLLINS

THE O'BRIEN PRESS
DUBLIN

First published 1993 by The O'Brien Press, 20 Victoria Road, Dublin 6, Ireland.

Copyright © Stephen Collins

10 9 8 7 6 5 4 3 2 1

British Library Cataloguing-in-publication Data
A catalogue reference for this book is available at the British Library.

ISBN 0-86278-349-6

Typesetting, design and layout: The O'Brien Press
Cover design: Neasa Ní Chianáin
Front cover photograph: The Star.
Separations: The City Office, Dublin
Printing: The Guernsey Press Co. Ltd.
The author and publisher would like to thank The Irish Press, The Irish Times, Donal Spring, Anna Spring and the Labour Party for the photographs used in this book. We also thank Gill and Macmillan Ltd. for permission to use quotations from Garret FitzGerald, *All In A Life*, Gemma Hussey, *Cabinet Diaries 1982-87*, Noel Browne, *Against the Tide*.

CONTENTS

Acknowledgements 6
Prologue 7

1 The Spring Family and the Labour Tradition

Founding a Dynasty 11
Left Turn 27
Labour in Coalition 38
Growing Up 48
In the Dáil 56

2 Thrust into Leadership

Triumph and Disaster 83
Unexpected Elevation 93
Squabbling Partners 103
Feeling the Cold 113
The Enemy Within 122
Dispute over Attorney General 132
Slow Disintegration 141

3 From Survival to Triumph

Staring into the Abyss 153
Winning the Party 162
Gutting Charlie 172
Bound for Glory 182
Power Play 193
Tánaiste Again 203
Future Goals 213

Bibliography 219
Index 220

Acknowledgements

I would like to thank all the politicians and the members of the Spring family who spoke to me in the preparation of this book; also my journalistic colleagues in Leinster House for their encouragement; the staff of the Oireachtas Library and the National Library for their help and courtesy.

Finally, thanks to Michael O'Brien and Ide O'Leary of the O'Brien Press for their advice and professionalism.

PROLOGUE

DICK SPRING WALKED into the Riverside Centre on Dublin's docks shortly after 11 p.m. on 27 November 1992, and the place went wild. The celebration to mark Labour's stunning performance in the general election had being going on for a couple of hours but everybody was waiting for Spring. From 8.30 p.m. when they had begun to arrive, the party activists who crammed their way into the Riverside recounted scarcely-believable tales from the most extraordinary election campaign any of them had ever experienced.

Party members, trade union officials, journalists recently converted to the cause and newly-elected TDs all jostled about in high good humour to celebrate an election triumph most of them thought they would never live to see. It was a night to remember. The final results were trickling in as the second day of the count drew to a close, and Labour had thirty-three seats in the bag.

The place was humming by the time Spring arrived and there was pandemonium when he made his appearance. Ruairi Quinn remembers being worried that things might get out of hand as the atmosphere of excitement mounted in advance of Spring's arrival. "It was pop-star hysteria stuff and I was afraid that Dick might get crushed when he arrived so a group of us waited at the door and formed a solid cordon around him."

Flanked by his director of elections, Barry Desmond, and principal advisor, Fergus Finlay, Spring slowly made his way through the room surrounded by a throng which included many of the new Labour TDs as well as the singer, Mary Coughlan. Ruairi Quinn took the microphone and got the crowd cheering wildly as he called all the TDs present to the top of the room to stand with the party leader.

When it was his turn to speak, Spring delivered a short address which brought an immediate hush. He joked for a few minutes, eliciting roars of delight as he predicted that Labour would soon be considering membership applications from the surviving Democratic Left TDs and even from Austin Currie, who had caused consternation in Fine Gael earlier in the day by saying that Spring, rather than his own party leader, John Bruton, should be Taoiseach.

Then he got down to serious business. "We have waited a long time for this evening, for this victory. It is important that this victory is the cornerstone of the future of this country. Two years ago we had a very successful campaign and that showed it could be done," he said, referring to the presidential election victory of Mary Robinson. "What we succeeded in doing in 1990 changed the face of Irish politics and that has been done by the most cohesive and organised party in the State. 1992 has laid the foundation stone for the Labour Party to become the major force in Irish politics."

Spring was cheered to the echo as he went on speaking without a script, which always shows him at his best. He finished on a deeply emotional note which may have passed over the heads of the recent converts to the Labour cause but which struck a chord with long-time activists. "I want to pay tribute tonight to all the people who have struggled on behalf of this party down the years, through the very difficult times when it was not easy to proclaim yourself a member of the Labour Party. Without them we would not be here tonight." There were tears in the eyes of some of the older people there who remembered all the long and hard campaigns stretching right back to the 1940s when, more often than not, Labour had struggled to survive.

1
The Spring Family and the Labour Tradition

FOUNDING A DYNASTY

IT WAS ENTIRELY APPROPRIATE, and hardly a coincidence, that the astonishing victory of 1992 should have been won by the son of a man who embodied that spirit of Labour endurance in hard times – Dan Spring, Labour Dáil deputy for North Kerry from 1943 to 1981.

The Spring political dynasty has occupied a Dáil seat in Kerry for fifty years without interruption. It is one of the most enduring family seats in the country and among the very few which did not begin with one of the founding fathers of the Independence movement. The Spring Labour seat in Kerry was hard-won and determinedly maintained. But no-one could have predicted its enduring quality when football hero Dan Spring first stood as a Labour candidate in 1943.

Dan Spring came from very humble origins in the town of Tralee. He was born in 1910, one of a family of fourteen children who lived in Strand Road in the working-class end of the town. Like most children of his background, he left school at the age of fourteen. He worked in a variety of jobs in his home town and in Limerick before becoming an official of the Irish Transport and General Workers' Union (ITGWU) in Tralee in the late 1930s.

Spring's road to fame began with his prowess on the football field. The Tralee O'Rahilly's football pitch was just behind his parents' house and from his earliest days he was a keen footballer. He was the star of the O'Rahilly's team and was picked for the Kerry team which won the All-Ireland in 1939.

Greater fame followed because the O'Rahilly's won the county championship in 1939 and Spring, as the club's representative, was captain of Kerry in 1940. The team carried all before it and Dan Spring had the honour of leading Kerry out onto the pitch in Croke Park for the All-Ireland final on 22 September 1940. Kerry beat Galway in a very tight game by seven points to a goal and three points in front of a crowd of 61,000 people. Spring, who played at full forward, got a point in the first half but was injured in the second and had to retire.

That didn't stop him from accepting the presentation of the Sam Maguire trophy. He was the first Tralee O'Rahilly's player ever to lead Kerry to victory in an All-Ireland final and that earned him an enduring reputation in his home town.

Dan's road to politics began through his involvement in the ITGWU. After his death in 1988, Con Houlihan recalled how it all started: "He began his working life as a bag carrier in a Tralee mill: his wisdom in council elevated him to the post of trade union official. He might never have gone farther but for his involvement with the bog workers in the first few years of Hitler's war.

"The county council treated them shamefully: they had no transport, no wet time, no shelter and were paid a pittance. Dan helped to organise a quiet revolution – although I must admit that on the evening of the famous first march in Castleisland I got a whiff of Paris in 1789.

"The success of the revolt encouraged Dan to stand for the next county council election. It seemed a forlorn hope; his predecessor had got only a few hundred votes. Dan was elected. When he stood for the Dáil he was again a rank outsider: he was never to lose an election in his long career."

That first election to Tralee urban district council and Kerry county council took place in 1942. Spring topped the poll with over 2,000 votes in the county council election and while he didn't top the poll for the urban council first time out he did so in every subsequent election until 1979.

The general election of 1943 was a much tougher proposition and few gave Spring a chance when he decided to put his reputation to the test by standing for the Dáil. It was a war-time election in which Fianna Fáil were on the defensive after eleven uninterrupted years of power, and the Labour Party put up a strong challenge in many parts of the country. In Kerry that challenge was spearheaded by two All-Ireland heroes – Dan Spring in North Kerry and Bill Myers in South Kerry. Spring had a running mate, J.J. Kelly, but from early on he was the front-runner and the party advertising in *The Kerryman* concentrated on the two footballer candidates. "Kerry Players in New Role" was the headline over the advertisement for Spring and Myers.

Spring campaigned strongly throughout the months of May and June 1943, travelling through the towns and villages of North Kerry. His son,

Donal, recalls that his father rarely spoke about his football achievements or his early days in politics but he often talked about his first act of that Dáil campaign. He took out his bike and cycled out to a bridge near Castlemaine with a roll of bills and a bucket of paste and there he put up the first "Vote Spring" posters seen in the constituency.

At a series of public meetings he attacked Fianna Fáil for ignoring the people for five years. *The Kerryman* quoted him as saying that now the election was called they were "moving about among their constituents asking to be thanked for neutrality and bread." According to Spring, speaking in Tarbert on 19 June: "The biggest portion of our people is just barely existing on relief and doles. Emigration has swept our finest manhood and womanhood into the war zone of England. Sanatoria all over our country are packed to capacity because our people have no proper living wages or proper housing conditions to give themselves the nourishment and comfort they deserve. The Labour Party will see that every man willing and capable of working will have work for adequate wages."

The heavy concentration on the plight of working people was a feature of Spring's campaign, along with the issues of neutrality and Republicanism. In his speeches up and down the constituency he defended the policy of neutrality and attacked Fianna Fáil for not being Republican enough. A Labour advertisement in *The Kerryman* conveyed the message:

> *Fianna Fáil – Proclaimed George VI King of Ireland.*
> *Fianna Fáil – Interned without trial 500 Republicans.*
> *Fianna Fáil – Banished 150,000 Irish youths to work and fight for the Empire.*
> *Fianna Fáil – Won't permit Irishmen threatened with Conscription to Return Home.*
> *Fianna Fáil – Have kept 100,000 people in Idleness and Poverty.*

The Spring campaign was a huge success, particularly in his home town of Tralee. On polling day he received 5,155 first preference votes in what was then a four-seat constituency. With his running mate J.J. Kelly picking up 2,352 and the total Labour vote coming to 25 per cent of the poll, he was home and dry and ended up with 8,440 votes. Myers in South Kerry wasn't as lucky but he polled a very respectable 16.5 per cent of the first preference total in a three-seat constituency.

Seconding the vote of thanks to the returning officer in Tralee, Dan Spring told the cheering crowd that he was very proud of the fact that he was the first Labour TD ever elected by the people of Kerry. Thanking all those who worked to ensure his election and those who voted for him, he said, "Anything I can do for anybody I will be only too glad to do."

Immediately after the election he placed a notice in *The Kerryman* thanking the Labour clubs around the county for ensuring that the cause of Labour was more evident than ever before. The notice contains echoes of a bygone age. "I wish to thank sincerely all those who, by their subscriptions, enabled me to defray the costs of my election and those who so generously lent me ponies and traps and other modes of conveyance on election day and enabled me to facilitate a little the very many supporters who had long distances to travel to the polling booths." Spring reserved a special thanks for his own townspeople. "I think a special word of thanks is also due to the people of my native town for the really magnificent support they gave me. I always felt that Tralee would stand firmly behind me and it is a pleasure to know that this belief was not unfounded."

Spring's breakthrough in North Kerry was symptomatic of Labour's success nationwide. The party pushed up its share of the first preference vote to a very impressive 15.7 per cent, a performance that was surpassed only in 1969 and 1992. The seventeen seats won did not fully reflect the number of Labour votes but, in a smaller Dáil of 138 TDs, it was a performance which gave the party hopes that a major breakthrough was around the corner. For Fianna Fáil, the 1943 election represented one of the party's worst-ever performances until 1992, but de Valera was able to continue in office as leader of a minority Government because the party won far more seats than its first preference votes justified, owing to divisions within the Opposition.

Labour's high hopes quickly turned to ashes, however, because of a bitter row in the party which was simmering in 1943 and erupted the following year. The row began in a conflict between the left, on one side, and, on the other, sections of the leadership who suspected a communist plot to infiltrate the party. These suspicions have always been dismissed as ludicrous by people on the Labour left and by historians, but recently-opened State archives show that military intelligence had uncovered a plot by a group of communists, including

James Larkin, junior, and John de Courcy Ireland, to win positions of influence in the Labour Party at the time.

The row between the left and the leadership reopened wounds which for the previous twenty years had split the Labour movement between the Irish Transport and General Workers' Union and James Larkin's Workers' Union of Ireland. In 1944, the general secretary of the ITGWU, William O'Brien, tried to have the Larkins senior and junior expelled from the Labour Party and, when that move failed owing to the strength of the Larkin influence in the Dublin Labour Party, five of the eight ITGWU Labour TDs broke away to form National Labour. Dan Spring was one of the ITGWU TDs who joined the break-away party, led by James Everett from Wicklow. (Everett's nephew and successor as Labour TD in Wicklow, Liam Kavanagh, was to play a pivotal role in making Dan Spring's son, Dick, leader of the Labour Party nearly forty years later.)

The division of the Labour Party in 1944 was acrimonious and there were bitter exchanges between the two factions. The split created an opening for Fianna Fáil who were struggling as a minority Government and de Valera called a snap election in May 1944, after a Dáil defeat on a Roads Bill. Fianna Fáil went on a determined offensive, with Seán McEntee in particular fighting a campaign on "Red scare" tactics.

Labour and National Labour between them lost five seats and the high hopes of the previous year crumbled amidst the recriminations. In North Kerry, however, Dan Spring stormed home to win a seat on the first count with 8,429 first preference votes. While other Labour TDs were squabbling over the "Red menace", he had built on his first-time election victory by hard constituency work and by continuing, as a trade union official, to represent the interests of workers in North Kerry, particularly the council and bog workers.

"My history for nearly twelve months as your representative in this Dáil can be shown as an open book – a book that will not tell of false promises nor false decisions. I have kept my friends and my promises," Spring told his constituents in an advertisement in *The Kerryman*. "I have carried the Labour programme into effect as far as it was possible for any one man to do and I will continue to carry the banner of the worker into every town and village that I enter. Since you elected me in June 1943, no man has worked harder nor fought harder than I to raise the standard of the working class."

He made no reference to the Labour split but an adjoining advertisement for National Labour emphasised his party's commitment to a united Ireland and to social justice achieved in accordance with Christian beliefs and principles. It said the party's TDs "have faced and will face the fury of elements whose underground dealings they have exposed and defeated. We stand neither for Moscow nor London but for Labour in Ireland and Labour in Ireland in true descent from James Connolly."

The split of 1944 was the culmination of tensions which had waxed and waned in the party since its foundation in 1912. The Labour Party was initially launched at the instigation of James Connolly at the Irish Trade Union Congress held in Clonmel in May 1912. The Congress was held a month after the introduction of the Home Rule Bill and Connolly's objective was to secure representation for Labour interests on all public bodies. Both Connolly and James Larkin, who was also at that 1912 conference, were Marxists, committed to a revolutionary brand of socialism. But other union leaders, like William O'Brien and Tom Johnson, who also participated in the formation of the party, had a very different agenda, one which was based on a more traditional trade union reformist approach to society.

Labour, although it polled well in a House of Commons by-election in Dublin in 1915 and almost took a seat from the Irish Parliamentary Party, was soon pushed to one side as the movement for Irish independence gathered steam. Connolly and the Citizen Army took part in the 1916 Rising, but the Labour movement as a whole adopted a tentative approach to the national question in an attempt to preserve working-class unity between its Protestant supporters in the North and its Catholic members in the rest of the country. In 1918 the Labour leaders were persuaded by Sinn Féin to stand aside from the general election to allow a clear decision by the people on the issue of independence. Many senior figures in the party later regretted accepting in 1918 that "Labour must wait" and they felt it permanently consigned the party to minority status.

Labour did contest local elections in urban areas in 1920, but it was not until the election which was held in the middle of the Civil War in June 1922 that the party entered national politics. Labour did very well in that election with seventeen of its eighteen candidates winning election to the Dáil. Tom Johnson was elected party leader and with the Republicans pursuing a policy of abstentionism, Labour became the main opposition to the Cumann na nGael Government of William T. Cosgrave.

A few years later, in 1927, Labour almost won control of the Government in very strange circumstances and Tom Johnson was on the verge of taking over the top job in the land. (Not until Dick Spring started talking about himself as a rotating Taoiseach in 1992 did a Labour leader come as close to leading the country.) Johnson was deprived of office by one of the most bizarre incidents in Irish political history. It involved a drunken TD being packed on to the Sligo train during a crucial Dáil vote and it happened in the aftermath of the general election of June 1927.

Labour had won 22 seats in that election, Cumann na nGael 47 and Fianna Fáil 44. It was Fianna Fáil's first election after the party's formation a year earlier, but its TDs stayed outside the Dáil because they wouldn't take the oath of allegiance to the British Crown. However, the picture changed dramatically a month later when the Minister for Justice, Kevin O'Higgins, was murdered on his way to Mass in Booterstown.

The murder prompted Fianna Fáil to enter the Dáil and Eamon de Valera offered Fianna Fáil's support for a coalition Government made up of Labour and some of the smaller parties for the normal lifetime of the Dáil. The main condition was that the Government would abolish the oath of allegiance; de Valera also laid down a number of other conditions.

In his biography of Tom Johnson, J. Anthony Gaughan recounts how in August 1927 the Labour leader put down a motion of no confidence in the Government and prepared to form a Government with the help of the Redmondite party, the National League, and a number of independents. Johnson and his key advisors travelled to the Powerscourt Arms Hotel in Enniskerry on Sunday, 13 August, where they spent the evening devising the Cabinet-to-be of the Labour-led coalition. The list of who was to have been in that Cabinet survived because of one of the biggest scoops in the history of Irish political journalism. After the Labour team left the hotel they went to the nearest bus stop to catch the 44 bus back to Dublin. At the stop they met Robert Smyllie of *The Irish Times*.

He immediately sensed that they were up to something and, having established where they had been, instead of boarding the bus he made his way to the hotel. He asked the owner where the Labour leaders had been meeting and was told they had spent three hours closeted in the summer house in the garden. Smyllie went there and discovered a pile of torn-up notes in the waste-paper basket. He poured the notes out on the table, ordered a bottle of whiskey and two hours later he had pieced together the Labour Cabinet. When the story appeared the following day the Labour leaders accused each other of leaking and didn't find out until years later how the story had got out.

Political tension built up, finally leading to a motion of no confidence on 16 August. It was generally assumed in the run-up to the debate that the Government would be beaten by 73 votes to 69. Even though the difference narrowed to 72-71 on the day, as some independents rallied to Cosgrave's side, the general expectation was that the vote would be followed by the installation of a Labour-led Government. It was then that Alderman John Jinks entered the stage – or rather, made a premature exit. A Redmondite from Sligo, Jinks was to have voted against the Government, but when the Dáil division was called he was mysteriously absent. As TDs tried to find him, some remembered seeing him earlier that morning in the bar along with the colourful independent TD and former Ulster Unionist MP for South Dublin, Major Bryan Cooper. It emerged later that Major Cooper had liberally plied Alderman Jinks with drink in Buswell's Hotel as he tried to dissuade him from voting against the Government. While accounts differ about what happened next it appears that Cooper called a taxi for Jinks, had him safely escorted to the Sligo train, and the hapless alderman was sitting on the train as it puffed out of Dublin when the division was called.

There was consternation in the Dáil when the vote resulted in a tie and the Ceann Comhairle gave his casting vote in favour of the Government. The world press picked up the story, Jinks had a brief moment of glory and Labour's prospects of leading a Government turned to ashes. Cosgrave then dissolved the Dáil and Labour suddenly found itself fighting a desperate battle just to survive.

Not only did the party have to fight Fianna Fáil and Cumann na nGael, it also had a bitter struggle with left-wing Labour opponents led by James Larkin. Larkin had left Ireland in 1914 and returned eight and a half years later to find that the ITGWU which he had founded was being run by a strong executive committee led by William O'Brien. After a bitter and unsuccessful struggle to regain control, Larkin founded the rival Workers' Union of Ireland.

Tension was running very high in the Labour movement in 1927 when Larkin and his son James Larkin, junior, led a group called the Irish Workers' League in an all-out assault on Labour. Abuse was heaped on senior Labour figures and this culminated in a public brawl at an election meeting in Rathfarnham. Tom Johnson's son, Fred, challenged remarks Larkin made about his mother and father, fisticuffs ensued and Larkin emerged with a cut over his eye. The tragic upshot from Labour's point of view was that the party lost nine seats and was left in a very weakened condition. Johnson lost his own seat in County Dublin, mainly because Larkin, junior, split the Labour vote.

Johnson was succeeded as party leader by Thomas J. O'Connell from Mayo, but he, in turn, lost his seat in a general election of 1932 when Fianna Fáil made its historic breakthrough and was able to form a minority Government with Labour support. In two successive elections, Labour had lost its leader. This time around, the party selected a young, dynamic trade unionist, William Norton, for the post. He took over at the age of thirty-two – the same age Dick Spring was when he became party leader in 1982 – and he stayed on as leader for nearly thirty years, growing increasingly conservative with age.

Norton faced an immediate political crisis with a hung Dáil, but he threw Labour's support behind Fianna Fáil and helped de Valera to rule as a minority Government. "Fianna Fáil at least promises that it will tackle the social and economic problems pressing with so much rigour on the workers," he told the Dáil. Norton had strong Republican views and during the 1930s he supported Fianna Fáil's social policies whilst trying to push de Valera in the direction of Labour's policy, often with some success.

Norton continued as party leader until 1960 and for much of that time he appeared to be more interested in the affairs of the Post Office Workers' Union, of which he remained general secretary, than of the Labour Party. Michael Gallagher, in his fine study *The Irish Labour Party in Transition 1957-82*, described him as "a highly intelligent man with a great interest in, though little sympathy for, left-wing parties and socialist thought in many countries. He became increasingly cynical towards the end of his life and his attitude towards some of the less articulate Labour TDs bordered on open contempt."

The election of 1944 came at an inopportune time for Dan Spring because it disrupted his plans to get married. Two years earlier, he had met Anna Laide, a nurse at St Finnan's Hospital in Killarney, when he visited the hospital to try to organise the workers there into the union. They were introduced by Bill Myers, who was a trade union official in Killarney.

Dan and Anna met a few times before they began going out together. Anna, the daughter of a small-farmer from Kilflynn in North Kerry, came from a relatively more prosperous background than Dan. A bright, intelligent girl, she didn't leave school at a young age like Dan but continued on to secondary school as a boarder at Mount Sackville in Dublin. After leaving school she trained as a nurse and returned to Kerry.

She recalls that in the 1942 local elections she voted for the Farmers' Party candidate like the rest of her family. But by the time the general election of 1943 came around she was going out with Dan Spring though few people knew about the relationship. She had told her mother, who voted for Dan, but her father wasn't aware of his daughter's relationship and voted as usual for Pat Finucane, the Farmers' candidate.

"I remember the day of the election – I was in Killarney because I didn't think I had a vote in North Kerry. But Dan rang me during the day to say it had been switched to my home place; you could do that in those days," says Anna Spring. "So I cycled the thirty-one miles to Kilflynn and made it by just about five minutes to cast my first vote for Dan."

The couple planned to marry the following year. "I handed in my month's notice to St Finnan's in May because we planned to marry on the first of June. But de Valera dissolved the Dáil on 28 May and we had to postpone the wedding until 29 June. Because it was a holy day, we had to get married at six in the morning. An uncle of Moss Keane's married us and he said Mass for us on our twenty-fifth and fortieth wedding anniversaries as well. After the ceremony, we had the breakfast at the Grand Hotel and we were on the half-nine train to Dublin."

Her own upbringing gave Anna Spring a keen understanding of the value of learning and she made sure that all their six children – three boys and three girls – were sent to boarding school and university.

"My one ambition was that they wouldn't be depending on public life for their living and I wanted each of them to have a career. It is not just that public life is hard but the insecurity of it makes things very difficult," says Mrs. Spring.

Anna had a profound influence on Dan and played a vital role in his political life, helping to ensure that he held on to his Dáil seat through all the political storms that were to come. "For her, politics is not a vocation, it's a way of life," Joe Revington, a family friend and long-time Labour activist in the constituency, told Brenda Power of *The Sunday Press* in December 1992. "Politics was what put bread on the table when she was trying to rear a big family on a TD's salary. So she made sure that the grass didn't grow in North Kerry without Dan Spring knowing about it. She has a photographic memory for people and pretty much an encyclopedic knowledge of North Kerry. She is a most remarkable woman."

Mrs. Spring says that she was effectively an unpaid secretary for her husband during his thirty-eight years in the Dáil. "TDs had no secretaries in those days. The pay was poor and there was no pension or free post." She did more than simply help her husband, though. When he was in Dublin she would deal with constituents' problems and keep an eye on local political developments. She became treasurer of the North Kerry Labour Party, a position she still occupies at the age of seventy-five at the time of writing.

The fact that he was growing up in a political family impressed itself on Dick Spring from an early age. "Politics was the order of the day and the whole basis of things was politics. I think it was more simple than it is nowadays, but it was an open-door business. We lived in a street house in Tralee and you knew from start to finish that you were involved in politics. It was highly likely that somebody would be in around breakfast time, somebody passing by with a query or somebody with a problem.

"Our first access to a telephone was in the nursing home next door, where my father would be called or messages left, that sort of thing. You were always very conscious that your father was somebody in the town. Still, he was a very modest man, just got on with his business, attended county council meetings, urban council meetings. You were also conscious of the fact that he was gone to Dublin every week.

Always for one or two days; he was never gone for three or four days. Another thing you would be conscious of was that included in his diary was the annual conference of the ITGWU. There were photographs of Bundoran, Killarney, Salthill, all those places where the conferences took place."

Anna Spring says that living on a TD's salary they couldn't afford holidays but she accompanied her husband to Labour Party conferences and to the annual conference of the ITGWU. "They were the only opportunities we had to get away. We were away for nearly a week and they were a great break." One other outing to which Anna Spring looked forward each year was the All-Ireland hurling final. In her part of North Kerry, hurling rather than Gaelic football is the more popular game and two of her brothers played hurling for Kerry. So did her son Dick, and she is almost prouder of that than of his more famous sporting exploits.

"Of course I was proud of Dan's achievements on the football field and Dick and Donal playing rugby for Ireland, but hurling is my game and I was happy as long as I got to the All-Ireland hurling final every year. I didn't mind missing the football if I had to."

Donal Spring remembers that they were the first family on the road to get a 'phone and there was always a stream of callers wanting to use it. "Even during the Christmas dinner people would be ringing up from America to talk to their relations and we would have to go and fetch them to the house. There was never any privacy in our house, which had two rooms downstairs and three bedrooms. That was one of the reasons we all went to boarding school. There would have been no room for us to work at home."

Donal also recalls his mother's interest in medicine and believes that if she grew up in today's conditions she would have been a doctor. "She had a huge interest in medical matters and I don't think it is a coincidence that her eldest child, Arthur, became a doctor. At home, as well as acting as Dad's unpaid secretary and local representative, she was also the person people on the street turned to for medical assistance. She was called on to deliver children, treat people for injuries and to lay out the dead."

The whole family participated in the basic political task of looking after the concerns of constituents. "All of us had to answer the door and take messages from people when Dad was away in Dublin.

FOUNDING A DYNASTY 23

Everybody came to us with their problems and they used to leave them with us, even when we were children and didn't understand half of what they were talking about," says Donal.

He remembers the hard work of his father and mother in coping with the everyday constituency work. Dan had a strict routine for sending off constituents' queries to Government departments and writing back to them with the replies he received. "My abiding memory of my father is of him sitting at the kitchen table writing letters in long-hand. As he finished each letter he put it in an envelope and, after addressing it, he would toss it into a big wicker basket kept for the purpose. When he had finished his mail he would rush out to the railway station to get the post on the evening train."

The Springs lived in a modest three-bedroomed terraced house on Strand Road, the same street where Dan had grown up. Anna Spring recalls that they lived for a few months in a flat in Rock Street before moving into the house where they spent all their married life. Dan never forgot his roots and to people who asked him in later years why he didn't move to a bigger house he answered: "A bird never flew so high that he didn't have to come down for water."

The secret of Dan's success, according to Anna, is that he was simply loved by the people of Tralee. "People sometimes think he was elected just because he was a famous footballer. But there are many other famous Kerry footballers who tried and failed to get elected, while he never lost an election in his life. He worked so hard for people he would get up in the middle of his Sunday dinner if there was a ring at the door. Of course he liked the respect people had for him, but he earned it."

He was an imposing figure, strongly-built and standing over six feet, and while he could be very tough-minded he had a wide circle of friends both in Tralee and in Dáil Eireann. People who knew him around Leinster House recall that he resembled his son, Dick, in his quirky sense of humour, but in Tralee they say that in personality he was like his youngest son, Donal, who is more outgoing and approachable than Dick.

After the election of 1944, Dan consolidated his position by standing by his neighbour and childhood friend, Charlie Kerins, who was condemned to death by de Valera's military courts. Spring had lived next door to Kerins as a child and the two were good friends and played football together. When he was arrested in June 1944, Kerins was the acting chief of staff of what remained of the IRA. Kerins was tried before a military tribunal in October for the murder of a Garda sergeant. He was found guilty and sentenced to be hanged. Spring joined fellow-Kerry TD, Pat Finucane, of the Farmers' Party, in drawing attention to the plight of Kerins and the two of them went to de Valera to plead for a reprieve.

Spring and Finucane were among the small number of TDs who raised the issue in the Dáil on 29 November 1944, but the Ceann Comhairle ruled out an adjournment debate. "Our point is that, in view of the peace and quietness in the country for the last few years, we believe it would serve no useful purpose to carry out this death sentence on Friday morning. Because we believe the young man got no fair trial," Spring told the House.

The following day, Spring, Finucane and James Larkin, junior, were expelled from the Chamber for persistently trying to raise the issue. None of them got the opportunity to make a major speech but Spring's interventions reveal the depth of bitterness on the issue.

> *Mr Spring: I stated last night, and I still state, that this young person did not get a fair trial.*
>
> *An Ceann Comhairle: That is quite disorderly.*
>
> *Mr Spring: This man is lying in Mountjoy awaiting execution in the morning. We have no-one to blame but the Taoiseach. I can certainly say the Taoiseach or any of his Ministers will not be too willing to address a meeting in Kerry in the near future.*
>
> *Minister for Education [Mr Derrig]: Is that a threat?*
>
> *Mr Spring: You can take it any way you like.*

With that Spring was suspended from the Dáil. The vote to expel him was seventy-five to eighteen with Fianna Fáil and Fine Gael combining against Labour and the Farmers' Party. Before he left the House, Spring had a parting shot at the big parties.

> *Mr Spring: I am leaving the House through a coalition vote between Fianna Fáil and Fine Gael.*
>
> *An Ceann Comhairle: By a decision of the House.*
>
> *Mr Spring: Fine Gael has seventy-seven murders in Kerry and Fianna Fáil has nearly as many.*

Spring's efforts on Kerins's behalf were to no avail because on the following morning, 1 December, the sentence was carried out by a hangman brought over from England. Nonetheless, Spring's role in doing everything he could to save Kerins cemented his position as TD for North Kerry and he held the seat through thick and thin after that. The defence of Kerins also stood to Finucane. He was returned for the Farmers' Party or Clann na Talmhan at every election from 1943 to 1965, despite the demise of both parties. The Republican folk-memory in the constituency never forgot the men who had stood by Kerins at his hour of death. (The name of the Tralee football team was changed to the Kerins O'Rahilly's and so it has remained until today.)

Meanwhile, the two wings of the Labour Party began to come together after 1948 when both helped to form the first Inter-Party Government in the State's history. By the time of the 1948 election, Fianna Fáil had been in power continuously for sixteen years and, while there was no clear alternative Government, all the other parties campaigned on the slogan "Put Them Out".

Between its two factions, Labour did quite well in that election but its fratricidal squabbles had weakened it as the leading party of reform. That mantle fell to Clann na Poblachta, led by Sean MacBride, which had a dizzying rise to success and an almost equally rapid descent into oblivion. The election result gave Fianna Fáil 67 seats, Fine Gael 31, Labour 14, Clann na Poblachta 10, Clann na Talmhan 7 and National Labour 5. All the Opposition parties combined had only the same number of seats as Fianna Fáil and they had to win the support of a majority of the twelve independent deputies to command a majority.

Despite the precariousness of the position, an Inter-Party administration was put in place, headed not by the Fine Gael leader, Dick Mulcahy, but by his party colleague John A. Costello. Both MacBride and the Labour leader, William Norton, objected to Mulcahy becoming Taoiseach and he accommodatingly stood aside while Costello took the position.

Labour got two Cabinet positions, with Norton taking over as Minister for Social Welfare. Another Labour TD, Tadhg Murphy, became Minister for Local Government, while James Everett, the leader of National Labour, was also appointed to the Cabinet. The participation of the two Labour Parties in the same Government brought about a *rapprochement*. Dan Spring acted as a mediator between the two sides, having kept up good personal relations with the official Labour Party TDs. He often claimed in later years to have been responsible for the formal re-unification in 1950.

The Inter-Party Government collapsed in a blaze of publicity over Noel Browne's Mother and Child Scheme in 1951. Browne's stormy relations with his Cabinet colleagues, particularly with his own party leader, MacBride, were partly responsible for the row and he received no support from the Labour Party. In the Dáil debate on the issue, Norton was the only Labour TD to speak. He criticised Browne's lack of judgement and suggested that he had been seeking a "head-on collision" with the Catholic Church.

Through these storms Dan Spring continued as a backbencher, gaining Dáil experience but keeping closely in touch with the concerns of his constituents in Kerry. The fact that he was a TD didn't stop him continuing to represent bog workers and council workers in the county. In an obituary after his death in 1988, John Rogers recalled one memorable clash in the early fifties when Spring was pursuing a claim for an increase of ten shillings a week for council road workers. The claim was turned down, and Spring brought all the road workers to a council meeting on the subject in Tralee. The assistant county manager opened the meeting by saying that the county manager could not attend because of illness.

Dan immediately withdrew with his contingent to the steps of the County Hall and called for the production of a doctor's certificate confirming the manager's condition. When a certificate was produced, Spring questioned its validity and a meeting of local doctors was called at which he was censured for impugning the certificate. The upshot of the affair was that, whatever about the validity of the manager's illness, the workers got their ten-shilling increase by the end of the day-long meeting – Dan was later presented with a radiogram "from the road workers of Kerry" and it still has a special place in the Spring home.

The second Inter-Party Government was formed after the general election of 1954. This time it was a tighter affair, composed of Fine Gael, Labour and Clann na Talmhan. It came to power in even more difficult circumstances than the first Inter-Party Government and found it difficult to cope with the economic depression of the 1950s.

In 1956, halfway through the lifetime of the Government, Dan Spring, who was now an experienced deputy with over a decade in the Dáil, was promoted to the position of parliamentary secretary in the Department of Education. He was delighted to have achieved the promotion, an equivalent to a junior ministry today. He had the honour of a State car but apart from that it did little to change his lifestyle or the way in which he looked after his constituents. Anna Spring recalls how pleased Dan was with the promotion; but it didn't go to his head and he worked as hard as ever. "I remember his Minister, Pa O'Donnell, remarking: 'I have only one thing to say about Dan. He works too hard.'"

Dick Spring tells a story which conveys his father's droll sense of humour and his attitude to politics. The seven-year-old Dick was with Dan, then a parliamentary secretary, at an official function in the Kerry Gaeltacht when the future Tánaiste first saw the tall, gaunt figure of Eamon de Valera, then leader of the Opposition. Dick felt sorry for de Valera and asked his father: "Why does he look so sad?" Dan thought for a moment and replied: "Because he's out of power."

LEFT TURN

THE PARTY FOR WHICH DAN SPRING was elected a TD in 1943 and 1944 was a different Labour Party from the party of today, although there are still some very clear lines of continuity between the two. The party of the 1940s and 1950s has received a bad press and has generally been dismissed, not only by urban intellectuals and left-wing ideologues but by many of its own members then and now. Much of the criticism, however, has come from the cosy perspective of college campuses and professional life, far removed from the harsh reality of working-class life in those uncomfortable decades.

Writing in the 1960s before he himself became involved in Labour politics, Conor Cruise O'Brien dismissed Labour as a party "dominated for years by dismal poltroons, on the lines of O'Casey's Uncle Payther." The historian Emmet Larkin was only a little more kind, describing Labour in 1964 as "the most opportunistically conservative Labour Party anywhere in the known world", while Brian Inglis wrote that it was "not recognisable as a Labour Party on the normal social democratic pattern."

This kind of criticism was written from the perspective of middle-class liberals who despaired of the party's refusal to challenge the Catholic Church on social and moral issues. Labour, however, was not a party of middle-class liberals, who were then very few in number in any case. It was predominantly a working-class party, representing the concerns of trade union members and the poorer elements of society, particularly outside Dublin. The party TDs naturally reflected the conservative Catholic ethos of their constituents and saw no contradiction between moral conservatism and a vigorous defence of the rights of the poor.

Dan Spring was a product of that environment. "Dan was a typical representative of the rural proletariat," says one Labour figure who knew him. "He and other Munster ITGWU TDs, such as Paddy McAuliffe, represented people like road workers, bog workers and railway porters, the people who were very much at the bottom of the pile in a conservative class-conscious society. Dan was deeply committed at trade union level and his political life was an extension of that. There was no great intellectual content but there was a sense of injustice at the plight of the poorest workers, the people who were treated as outsiders by the broader Irish society."

It is virtually impossible for people living in the Ireland of the 1990s to visualise the depth of poverty that existed in the forties and fifties. Heinrich Böll in his beautiful and evocative *Irish Journal*, describes that Ireland, a country which in many ways is utterly foreign to us now, but his account gives an idea of the kind of grinding poverty which afflicted the people Labour TDs tried to represent. Böll writes about the hordes of bare-foot children whose tattered clothes were held together by safety-pins. An account of a day in Limerick is typical:

> *Dim lights burned in the bookies' offices, drunks staggered through the gutters and the children who that morning had swung from sides of beef in butcher shops now showed that there is a level of poverty for which even the safety-pin is too expensive: string is cheaper and it works just as well. What nine years ago had been a cheap jacket, but new, now served as jacket, overcoat, trousers*

and shirt in one; the grown-up sleeves rolled up, string
around the middle and held in the hand.

A German friend who accompanied Böll on that trip to Limerick found the level of poverty overwhelming and frightening.

> *My companion was trembling; he was a victim of the most*
> *bitter and stupid prejudice of all; that people who are*
> *badly dressed are dangerous – more dangerous anyway*
> *than the well-dressed ones. He ought to tremble in the bar*
> *of the Shelbourne Hotel in Dublin at least as much as*
> *here, behind King John's Castle in Limerick. If only they*
> *were more dangerous, these ragged ones, if only they were*
> *as dangerous as those in the bar of the Shelbourne Hotel*
> *who don't look dangerous at all.*

Labour TDs like Dan Spring had to cope with the reality of trying to improve conditions for those ragged ones that Böll met on his visit to Limerick and other Irish towns. "Dan regarded his Dáil role as representing his individual constituents. His correspondence was voluminous and he didn't take his eyes off it. While he had a strong sense of the Labour movement he had no interest in the abstract – for him it was very much about individual people and their problems," says a Labour source.

This adherence to the practical reality of trying to make gradual improvements in the lives of working-class people, generally on an individual level, rather than campaigning for State socialism or tilting at the windmill of Church influence annoyed left-wing radicals. One of them was Noel Browne, who had a love-hate relationship with Labour when he turned to the party after a time in Fianna Fáil and a spell with the fledgling National Progressive Democrats. In his autobiography *Against the Tide*, he cruelly dismisses almost every single one of the Labour TDs he ever met. His description of Labour leader William Norton is particularly savage and the amount of vitriol used says more about Browne than it does about Norton. Part of his description is as follows:

> *His childish enjoyment at table evoked feelings of amuse-*
> *ment and revulsion. My wife and I would watch incredu-*
> *lously as he would call for a second helping of his*
> *favourite sweet, a spun sugar confection which stood*

*about four inches high and was shaped as a bird's nest.
With his table-napkin tucked firmly into his straining
white collar, his flickering brown monkey's eyes would
lovingly follow the waiter and his spoon as he loaded the
plate down for the second time. Spoon and fork filled the
sugary syrup into his mouth until there remained only
the melted warm honey mixture on his plate. This too was
greedily scooped into his now slobbering mouth. Like a
hungry suckling piglet, frantically probing the fat sow's
belly, spoon and fork were followed by his chubby fingers
and last of all his thumbs, each of them lovingly and
lingeringly sucked dry.*

What Browne omits to mention is a fact well-known in Labour
circles. Norton was a diabetic. That certainly helps to explain his
obesity and his craving for sweet foods but it is not something that is
alluded to in the bilious description of his shortcomings.

Browne is also scathingly dismissive of Dan Spring. "One other
National Labour deputy, a well-known footballer with little else to
offer, was given a parliamentary secretaryship; his name was Spring,"
is his summing up. In another passage, Browne disparagingly refers
to "the culchies" of the party. "These were the cute rural deputies,
Spring, Coughlan, Michael Pat Murphy and others who could, with a
practised ease, build a nest in your ear while minding mice at a
crossroads."

Such a condescending dismissal of Spring and the other rural TDs
by a well-heeled radical doctor like Browne was typical enough of an
attitude to Labour which persisted until the mid-1960s and recurs
regularly among urban liberals when Labour goes out of fashion.

John Rogers provided a more accurate measurement of Dan Spring's
achievement when writing his obituary in *The Irish Times* in 1988.
"Politically his greatest achievement was to take and keep secure a
Dáil seat for Labour in North Kerry. He made it possible to present
Labour politics at a time when the mood of his countrymen was to
reject such radicalism. His method was to rely on providing action and
leadership on issues, rather than rhetoric or ideology."

In the mid-fifties Spring was the father of a young family. He had
six children – Arthur, Kay, Dick, Maeve, Donal and Noelle – and they
all lived in the small house in Strand Road until the older children went

to boarding school. The boys attended the local Christian Brothers' school and Anna Spring made sure that they all studied hard and did their homework.

"I remember I was quite strict on Dick and on one occasion I wasn't satisfied that he was doing enough at school. So I went down to see the teacher, Master Hayes, to ask if he was working hard enough. He was surprised at me and said that Dick was well able for all the work; not only that but when he had to leave the class for any reason Dick was the one he would put in charge. 'He'll be a leader of men yet,' the teacher told me and I remember his words until this day."

As the depressing fifties gave way to the more hopeful sixties, things began to change in Labour. The party's participation in the second Inter-Party Government had disillusioned many of its supporters and its performance in the 1957 election was the worst since 1933. The party won just 9.1 per cent of the vote and only eleven TDs were elected to the Dáil, although the strength was brought up to twelve by the Ceann Comhairle, Paddy Hogan. Dan Spring held on without much bother and increased his vote compared with the previous election in 1954. It was not the first or last time he was to buck the national trend on the basis of hard constituency work and a keen nose for political reality.

In a mood of deep disillusionment, Labour held two delegate conferences in the space of eight months in 1957-58 and came up with the crucial decision not to participate in another Inter-Party Government but to remain in opposition until it had built up enough support to form a majority Government. Party chairman, Jim Tully, told delegates that they had gained little and lost a lot by taking part in previous coalitions. In future, they should stick to their own programme, put up enough candidates to form a Government and not deviate one inch until their goal was reached.

The anti-coalition policy was to mark a new phase in the development of Labour, with a gradual build-up of support until the heady days of the late 1960s and the confident belief that "the seventies will be socialist."

William Norton's long leadership of the Labour Party was effectively ended by the 1959 annual conference when he was subjected to fierce criticism from a number of speakers, including James Larkin, junior. Norton's attempt to drag up Larkin's communist past back-fired as the delegates just didn't want to know. Among the fiercest critics of Norton at the 1959 conference was a fiery young radical from Cork called Michael O'Leary, who himself was hounded from office at a party conference more than twenty years later. In fact, the history of the Labour Party provides a regularly recurring pattern of party elders being devoured by their left-wing opponents, who take office only to be devoured in their turn by a new set of left-wing critics.

Following the humiliation of the 1959 conference, when he was so widely attacked from the floor, Norton stepped down in 1960 and was replaced by Brendan Corish. Under the new leader, the party stuck to its anti-coalition stance and gradually began to adopt more left-wing policies. This widened the party's appeal and a growing confidence that its hour was close at hand developed in its ranks as the decade progressed.

Corish held the Labour seat in Wexford that his father before him had filled since the foundation of the State. In some ways, he appeared to be a typical enough Labour TD in occupation of the family seat. His statement in 1953 that "I am an Irishman second, I am a Catholic first" appeared to confirm the traditional image and was regularly thrown in his face by Noel Browne and other left-wingers.

He did have a wider vision, however, of his party's role than his critics often gave him credit for and during the 1960s he moved it decisively to the left. He was not afraid to call himself a socialist and by appearing to be in tune with the mood of the times attracted a whole new generation into the party. Noel Browne joined Labour for the first time in 1963, against Corish's wishes, when the National Progressive Democrats merged with Labour.

"Corish in full flight on a platform was a charismatic figure. He was a great orator, one of the finest around after James Dillon, and he had a tremendous public appeal," says one Labour figure who was active at that period.

Changing the party's fortunes took time. In one of the dullest general elections in the State's history in 1961, Labour improved its share of the vote and increased its number of Dáil seats from twelve to sixteen. The election of 1965 saw a more dynamic party make an even bigger improvement to 15.5 per cent of the vote and twenty-two Dáil seats. Among the newly-elected TDs that year were Michael O'Leary, who was elected in Dublin's inner city; Frank Cluskey, representing a new breed of Dublin trade union official, and the mercurial Dr John O'Connell. It seemed the party was on the verge of a major break-through.

By 1967 Corish had firmly identified Labour as a socialist party. John Horgan recalls how at the annual conference that year Corish's proclamation of socialism as the creed of the party led to a kind of euphoria. "Speaker after speaker at that conference followed the Corish line by prefacing their remarks from the platform with the phrase 'Speaking as a socialist ...' as if they were caressing a shiny new toy, whose inner workings had not been, as yet, fully examined. But the fillip it gave to the party, not least in the media – excited by the student revolution of that year and by the general sense of movement and unpredictability which characterised the sixties as a whole – was undeniable." Brendan Halligan had been appointed as general secre-tary that year and Corish, who came increasingly to rely on him, addressed the conference on the twin themes of "Let's build the New Republic" and "The Seventies will be Socialist". It was heady stuff for the Labour delegates but they loved it and revelled in the whole new mood of confidence. Halligan was a dynamic general secretary who set out to remodel the party from top to bottom.

Dan Spring, however, did not fit easily into that new-model Labour Party and he had little faith in the promise of a socialist dawn. He continued to work for his constituents as he had done for twenty years and relied on that, rather than on ideological dreams, to get him elected.

While Dan may not have been overly impressed by the develop-ments in the party, down in Kerry he expanded his own Labour organisation. Anna Spring says that when he was elected first there were just two or three clubs, as branches are called in Kerry. By the 1990s there were thirty-one clubs and a very formidable organisation. "Dan started off organising the clubs and he put a very firm structure in place," says Anna, who was very actively involved in the whole process. "We organised so well that we were able to get two people on to the Administrative Council (AC) at annual conference long before Dick became leader."

In fact, the Kerry buses, which, from the 1960s on, brought one of the biggest constituency delegations to annual conference became one of its features and they were crucial to the party's decision-making process. The Kerry delegates regularly played a pivotal role in protecting the leadership on critical occasions. They voted as a bloc on major issues and in the elections to the various officerships. Dan and Anna saw to it that the votes went the way they were supposed to go.

The mood of euphoria in Labour was heightened during 1968 with an influx of new members, including Conor Cruise O'Brien who was regarded as a very important catch. O'Brien, who had been so critical of Labour as a conservative force only a few years earlier, now argued that Ireland was about to take a decisive shift to the left under the direction of Labour. Fianna Fáil now began to attack Labour furiously. This showed how worried they were, because the tactic for a number of years had been to dismiss the party more in sorrow than in anger, most famously in Seán Lemass's remark that "the Labour Party are a nice, respectable, docile, harmless body of men, as harmless a body as ever graced any Parliament." Fianna Fáil reverted to the Red scare tactics of the 1940s, typified in Kevin Boland's reference to "Conor Cruise Cuba God Bless Albania O'Brien".

The 1969 annual conference was suffused with optimism. Speakers, including Corish, talked enthusiastically about what a "Labour Government" would do and the party's anti-coalition policy was restated. Corish went so far as to say that, if a future conference were to decide in favour of coalition, his "continued support for socialism will be from the backbenches". According to John Horgan, Corish made this statement only when pressed by the proposer of the anti-coalition resolution, none other than Michael O'Leary, to throw his weight behind it in case it was lost. It was a statement that, along with his reference to being a Catholic first, was to haunt Corish for the rest of his political life. Noel Browne in particular was to raise both statements at every opportunity in order to embarrass the leader.

Labour entered the 1969 election not just with high hopes but with undisguised confidence that it was about to shatter the mould of Irish politics. There was a strong feeling that it would at least overtake Fine Gael as the second party in the State and supportive media coverage, particularly from *The Irish Times*, encouraged Labour activists to believe that they were on the point of an historic breakthrough.

Conor Cruise O'Brien was joined by other high-profile candidates. The star of RTE's current affairs programme *Seven Days*, David Thornley, who also was a politics lecturer in Trinity College, announced a month before the election that he was standing for the party. Another TCD lecturer, Justin Keating, who was widely known for his farming programmes on television, was also a candidate, while Dr Noel Browne, Dr John O'Connell and UCD economics lecturer, John O'Donovan, added to the glamour of the Labour ticket. Former Irish Farmers' Association (IFA) president, Rickard Deasy was another well-known convert, while the endorsement of Labour's agriculture policy by General Michael Joe Costello of Sugar Company fame was an additional string to the party's bow.

In the expectation of a massive swing in its favour, Labour headquarters decreed, on foot of a resolution passed by the 1967 annual conference, that a minimum of two candidates should run in every constituency. This was a vital part of the strategy confidently designed to make Labour at least the second largest party in the State. Some rural Labour TDs had misgivings. Paddy Tierney in North Tipperary even refused to stand rather than obey the ruling. Most, however, went along with it, their misgivings swept aside by the wave of euphoria which enveloped the campaign. Dan Spring was one of just two sitting TDs who refused point-blank to go with the two-candidate strategy, which he regarded as electoral suicide. Michael Pat Murphy was the other.

Anna Spring remembers that Tadhg Harrington came down from Dublin as an emissary from headquarters to persuade Dan to agree to a second candidate. "Dan argued against it and the discussion was going on for some time when I said: 'You can put up two candidates if that's what you really want but Dan Spring won't be one of them.' That was the end of that and we heard nothing more about it," says Mrs. Spring.

It wasn't just the candidate strategy which upset Dan. His keen political nose told him that all the confident predictions from headquarters were nonsense and he dissociated himself from the whole 1969 project. He fought his own traditional campaign and ignored the media hype and the promise of a new socialist dawn. He hardly mentioned the Labour Party at all in his advertisements, which merely stated that he had worked for the constituency for twenty-six years and urged: "He helps you. Now you help him."

Spring's caution was legendary and he was always careful not to get out of step with his constituents. He was unequivocal in the opinions he held but he was careful about expressing his views either in the Dáil or to the media. One newly-elected deputy in 1969 recalls how he carefully prepared a speech and delivered it in the Dáil. Afterwards he met Dan Spring and asked him what he thought of it. "There's many a man talked himself out of a good job," was Spring's cryptic reply.

In 1969, Spring was determined that, whatever his colleagues intended to do, he was not going to talk himself out of his job. He had a young family who were now attending boarding school. Politics was his life but it was also his job and his only source of income. The Dáil salary was what put bread on the table and paid for his children's school fees and he had no intention of jeopardising his hard-won livelihood by chasing a socialist rainbow.

While Dan regarded politics to a large extent as a job he had a code of practice to which he rigidly adhered and on which he would not compromise. "Dan never took money from anybody he had helped, although it was often offered," says Anna. "There is a lot of talk nowadays about political contributions but he had an iron rule. He wouldn't accept money. At election times the clubs raised some money, we spent some of our own and the union made a contribution. That was it."

Thus in 1969 he campaigned as he always had, relying on the respect and affection of his constituents to return him to the Dáil. "Dan Spring was a professional politician with a sure instinct. He could smell the wind before it even blew," was how one Labour activist recalled that election campaign.

Fianna Fáil fought a furious campaign against Labour, alleging that its policies were communist and alien to Ireland and that they involved an attempt to undermine the Catholic Church. Michael Moran, the Minister for Justice, in a famous outburst, referred to "the new left-wing political queers who have taken over the Labour Party from the steps of Trinity College and Telefís Eireann." Seán McEntee, father-in-law of Conor Cruise O'Brien, said Labour stood for Lenin, Stalin and "the red flames of burning homesteads in Meath". Cuba was referred to again and again by Fianna Fáil speakers, following on from a remark by Cruise O'Brien that Ireland should consider opening an embassy there while closing the one in the Vatican.

When the votes were counted, Spring's scepticism was proved

correct and most Labour candidates found to their astonishment that they had suffered a devastating rebuff. The party won just eighteen seats, a loss of four on 1965 and a far cry from the confident hope of becoming the second party in the State. In fact, Fine Gael, which had been written off by the media, won three extra seats to push its total up to fifty in the new Dáil.

Despite the deep disappointment, there were some encouraging trends for Labour. The party's percentage vote was the highest ever, due in some measure to the record number of candidates, while in Dublin, Labour overtook Fine Gael in total votes won and took eight seats. However, in rural Ireland, particularly in Munster, the result was a disaster. In Waterford, Cork and Tipperary, Labour seats were lost.

Dan Spring, Michael Pat Murphy and Stevie Coughlan held on in the teeth of the disaster but significantly both Spring and Murphy had defied the two-candidate edict and won by doggedly personal election campaigns which virtually ignored the fact that they were Labour candidates. In Kerry North, Spring just barely survived the rout of Labour in Munster. His vote was down to just under 5,000 but he won enough transfers to squeeze past Kit Ahern of Fianna Fáil who was more than 300 votes ahead of him on the first count.

During the campaign, according to John Horgan, Halligan had threatened to expel Spring for refusing to accept a running-mate. When the two met after the election, Spring brought it up: "Are you going to expel me?" he asked defiantly. Of course he was left severely alone.

On the national level, a striking feature of the 1969 election result was that Fine Gael and Labour had enough votes between them to put Fianna Fáil out of Government. The absence of an Opposition transfer deal allowed Fianna Fáil under Jack Lynch to slip through to power again. It was the party's third successive election victory and the galling aspect of it from the Opposition's point of view was that Fianna Fáil could easily have been deprived of a majority if there had been any kind of reasonable transfer arrangement between Fine Gael and Labour.

The collapse of its grandiose hopes in 1969 and the realisation among Labour TDs that, unless they changed tack, Fianna Fáil might continue in power indefinitely, prompted a fundamental rethink of the anti-coalition policy over the following twelve months. It also opened up wounds in the party which took twenty years to heal.

LABOUR IN COALITION

APPROPRIATELY ENOUGH IT WAS in 1970 that Labour abandoned the notion that "The Seventies will be Socialist". It was not simply the failure to win office but the shattering of such confident hopes which led to the need for a fundamental reassessment of the party's strategy. The Arms Crisis which rocked the Fianna Fáil Government in the spring of 1970 helped to force a rethink on the basis that some form of alternative to a Fianna Fáil Government would have to be put before the people at the next election. By the summer of 1970, the Labour leadership was determined to escape from the anti-coalition straitjacket in what Cruise O'Brien termed "Operation Houdini".

A special delegate conference was held in Cork in December 1970 to consider the issue. It was one of the most passionate, bitter and divisive conferences ever held by the party – and that's saying something. Almost all the eighteen TDs were in favour of dropping the ban on coalition but intense opposition to a change in policy was led by the charismatic figure of Noel Browne, who was adored by those on the left. Ironically, Browne was the only Labour TD, apart from Corish, who had actually served as a Government Minister but he was by now virulently opposed to coalition with Fine Gael. He had already raised the ire of his parliamentary colleagues by a newspaper article in which he said he preferred "Marxist-based revolutionary socialism" to social democracy and called for the provision of divorce, contraception and abortion facilities.

Throughout the seventies, Browne was the *bête noire* of the Labour establishment. His speeches at annual conference were often the highlight of the weekend and the mesmeric effect he had on many delegates had to be seen to be believed. The appearance of this striking pallid figure, with his jet-black hair, on the speaker's podium was enough to send a thrill through the audience and when he spoke, his voice dropping to a hoarse whisper as he reached a climax, the emotion in the hall was palpable. Often Browne appeared to be on the point of bringing the entire conference behind him and sweeping the leadership away as the delegates responded to his emotional appeals. He had the habit, however, of suddenly breaking the spell he himself had woven by snarling vicious insults at some prominent figure, particularly Corish.

At the Cork conference he was in tune with the views of many of the ordinary members, particularly those from Dublin, who had been attracted to Labour in the heady atmosphere of the late 1960s. Michael Gallagher estimates that 90 per cent of the Dublin speakers at the conference were against coalition while those from outside Dublin were evenly split. The 858 delegates who attended the conference attacked each other in violent language, which struck most impartial listeners as the nearest they had come to watching a civil war.

"Shame! Shame!" shouted Browne at one stage during a speech by Corish, to which the party leader replied: "I never shouted 'Shame' when you voted to abolish food subsidies" – a reference to Browne's support for Fianna Fáil's abolition of subsidies in 1952. When the coalition issue was put to a vote, after various procedural wrangles, the pro-coalitionists won by two to one. Browne then led a walk-out of anti-coalitionists. The television cameras were there to record the event and bring the split in Labour to a wider public.

Following that conference Labour was riven by further bitter divisions, most of them having nothing to do with the coalition issue. The parliamentary party was split between rural and urban TDs, between liberals and conservatives and between nationalists and anti-nationalists. Not all of the cleavages were on the same lines but many of them involved the same personnel in either camp. Dan Spring remained resolutely on the side of rural conservative Labour with an unashamed attachment to Republican ideals.

The year after the pro-coalition decision there was a bitter row at the party conference on the contraception issue and another one over a motion to expel the colourful Limerick TD, Stevie Coughlan. Spring made no secret of his anti-contraception views and he also opposed the move to remove the whip from Coughlan.

Corish had accepted the need for constitutional change on issues like divorce and the introduction of family planning but he wanted to move gradually and bring the rural TDs along with him. Browne, however, alienated them by a series of violent attacks on the Catholic Church. In a speech at Tramore, Co. Waterford, he described the Church as a "sectarian and bigoted politically conservative pressure group". He also said that many priests had chosen celibacy because "they find the whole subject of sex and heterosexual relationships threatening and embarrassing". It was not only the rural conservatives who were annoyed. The parliamentary party issued a statement expressing regret for the offence Browne had caused and described his comments on priests as an insult. Browne himself objected to the apology.

In 1972, Browne and John O'Connell introduced a private member's Bill in the Dáil to make contraceptives and birth control literature available. There was opposition to the Bill in the parliamentary party and it was refused a first reading in the Dáil. Spring, Coughlan and Michael Pat Murphy voted against it, along with eight Fine Gael TDs and Fianna Fáil, to defeat the Bill by seventy-five votes to forty-four. An emergency motion was put down for the 1972 conference to have the three TDs expelled for their action, but delegates voted not to debate it.

Dan Spring's views on contraception were deeply held. He was a devout Catholic although, typical of him, he always stood at the back of the church with his working class friends during Mass and only took a seat when arthritis caught up with him in old age. He was not at all unusual for a person of his age and background, but many of the newer Labour TDs and the bright new party members found it difficult to come to terms with someone of such fixed views which ran counter to the way the party was evolving at that stage.

"Of course Dan was a conservative but he wasn't authoritarian. For instance, he allowed his children to develop their own ideas and could accept that a younger generation would hold different views to his," says a Labour activist who knew him.

The next election in 1973 was totally unlike that of 1969 and, for that matter, of any other election campaign since. With the anti-coalition policy dropped, Labour was in a position to fight a different type of campaign. Some exploratory talks had taken place before Jack Lynch dissolved the Dáil on 5 February but, immediately afterwards, Corish met Liam Cosgrave and agreed to fight the campaign on a common platform under the banner of a "National Coalition". It was agreed that

Cosgrave would take over as Taoiseach and Corish as Tánaiste if they came out on top. An election manifesto was drafted by an eight-man team in the space of just three hours and this fourteen-point manifesto was the cornerstone of the campaign.

The coalition strategy worked, even though there was a last-minute swing back to Fianna Fáil when the party promised in the dying days of the campaign to abolish rates. While Labour and Fine Gael combined lost votes compared with 1969, they won more seats because of much better transfers. There had been no agreement in advance on Government posts and, on a strictly proportional basis, Labour with its nineteen seats to Fine Gael's fifty-four was entitled to four of the fifteen Cabinet positions. When the two leaders met, however, Cosgrave immediately offered five Cabinet posts to Labour. The party also got two of the seven junior ministries (or parliamentary secretaryships, as they were then called) while Labour's Sean Treacy was made Ceann Comhairle. Apart from Corish as Tánaiste and Minister for Health and Social Welfare, the other Labour Ministers were Conor Cruise O'Brien (Posts and Telegraphs), Justin Keating (Industry and Commerce), Jim Tully (Local Government) and Michael O'Leary (Labour). Frank Cluskey and Michael Pat Murphy got the junior posts.

It was a big disappointment for Dan Spring. Having served as a junior Minister for the last year of the previous coalition, sixteen years earlier, he had hopes of getting another junior ministerial post. Brendan Corish passed over his longest-serving TD in favour of Michael Pat Murphy from West Cork and it was a bitter blow for Dan.

Twenty years later, when his son Dick was in the position of handing out the jobs in the Labour-Fianna Fáil Government, some long-serving TDs expressed their deep annoyance at being passed over. "I understand how you feel. I knew what it was like to be in a house where somebody was passed over for the job they believed was their due," Dick Spring told one of the senior people disappointed by his decision.

Donal Spring recalls the dismay in the family at the fact that his father was passed over in 1973. "He was very disappointed because he felt that as the senior member of the party he was entitled to a post. He saw people who had joined up when the party was on the crest of a wave getting senior positions and of course they were as quick to leave when the going got rough again."

For all his discontent, Dan Spring didn't react by rocking the boat for the new Government. Other Labour TDs, like David Thornley, John O'Connell and Stevie Coughlan, caused trouble for the party and embarrassment for the Government, but that wasn't Spring's style. With a trade unionist's strict sense of discipline, he swallowed his disappointment and loyally backed the Government.

At Labour's annual conferences, the Kerry buses arrived as usual with their large number of delegates and they backed the leadership against the left-wingers and those like Noel Browne who sought to overturn the coalition. "Dan didn't have much time for Corish and maybe that's understandable," says one Labour TD, "but he didn't consciously position himself in opposition to the leadership in the way that other conservatives like Sean Treacy and Stevie Coughlan did."

The National Coalition was initially dubbed the "Government of all the talents" and it had a long honeymoon period during which a number of popular measures were introduced. Things went so well in the beginning that Michael Gallagher wrote a few years later: "Some of the early press comment, indeed, was almost embarrassingly sycophantic." The Government's first budget, which contained a wide range of social welfare increases, met with a very positive welcome and Gallagher quotes *The Irish Times* comment that it was "the most progressive budget yet".

The end of sixteen years of Fianna Fáil rule had prepared the electorate for a different style of government, but it was the Coalition's bad luck that the Arab-Israeli war of 1973 suddenly blighted its high hopes by bringing about a worldwide energy crisis. Oil prices rose by 500 per cent in the aftermath of the war and the result was massive inflation and rising unemployment throughout Europe. Ireland, which was almost totally dependent on imported oil for energy, was badly hit.

Prices doubled during the Coalition's term of office and were brought under control only towards the end when the Government's political doom had been sealed. Justin Keating as Minister for Industry and Commerce was dubbed the "Minister for Prices" on Frank Hall's satirical television show *Hall's Pictorial Weekly*, and the tag stuck. In fact, that television programme mercilessly caricatured the Government and its Ministers. The Minister for Finance, Richie Ryan, was called "Richie Ruin" and the nickname nearly destroyed his political career.

Within the Government there was a high degree of cohesion

between the Fine Gael and Labour Ministers. The only real animus was between Liam Cosgrave and Garret FitzGerald. Labour Ministers were very impressed with Cosgrave who, despite a dour public image, proved an excellent Cabinet chairman. His style of Government was to let Ministers get on with their job and he placed the same degree of trust in his Labour Ministers as in his Fine Gael colleagues.

"From the very beginning, Cosgrave behaved impeccably. His initial move to offer us one more Cabinet seat than we were entitled to showed generosity and a grasp of politics that his detractors would never match," says one Labour figure who was involved in that Government.

Cosgrave and Corish got along very well on a personal level in Government, despite the fact that they had had their differences as Opposition leaders in the Dáil. They had a practice, whenever things were getting a bit tense, of retiring for a few hours to the Taoiseach's office, closing the door behind them and opening a bottle of whiskey. Over a few drinks the problems between them would be threshed out before they had a chance to sour the atmosphere around the Cabinet table.

Cosgrave also got on well with Conor Cruise O'Brien and the two men learned to respect each other. Although O'Brien was Minister for Posts and Telegraphs, his most notable contribution to politics during the Government's lifetime was his constant critique of the traditional nationalist approach to Northern Ireland. This provoked great hostility from many quarters and O'Brien engaged in regular jousts with the media. But Cosgrave stood by his Minister.

The escalating violence in the North was another stroke of bad luck to add to the Coalition's woes. The necessity for strict security measures made the Government unpopular and the Sunningdale Agreement, which was painfully negotiated in 1973, unravelled the following year because of the hostility of grassroots Unionists and the cowardice of British Prime Minister Harold Wilson in the face of the Ulster Loyalist workers' strike.

The Coalition was also heavily criticised for its record on jobs. When it took office, unemployment was just 71,435 but this had risen to 115,942 by the time it left in 1977. Although the 1977 figure looks very respectable by the standards of 1993, it was regarded as a major failure to add to the spiralling prices of household goods. Government

borrowing had increased dramatically to cope with the effects of the
oil crisis and, while this was being scaled back by 1977, it was another
nail in the Coalition's coffin.

There were a number of positive achievements to its credit after the
first year. Jim Tully ensured that an incredible 100,000 houses were
built during the four years. In the social welfare area, Labour delivered
a massive extra allocation of resources, with increases in all benefits
much greater than the rate of inflation. Unmarried mothers, prisoners'
wives and single women aged over fifty-eight all received benefits for
the first time. There was also a major reform of labour law, with
workers' rights being expanded significantly.

Dan Spring had no difficulty in supporting the main thrust of
Government policy but he found himself alienated on two fronts. The
first was Northern policy, where Labour's approach came increasingly
to be dominated by Cruise O'Brien. The escalating violence in the
North since 1968 had prompted a reappraisal of attitudes among many
people in the Republic and Labour made a decided shift in policy away
from the traditional rhetoric about a thirty-two county socialist Republic
to a recognition of the validity of the two traditions, Unionist and
Nationalist, on the island.

Spring was totally out of sympathy with the new policy and had
little time for O'Brien. He took an old-fashioned Republican line, along
with other traditional Labour TDs like Sean Treacy and Stevie Coughlan. There had already been fierce rows within the Labour party over
the previous two years as the O'Brien line had gradually come to be
accepted, though not without acrimonious debates, at annual conference. Now after the 1973 election, some of the new TDs like David
Thornley and John O'Donovan were also out of step with the new
direction on the issue.

An incongruous alliance developed between Thornley and the old
Republicans and it was not just confined to the issue of the North. John
Horgan records his fascination at this link-up between Thornley and
TDs like Spring and Coughlan on the Republican side. "He saw their
power-base as essential, he once said, to thwart the efforts of Noel
Browne and others on the doctrinaire left who might take the party
on a pilgrimage to frustration." One TD recalls how, for a jape,
Coughlan once stuck a picture of Cruise O'Brien on the partition wall
over Spring's desk. When Dan came into the room and saw the picture,

he promptly put his fist through it and through the flimsy partition wall into the next room. That expressed what he thought of Cruise O'Brien.

During the Cosgrave coalition, Thornley, who was also bitterly disappointed at not achieving office, took a more and more Republican line, appearing at one stage on a Sinn Féin platform in O'Connell Street and also harrying the Government over its security measures. Despite Thornley's support for them in previous tight spots, Spring was the only one of the rural conservatives to reciprocate and to stand by Thornley. Along with Michael D. Higgins and John O'Connell, he opposed the removal of the whip (which was ultimately taken away from Thornley).

Most of the urban TDs – anti-Republicans like Conor Cruise O'Brien, Barry Desmond, Frank Cluskey and Michael O'Leary – were also divided from their rural colleagues on liberal agenda issues. It was social issues, particularly contraception, that were to drive a further wedge between rural deputies like Spring and their more liberal colleagues. In the landmark McGee case in 1973, the Supreme Court decided that the ban on the importation of contraceptives was unconstitutional, despite the 1935 Act which made both sale and importation illegal.

The Government responded by authorising the Minister for Justice, Pat Cooney, to bring forward legislation to regularise the position. In June 1974, the Government introduced the Control of Importation, Sale and Manufacture of Contraceptives Bill which would have allowed contraceptives to be sold under licence by chemists to married people only. The Government parties allowed a free vote but Fianna Fáil did not. Des O'Malley led the Fianna Fáil assault on the legislation in the Dáil and ridiculed the Coalition for trying to legalise contraception. Meanwhile, the Catholic hierarchy had declared that it was up to the legislators to decide if the law should be changed though the Church taught that the use of contraceptives was wrong.

When the vote was taken on 16 July on the second stage of the Bill, it produced one of the most sensational episodes in the history of the Dáil. Not only was the Bill defeated by seventy-five votes to sixty-one, but the Taoiseach actually voted against his own Government's legislation. Cosgrave did not inform any of his colleagues beforehand of what he was going to do and the Government chief whip, John Kelly, was under the impression that he was going to support the Bill.

Kelly was shocked beyond belief by the Taoiseach's action because he had reassured some nervous conservative backbenchers that Cosgrave supported the measure.

The Minister for Education, Dick Burke, and five Fine Gael backbenchers, including Oliver Flanagan, also voted against the Bill. In what was effectively an abstention, Dan Spring did not travel to Dublin for the vote and many of his colleagues were furious with him.

Journalist Vincent Browne asked Spring a few days before the vote what he was going to do but all Dan would say in reply was: "You'll have to come into the press gallery on the day to find out." Spring had to attend a civil court case in Cork on the day of the vote and that was the ostensible reason for his absence, but his colleagues had no doubt that it was a political statement on his part.

Relations within the Labour parliamentary party were also frequently strained on other issues during the lifetime of the Cosgrave Coalition but there was no alternative leader waiting in the wings to take over. On one occasion, Corish walked out of a difficult parliamentary party meeting, threatening to resign. Frank Cluskey looked around the remaining eighteen TDs in the room and remarked: "The only trouble about electing a replacement is that none of us is capable of finding a seconder."

During the lifetime of the Coalition, Labour attracted some more new recruits. Two talented university senators, Mary Robinson and John Horgan, joined the parliamentary party. Horgan was later elected as a Labour TD but lost his seat in Dublin South after one term and returned to the world of academia and journalism.

Mary Robinson found Dáil politics more difficult still. She contested Rathmines West in 1977 but had to endure a bitter campaign clouded by personal rivalries after she had been added to the list of approved candidates by the Administrative Council. She failed to get elected by only 406 votes – the closest she ever came to a Dáil seat. "I could have handled it with more sensitivity at the time. I was unprepared for that kind of faction in-fighting and perhaps I assumed my welcome would be greater than it was. I took things for granted that I should have worked harder at," she said eight years later.

The 1977 election was a disappointment for others as well as for Mary Robinson. The "Government of all the talents" came crashing to earth in spectacular style. The leading Labour intellectuals and Government Ministers, Conor Cruise O'Brien and Justin Keating, lost their seats and departed the national political scene. Fianna Fáil swept to a landslide victory because of the redrafting of constituencies by Jim Tully – as part of a grand design to ensure that the Fine Gael-Labour coalition would be unbeatable!

In Kerry North, Dan Spring again survived the deluge. While the big Labour names were toppling like ninepins, he came through again to win his tenth election on the trot. It was a remarkable achievement because the first-count figures were very ominous for him. The constituency had been reduced from four to three seats in 1961 and Spring's demise had been forecast at that stage. He had survived again and again in tight situations but in 1977 he was well behind the two leading Fianna Fáil candidates and 200 votes behind the Fine Gael candidate, Ger Lynch, on the first count. Not only that, but Lynch had a running mate who polled nearly 2,000 votes, so the news looked very bad for the great survivor.

Dan traditionally stayed in the house on Strand Road during most of the count and went down to the count centre only for the concluding stages. Donal Spring recalls that in 1977 they were all in a tizzy when the news was brought to the house about the state of play on the first count. "Dad refused to panic at the figures. He just remarked 'Don't worry, the votes will come back. They won't continue their preferences without coming to me first.' The remarkable thing was that he was right." The percentage figures show what an amazing result it was. Fianna Fáil with 57 per cent of the vote got two seats, Fine Gael with 24.5 per cent got none, and Labour with 18 per cent got one. Dan Spring had done it again, despite a Labour disaster, but it was to be his last hurrah.

GROWING UP

AS DAN SPRING SOLDIERED ON through election after election his family were growing up. Two of his sons, Dick and Donal, were boarders at Mount St Joseph's secondary college in Roscrea. As it was on the road to Dublin, Dan was often able to call in to see them on his way to the Dáil.

It was at Roscrea that Dick Spring started to play rugby, a game which was to have an enormous influence on his life. "Funnily enough, for about two years there I refused to play rugby. You had options – there was hurling, football, rugby and athletics. You name it, they did everything. But by my third year in the school, I had played on every team that was possible in hurling and football, even under-age; it didn't matter. We were knocked out of the senior hurling in about October 1966, and one of the lads said to me: 'Why don't you come and play rugby?'

"It was great crack. It meant Donnybrook and hot showers after a game as opposed to Abbeyleix and a cold tap when you came off the hurling pitch. So I tried the rugby then and I must say I never looked back. The first day ever, I played as a centre. Sixteen guys turned up so they put me in as a third centre and the very first ball I caught I put it over the bar, Gaelic football style. I forgot to drop it or anything; just kicked it over the bar and then I ended up being out-half. The guy who was playing at out-half on the junior team, who had to move when I came in, was Mick Sherry. He ended up playing for Ireland as a wing forward.

"Roscrea was a sportsman's paradise. We played sport morning, noon and night. We used to train after breakfast. At lunchtime we'd get the backs out training and then we played rugby for the afternoon. We'd sketch out team plans during study. But you had really to study. I mean the fact that you were confined from six p.m. to eight and from nine to ten-thirty p.m. meant that at least you were going to bed with some study. So I enjoyed it. The monks weren't particularly obtrusive or anything like that. It wasn't as rigid as one was led to believe. The Cistercians were fairly laid back. No problems."

When he first took up the game in Roscrea, a Labour Party supporter heard about it and went to Anna Spring to express his disquiet. "I remember when this fellow came to my mother some time in the 1960s and said that Dick playing rugby would cost Dad his seat," recalls Donal. "My mother replied that she would regard it as a great honour if Dick continued with the game and played for Ireland one day. Of course she had no notion at the time that this was going to happen."

When he left secondary school, Dick went on to university in Trinity College. That again was an unusual step at a time when Trinity was still regarded as something of a "West British" institution and Catholics in most dioceses still required the permission of their bishop to go there. Why did Spring opt for Trinity?

"They paid me to go there," he says with a smile. "There is a bursary for impecunious Kerrymen – a Reid sizarship, actually; it's still there – and five of us did the exam and I got first place so they gave me £50 a year plus commons, which meant I had a hot meal every day, which was a luxury in those days. I have to say the odd commons ticket was auctioned for a few pints.

"There was also the fact that about twenty-four people from Roscrea were going to university and most of them were going to UCD. I had this notion that UCD would just be like continuing on with boarding school, so I wanted to go somewhere different. Three or four of that year went to Trinity. I enjoyed Trinity. I had been inside it just once before, to do an entrance exam.

"I was intrigued when I got there first to find there were just twelve hours of lectures a week. By the second or third week, you were finding it hard to make it along to lectures, you know. I did a bit of study but I didn't do enough, to be honest. I got very involved in rugby."

Dick Spring says he had always wanted to be a lawyer. "It was in my mind all the time, though I wanted a general education as well. I started out with economics and politics but I failed my first year exams. I had the choice of staying back and repeating them or going ahead so I switched and went ahead in general studies. I did English, History and Economics. I was quite happy to doze along. The real purpose I had was to go and do the bar anyway.

"I think the combination of law and politics was probably the attraction. They seemed to go hand-in-hand. There was a very strong insistence by my parents, my mother particularly, that if you were going into politics you should have a qualification. For two reasons – one, it gave you a standing in politics and secondly it was a fall-back position. My father's fall-back position was going back to the trade union as a branch secretary. After an absence of twenty or thirty years that would be a bit ridiculous because obviously other secretaries had been appointed. Whether or not the union would have put everybody down one ranking was uncertain and a bit impractical anyway. We were living on the margin in that respect. So that was the motivating reason."

Initially Spring took some interest in student politics but it soon faded. "I was involved in politics in Trinity after seventeen days. The Student Representative Council had been disbanded the year before because of internal problems so they had elections within three weeks of my moving into college and I contested. But I found it to be absolutely tiresome, and after a few meetings I said: 'For God's sake this isn't for me at all.' So I gave up after a while."

Spring also became involved in the Labour Party in Trinity "but again, I was never one for sitting around theorising for long periods of time and I ended up running the rugby club for a number of years, taking up various positions like secretary and captain of various teams. So that became the thing I did when I first went to Trinity." He devoted a lot of his time to the sport and captained the Trinity team to an historic colours victory over UCD.

Another significant feature of his student days was that Spring struck up a friendship with a fellow-student, John Rogers from Dublin, and the two young men shared rooms at the college. At that time, Rogers was a supporter of the liberal "young tigers" in Fine Gael and was no more inclined than Spring to support radical causes.

While he may not have been active in politics in university, Dick, like the rest of the family, campaigned for his father whenever elections came around. When he came home on holidays there was often discussion of political events in the family and as the children got older they, in common with other Irish people of their generation, began to challenge the views of their parents.

"In our house we had our dinner in the middle of the day," says Donal. "I remember we always turned on the radio to hear the news at 1.30 p.m. and nobody dared open their mouths while it was on. I can remember that when Dick would come home from college and there was some item on about contraception or divorce, fierce arguments would develop at the kitchen table. Dick, in particular, would challenge Dad's views, but we would all pitch in."

As their family grew up, Dan and Anna never had much money. They continued to live in the house on Strand Road, which they rented until they bought it late in Dan's career. "Everything my father earned was spent on us and he never had a penny to the day he died," says Donal. He recalls that Dan's favourite pastime was to cut turf in the bog in the summer. "He would remember a year when the turf was good and he could judge the quality the way a connoisseur will know a good bottle of wine. He just loved going to the bog and people he had done things for would go out and help him and that would make his day. I often remember him sitting on a rick of turf taking notes as people came to the bog to look for help with their problems."

Anna Spring recalls those days with fondness. "Dan loved the bog. We would cut and save our own turf every year. In later years we got the machine in to cut the turf but we still saved it ourselves. We'd take a picnic out and spend the day there." Such was his love of the bog that, after Dan died, Anna had heather planted on his grave.

After Trinity, Dick pursued his ambition to become a lawyer and, along with John Rogers, went to the Kings Inns to study for the bar. Spring was by this stage getting restless with student life in Dublin. "Life got a bit confused in those days. I went driving steamrollers in London, while waiting to finish my exams. I remember coming back one time to do my finals at the bar and the course had changed. So I went up to Charles Lysaght, the examiner, and I said: 'This is ridiculous. This question wasn't on the course when I did it last year' and he said: 'Well, if you hadn't been driving steamrollers in London, you might have the knowledge required.' 'OK,' I said, 'I'll see you in October.' They used to call it the Autumn Handicap.

"Summers around Dublin, especially for students, were no good at all," Spring found. "We used to make ourselves available as a rent-a-crew in Dun Laoghaire. There was a very nice man there, who had a big yacht, and we used to go off and crew for him. The first few trips were unbelievable. Somebody would say: 'Will you go up there and pull down the halyard.' And you'd say 'Wha?' '– the rope.' We used to go off for weekends, cruising around the Irish Sea, pretending we were big men, you know.

"But you can take so much of that. You have to get on with it, so I went off to England for a while. I arrived in London on the morning after the Birmingham bombs. I remember leaving Euston Station to try to make contact with the friend I was going to stay with. He didn't have a 'phone in the house and I had to wait around till he came home from work. The tabloids were full of 'the bloody Irish'.

"That was on a Thursday morning and I played rugby on the Saturday for London-Irish out in a place called Camberley – a nice settled respectable place. We got terrible abuse. People were inside drinking beer and watching the television which was showing Ireland playing New Zealand in Lansdowne Road. Every so often they would come out and start shouting at the Irish. It was understandable, I think, in the context of the Birmingham bombs." After finishing his exams, Spring spent another spell in London and then decided go further afield to the United States and on to New Zealand.

"I had one of those long trips planned. And, in fact, when I was in London I had discussed with a number of guys a plan to sail around the world. But I never did."

In New York, he got a job as a waiter-cum-barman in the Mad Hatter pub. "I was there for two years. It was great fun. I worked by night, played by day; what more could you want in life?" Spring wanted a break from rugby having played the game for more than ten years but he found the pub-owner had hired him specifically so that he could play for his team. In the event, he enjoyed playing in New York and could have played for the United States. He was called for the US final trial but couldn't make it.

It was there in the Mad Hatter in 1976 that he met his wife, Kristi Hutcheson. Kristi was originally from Hampton in Virginia and worked as a teacher for a time after graduating from college before becoming an air hostess to see the world. The couple got married in New York a year later. "He'd explained to me that his father was a TD and that he himself had three goals to come back to Ireland for: to practise at the bar, to win an international rugby cap and to be elected to the Dáil," Kristi told a newspaper interviewer a few years later.

In fact, Irish politics intruded on the couple even as they were getting married. "We got married in June of 1977 on a Saturday and I was canvassing in North Kerry on a Monday," says Spring. "My family were all due to come out and everything but Mr Cosgrave spoiled my wedding. It was history repeating itself to an extent. My parents had to cancel their wedding for an election. So we got married on a Saturday, had twenty-four hours of a honeymoon and I went to Ireland on the Monday while Kristi went back to work. We met, I think, three weeks later."

When Dick flew home to help in his father's campaign he joined other members of the family on the hustings. "It would be worse than giving up your religion not to turn up to a campaign. Politics in Ireland is so personal anyway and in rural areas all the more so. I mean, if a member of a family wasn't there people would wonder why. Now my returning four days before the election was token more than anything. When my father saw me arrive in my cream suit and with my unshaven face, I think he told the lads: 'Get him off the street.' He was not impressed, but I was then in what I describe as my 'gaucho' days."

During the tense count Dick Spring became involved in a row with a photographer, which might appear to indicate that he lacked the temperament for Irish politics. "We had a row during the count. The photographer was following me around, wanting to get his picture and I didn't particularly want to be photographed. I looked up at a big window and said: 'If you don't stop following me around everywhere with that camera you'll go out through it.' He didn't, of course. I believe if you don't want to do these things you should be entitled to your privacy. Mind you, if you are inside in the middle of an election count it is hard to insist on it. Poor man, he was around Leinster House for years afterwards. I talked about it to him later and he said he understood it at the time."

A few months after that election, Dick and Kristi decided to come to Ireland for good and initially they lived in Dublin. "I started to play rugby for Lansdowne who had a disastrous season. We were beaten by Terenure in the first round of the cup. I broke my finger the only time I even attempted a tackle. So I started practising law. Kristi got work in St John of God's teaching English.

"She was very good with the kids but she couldn't get a permanent appointment. I was leaving Dublin every Tuesday morning at half past five or six o'clock and going down to Limerick, Killarney, Ennis and Kilrush, following the court on the south-western circuit and trying to get back up to Lansdowne for training at six p.m. on a Thursday. I'd always be late for training and the lads would say 'God, where were you?'

"They didn't realise how far Killarney was from Lansdowne Road until I took them down one time for a match and they thought once you arrived in Limerick you were in Kerry. They didn't realise the journey was only starting.

"That was the first year in Lansdowne. The team was in such a mess that I took on the captaincy. We organised the club and I put a team together. There were a lot of guys who said they were worn out after ten or twelve years and were finished playing at twenty-seven or twenty-eight. I got them back playing.

"Some guys had a tendency to put on weight and you had to get them training long before the season because they would never get fit during it. So I had them out in Belfield doing cross-countries twice a week all during the summer. By September it was obvious we were going to be a side to take notice of. We lost out in the league by a try differential but we won the cup."

Spring's performances for Lansdowne brought the fulfilment of one lifelong ambition. He was selected for the Irish team. "I had intended doing it before I was twenty-eight years of age, mind you, but something went wrong along the way. I was a sub in 1974 on three occasions. On one occasion we went to London without Tony Ensor, who stayed back to do an exam. I was praying that there would be a fog in Dublin or something so he couldn't get to London but he went out and played a blinder – both he and Mike Gibson, the same day."

Spring's international experience was blighted by one incident in 1979 which has gone down in folklore. He dropped a high ball near the Irish line in Cardiff Arms Park and Wales scored a try. "One up, one down and one to go – that describes my sojourn with the Irish team. It didn't work very well. The next time I drop a ball I should drop it in the back pitch in Lansdowne Road and not the front pitch in Cardiff Arms Park. But the irony is that I had never had a difficulty in my career. One of my strong points was catching the ball and on this glorious occasion, for various reasons, one drops the ball! We have to live with that, but playing for Ireland was a great honour. Everyone wants to do it and I was very honoured to get the opportunity."

Dropping the ball was a psychological blow which stayed with Spring for a long time. "Dick has a good sense of humour but you didn't make jokes about dropping the ball for a good few years afterwards," says a friend.

Even at the Labour conference of 1993, when party chairman, Jim Kemmy, made a crack about the dropped ball while introducing his leader before the keynote address, Spring put aside his speech for a moment to respond: "I have always said that I will take criticism on that point from anybody who has played rugby for Ireland and hurling and football for Kerry, but I doubt if there is anybody else who has," he said before delivering his prepared speech on live television.

IN THE DAIL

LABOUR EMERGED SHOCKED and confused from the defeat of the Cosgrave Coalition. The party had lost its big stars like Cruise O'Brien, Keating and Thornley, was deeply demoralised and badly in need of a new direction. The first task was to select a new leader because Brendan Corish followed Liam Cosgrave's example and stepped down after the election disaster. He had been seventeen years in the job.

There were two candidates for the succession. One was Frank Cluskey, who presented a dour Dublin image to the public but who, in reality, was humorous, witty and capable of devastating repartee. The other was Michael O'Leary, a much more flamboyant character, who was a brilliant campaigner but regarded by many of his colleagues as being over-ambitious and unreliable.

"Frank was great with the party but not with the public, while Michael was great with the public but a disaster in the party. If only one person could have combined both their talents," sighs a Labour TD.

When the contest took place in the summer of 1977, the sixteen Labour TDs split evenly and the candidates received eight votes each. While the vote was completed by secret ballot, there was no secret about who had voted which way. Those backing Cluskey were Brendan Corish, Barry Desmond, Eileen Desmond, Ruairi Quinn, Joe Bermingham, John Ryan and John Horgan.

The O'Leary supporters were Dan Spring, Liam Kavanagh, John O'Connell, Seamus Pattison, Michael Pat Murphy, Jim Tully and Pat Kerrigan. The split was interesting in that the rural deputies, including Dan Spring, tended to support O'Leary while Cluskey was more attractive to urban TDs. This was also a breakdown along old ITGWU-WUI lines, reflecting the history of the party and the breach between Labour and National Labour in the forties.

After the tied vote the names should have gone into a hat but Ruairi

Quinn, who was a new TD, suggested another ballot. This time around, one of the TDs changed sides and Cluskey won by nine votes to seven. O'Leary was then chosen as deputy leader. The effect on the party of such a close contest was damaging because neither Cluskey nor O'Leary accepted the result with good grace. Cluskey remained darkly suspicious of O'Leary and fancied he was plotting at every hand's turn, while O'Leary virtually opted out of parliamentary politics and didn't really come to life until the European election campaign of 1979, when he was a candidate for Dublin along with John O'Connell.

Under Cluskey's leadership after 1977, the Labour party at times presented a vigorous opposition in the Dáil to the whopping Fianna Fáil majority. But it failed to change with the times and present a new image to the public or to get its own house in order and stop the incessant squabbling which characterised the party.

Opposition politics came to be increasingly dominated by a revitalised Fine Gael party under Garret FitzGerald. Garret toured the country, presented Fine Gael as the party of modernisation and gradually took much of Labour's social democratic clothes for himself. Fine Gael managed to achieve that indefinable thing in politics and became the fashionable party. Labour, despite dogged and persistent performances in the Dáil by Cluskey and other leading TDs like Barry Desmond, particularly after the accession of Charles Haughey, failed – apart from one notable occasion – to click with the public.

That occasion was the European elections of 1979 when John O'Connell and Michael O'Leary managed to win two seats out of four in Dublin while Liam Kavanagh won a seat in Leinster and Eileen Desmond one in Munster. The campaign showed that popular Labour candidates could pull it off in elections but the party failed to build on the achievement. Ironically, the two Labour victors in Dublin left the party in the next few years. After a number of vicissitudes, O'Leary joined Fine Gael and O'Connell Fianna Fáil. With the approval of the 1981 election, it was Fine Gael who were making the running on the Opposition side.

As Labour struggled to keep pace with a revitalised Fine Gael, Dan Spring was drawing towards the close of his political career. Like many TDs of his age in all Dáil parties, he still retained his deeply conservative views on moral issues. When Charles Haughey introduced in 1979 a Family Planning Bill to legalise the sale of contraceptives to married people – "an Irish solution to an Irish problem" – it was opposed by the Labour Party. Most Labour TDs objected on the grounds that it was far too conservative, but Dan Spring and Michael Pat Murphy disapproved of legalising contraception in the first place.

With the party split on the issue, it became clear that it would be impossible to devise amendments to the Bill with which all TDs could agree. Labour decided not to table any amendments at all, on the basis that the Bill was so bad that it was beyond improvement. Fine Gael were similarly divided and didn't seek to put forward any substantial amendments.

In 1980, the parliamentary Labour Party gingerly approached the divorce issue by producing a private member's motion in the Dáil. This called for the establishment of an Oireachtas committee to report on the appropriate form of amendment to Article 41 of the Constitution. Fianna Fáil came out firmly against the introduction of divorce and Fine Gael, divided on the issue, sought to amend the Labour motion. However, when the Labour motion was put to the House, two of the party's own TDs, Dan Spring and Michael Pat Murphy, were again found to be at loggerheads with party policy and they abstained on the vote. Fine Gael also abstained on the main motion which was defeated by sixty-two votes to fifteen.

Dan Spring was sixty-seven years old when he held his seat for the eleventh consecutive election in 1977 and he decided that he would not run again. Unlike many veteran politicians, he knew when it was time to go with dignity. As he came to the end of his political career, a decision had to be made about which of his six children would try to hold the Labour seat in North Kerry. By 1979, when the local elections came around, decision time had arrived.

"I had a terrible choice to make," recalls Dick Spring. Even though the season had gone badly for me on the national team, we had won the cup at Lansdowne and I had played well so I had kind of got my confidence back. There was one particular semi-final in which Van Esbeck even wrote favourably about me! Even after a bad season, I sort of won the match for Lansdowne almost single-handed.

"I was out in the Belvedere sevens on a Sunday afternoon and the Irish team was being put together for Australia for a six-week tour. I was approached and asked if I was available for the tour. The Kerry county council convention was taking place a few days later. So I had to do a bit of thinking about it and the fact that the Belvedere sevens were on the day after we had won the Leinster Cup might have had an effect on my thinking that day. So I said 'no' I wasn't available. I probably wasn't available anyway because Kristi would have been on her own for six weeks, so it just wasn't on. We were just settling in here, trying to find our way. So the options were Australia or Kerry county council and I settled for Kerry.

"Timing-wise, the family was beginning to get very conscious that my father was sixty-nine years old and very obviously tiring. We thought also that he needed a break from the monotony of the old Kerry-Dublin rail journey which he had been doing for thirty-six years at that stage."

Dick emerged as the likely successor almost by a process of elimination. "Arthur was interested in politics but never for a moment did any of us think he was going to make himself available. I just think it fell my way but I probably would have been the most political of them. I had always been available to go to by-elections and I enjoyed politics.

"So we had the selection convention. As we hadn't informed the branches, there was a small bit of consternation, not so much that I was being proposed as that my father was resigning from the council. Then people saw a whole generational thing unfolding before their eyes. And for people who had been involved for thirty or forty years, it was a big change. I suppose one should have been a bit more considerate in terms of breaking the news but it worked OK. I contested the elcction and was elected to Kerry county council and Tralee urban council."

Anna Spring had mixed feelings about seeing Dick become involved in politics. "My one ambition was that none of them would have to depend on public life because it's much too precarious a way to earn a living. That was the thing that made me a bit reluctant to see Dick get involved but he was always more interested than any of the others. Of course they all helped Dan at election times but Dick was more committed to politics."

He was soon embroiled in controversy over an incident at the council which has since passed into folklore as a refusal to stand for the Angelus. In fact, the issue was much more complicated. "The chairman of the urban council proposed one night that there be a vote of sympathy to Gardaí who had been shot. I was fully supportive of that but the chairman decided to say the prayer, the Hail Mary. There was a non-Catholic member on the council and I thought if you are going to do something like that it should involve all sides, with nobody worrying whether it was offensive to one side or the other. That was the reason I refused to stand for the prayer, but it was all misconstrued.

"I got some very bad vibes from Gardaí at the time and I privately made known what had happened. They now know my attitude to the paramilitaries and violence. And then, of course, it became the Angelus I wouldn't stand for. It was all nonsense, they don't stand for the Angelus at Kerry county council. Vincent Browne ran that story a few times. Like all these things, do you correct it? It just ends up a farce so I forgot about it."

Still, such a stance did not fit easily with the traditional religious beliefs held by Dan Spring and there were doubts about how the voters of North Kerry would react to Dick when he stood for the Dáil. He didn't have a lot of time to show them what he was made of. "It was really a question of getting stuck into politics, which was difficult enough because I was also practising at the bar and I ended up in silly situations. I was doing a case in Dublin one time and I thought it would last for one day, a Monday. I had arranged branch meetings in Kerry for Monday night, Tuesday night, Wednesday night, three nights in a row. And I ended up commuting from Kerry to Dublin and back down for branch meetings. Driving to Mallow; getting on the train at Mallow, getting up to the Four Courts. That sort of thing made me realise how impractical it was. So we moved down to Kerry. And I started to work more towards the circuit rather than coming up to the High Court, but ultimately you have to travel to Dublin anyway."

The election came in 1981 when Charles Haughey dissolved the Dáil in June of that year. The tide was not exactly running in Labour's favour and there was no knowing whether the voters who had supported Dan Spring for so long would carry forward their support to his son.

"That first one was very tough. Dick was an unknown quantity as far as most of the electorate were concerned," says Donal Spring. "Political dynasties had been getting a very bad press and Dick had to prove himself in that election." The Spring family, as usual, were out in force on the campaign and the Labour clubs rallied around.

The Labour organisation in the constituency is inseparable from the family. Anna Spring's long-time position as treasurer means that nothing happens in the organisation without consultation with her. At election times, almost every canvassing team in North Kerry has a member of the Spring family with it, if not a brother or sister, then a cousin or uncle. On Dick's election debut, no-one in the family or in the organisation was sure whether the torch could be passed on to a new generation.

"For a long time beforehand the main thing was getting ready for the election. My father and myself both applied ourselves, I suppose fairly assiduously, to the organisation and to the campaign," says Dick.

At a national level, the campaign was a shattering experience for Labour. The party found itself marginalised as the first round of the titanic struggle between Garret FitzGerald and Charles Haughey grabbed the public imagination. Fine Gael, with a popular leader, a revitalised image and a huge injection of cash from the business community, were full of confidence and Labour was completely overshadowed in the scramble for votes.

An added ingredient to the campaign was the intervention of H-Block candidates, who were on hunger-strike in the Maze prison in Northern Ireland. The hunger-strikers were a threat to Fianna Fáil's chances of winning an overall majority, but in some areas they also took a sizable slice of the Labour vote. North Kerry was one of those constituencies because the Spring vote had always contained a significant Republican element.

"I suppose it was a sign of the times that despite both of us working at it and working very hard, I survived by only 144 votes," says Dick. "Actually, when I left the house to go down to the count, I was told I had been defeated. Tallying wasn't that sophisticated in those days. When I went down I had a speech written to thank them for voting for my father for thirty-eight years. When I arrived down they said it had swung back my way. So, it was 144 votes at three o'clock in the morning. I think there was a recount ordered. I was asked: 'What if the recount goes wrong?' and I said: 'Ah, sure, I can always say I was a TD for a few hours.' The base vote was there. I think I polled something like 5,600.

"The H-Block candidate polled 11 per cent and he gave me 918 transfers, the most of all the candidates. This was funny because I hadn't marched in the H-Block protest though other North Kerry candidates had. I think a lot of the young people probably voted for me and some of the traditional Dan Spring voters might have gone and then come back. I think I polled very well, around 16 per cent in that election, which would have been my father's kind of figure. In 1969, 1973 and 1977 he was struggling. He was quite lucky at times. Never having fought with anybody I think that is why he got the transfers."

Looking at the figures it is easy to see why the Spring camp felt the seat was going to slip away from them at one stage during the count. The H-Block candidate received a very substantial 3,860 first preferences. Spring did well, receiving 5,685 votes on the first count but, as in 1977, Fine Gael outpolled Labour and it was difficult to see how he could pull through. On the second count, Spring was 500 votes behind the Fine Gael candidate, Ger Lynch, and looking to be in trouble. However, transfers from the H-Block candidate narrowed the gap to 100 votes. What saved the Spring family seat and Dick Spring's budding career was the surplus votes of Fianna Fáil TD and fellow-Tralee man, Tom McEllistrim, which helped him to squeeze past Lynch.

The big shock for Labour on a national level was that the party leader, Frank Cluskey, lost his seat in Dublin South Central as a result of a row with Dr John O'Connell, who had left the party but had run in the same constituency. Fianna Fáil's chances of an overall majority were ruined by the H-Block candidates; Fine Gael did very well and Labour trailed in a very bad third. The outlook for the party and its youngest TD, Dick Spring, was problematical, to say the least.

Labour emerged from the 1981 election in a curious position. The party lost votes, lost seats and lost its leader, yet it was presented with the opportunity of going into Government with a resurgent Fine Gael under Garret FitzGerald. There were divided views within the party about what to do. After four years of Opposition, at a time when it should have been in a position to gain votes and seats, it had lost out badly. The number of TDs had been cut to fifteen and the national share of the vote slipped under 10 per cent. Apart from 1957, it was the worst result for Labour since 1933.

In Dublin, the party's showing was terrible. Frank Cluskey, Ruairi Quinn and John Horgan lost their seats in what amounted to a rout. Only Michael O'Leary and Barry Desmond had held on and were joined by Mervyn Taylor, who was elected for the first time in Dublin South West. Party members in Dublin made wry jokes about the fact that they were represented in the Dáil by "two Corkmen and a Jew".

The first thing to be done was the selection of a new leader. O'Leary was chosen unanimously to fill the post. The next issue was what the party intended to do about the formation of a Government. O'Leary opened negotiations with Garret FitzGerald, although both parties combined did not have enough Dáil seats to command an overall majority. The two party leaders, with some back-up assistance, worked out a joint programme containing a number of concessions to Labour while retaining Fine Gael's tax proposals from the election manifesto. The concessions to Labour included a 1 per cent income levy to create youth employment, a National Development Corporation with re-sources of £200 million and increases in capital taxation. O'Leary asked for a commitment to a divorce referendum but did not get it.

A special Labour delegate conference was fixed for 28 June in the Gaiety Theatre in Dublin to consider the issue. Most of the Labour TDs backed the proposed coalition. Most critically, Frank Cluskey seconded O'Leary's motion that the deal be accepted. Nonetheless, three newly-elected TDs – Michael D. Higgins, Mervyn Taylor and Toddy O'Sullivan – opposed the deal. Mary Robinson, then a Labour senator, took a hardline left-wing attitude, telling the conference that Labour would be absorbed into Fine Gael in a coalition Government and that the party needed time "to develop its socialist policies and its distinctive identity and organisation".

Dick Spring took a completely different line, making a strong speech in favour of coalition and urging delegates to back the leadership on the issue. More important than his speech, he delivered the Kerry votes for the coalition deal. "I remember standing outside the Gaiety watching this young new TD, Dick Spring, as he organised the Kerry delegates," recalls a Labour TD. "As the Kerry people got off their buses, their names were ticked off and Spring issued them with their delegate cards. From the word go, it was clear that this guy was no novice and he knew what the reality of politics was all about."

"We had the usual thorough briefing from Michael O'Leary on the Sunday morning up in Labour head office which most of us couldn't find at the time," Spring remembers wryly. "We had the conference in the Gaiety. It broke down along very clear lines, for or against coalition.

I can't remember whether I spoke that day but I probably did. I always wanted to be on the stage."

As usual there was vociferous opposition to coalition from Dublin delegates who had failed dismally to get people elected to the Dáil. The loudness of the anti-coalition faction frightened the leadership and they thought the vote was going to be very close. Spring ensured that the Kerry buses did not go home as early as planned and that every last one of his delegates stayed to vote solidly for the deal. It was a gesture that did not go unnoticed by O'Leary. In the end the coalition motion was carried relatively comfortably by 737 votes to 477 but there was little comfort to be taken from the fact that 40 per cent of the conference was opposed to the deal.

Dan Spring, captain of the Kerry football team, brings the Sam Maguire cup home to Kerry in 1940. This photograph was taken in his mother's kitchen; she is left of Dan in the photograph.

Dan Spring and Anna Laide on their wedding day, June 1944.

*Dick Spring as a young child (centre) with his parents Anna
and Dan, brother Arthur and sister Kay.*

*The Spring family. Front, from left: Dan, Donal, Dick, Anna, Noelle.
Back, from left: Kay, Maeve, Arthur.*

Schoolboy Dick Spring, right, with two of his classmates.

Dan and Anna Spring in 1987, the year before Dan died.

Dick Spring at the age of twenty-six, in 1977, at his father's last election count.

Left: William Norton, Labour Party leader from 1932 to 1960.
Below: Brendan Corish, leader of the Labour Party from 1960 to 1977, campaigning in front of the Labour slogan of the sixties.

Right: Michael O'Leary, Labour leader from 1981 to 1982, when he left the party and joined Fine Gael.
Below: Frank Cluskey, who led the party from 1977 to 1981, when he lost his Dáil seat.

Dick Spring was elected leader of the Labour Party in 1982 and led it to its greatest triumph in the 1992 election.

Above: Mary Robinson ran for Labour in Dublin West constituency in the election campaign of 1981. She is photographed here with her running candidates Anne McStay and Eamon Tuffy. None of them was elected.

Right: Dick Spring on being elected party leader in 1982.

*The 1987 election campaign, with Dick Spring, Barry Desmond, Mervyn Taylor and
Eamonn Walsh. Lack of funding for health was one of the main reasons
for the break-up of the Fine Gael-Labour Coalition Government.*

*The all-male Labour parliamentary party in 1987. Left to right: Frank Cluskey,
Toddy O'Sullivan, Michael D. Higgins, Mervyn Taylor, Liam Kavanagh,
Seamus Pattison, Dick Spring, Barry Desmond, Ruairi Quinn,
Michael Bell, Brendan Howlin, Emmet Stagg.*

Celebrating the presidential election victory 1990 with Mary Robinson.

Dick with his mother in 1992.

Attending the Beef Tribunal in 1992, Dick Spring with (left) his brother Donal, solicitor, and his personal assistant Fergus Finlay.

Victory in the 1992 general election, Dick with his mother and his wife.

*After the election of 1992, negotiations open between the Labour Party and Fianna
Fáil. Dick Spring and Albert Reynolds meet at the Berkeley Court Hotel, Dublin.*

Dick Spring, Labour, and Albert Reynolds, Fianna Fáil, leaving the negotiations room at the Berkeley Court Hotel during the discussions which led to the formation of a coalition government in 1993.

The Spring family. Left to right: Kristi, Laura, Dick, Adam (in front) and Aaron.

2
Thrust into Leadership

TRIUMPH AND DISASTER

DICK SPRING WALKED INTO THE DÁIL chamber as a TD for the first time on 30 June 1981, and was made a Minister of State on his first day. He was still a couple of months short of his thirty-first birthday. Most Irish politicians who attained office so easily came to grief later but Spring was to prove the exception. When it came to forming the Government, O'Leary sought five Cabinet posts as in 1977. As the proportionate strength of the two parties had changed since then, FitzGerald refused and initially offered only three. There was a compromise on four Cabinet posts and three junior ministries. Apart from O'Leary, the Cabinet posts went to Liam Kavanagh, Eileen Desmond and Jim Tully.

The surprise omission was Barry Desmond who had to be content with a junior Ministry, Economic Planning. The parliamentary party chairman, Joe Bermingham, got the Office of Public Works, and the third junior ministry, Law Reform, went to Dick Spring. His father had spent thirty-eight years in the House and had held office for less than two years but Dick walked right into office on his first day to much general surprise.

"I remember having a very pleasant conversation with Michael O'Leary a few days before the Government was formed," says Spring. "I had known Michael fairly well. I would have been in his wing of the party, I suppose, prior to having been in the parliamentary party. I met him on the back steps one day as I was leaving Leinster House and he said: 'How are things?' and I said: 'Just fine, catching up with the work.' I said to him: 'Look, my seat is fairly marginal down there so, if there are any appointments around, just keep me in mind. No offence taken one way or the other.' I didn't put any pressure on him. And I met Vincent Browne the day the Dáil was resuming and he told me I was going to be a junior Minister. Vincent Browne told me! That's the way things work in Ireland."

His appointment was due to a number of factors, one of them being that Labour desperately needed to find a youthful face and Spring provided that in a party which was growing increasingly middle-aged. Spring was also regarded as a safe pair of hands, despite his youth. He hadn't been prone to adopt left-wing poses or to cause trouble within the party. His education and political background appeared to indicate somebody who could be trusted by the party leadership and he had delivered the votes at the conference when the call went out.

"So I became a junior Minister. Nobody hands you an envelope with your instructions. You're on your own. I arrived up to the Department of Justice the following morning and parked my car, which I had bought on the strength of becoming a TD. I think it was a second-hand Opel Ascona, a big step up in the world! I parked the car on a double yellow line and was just going up the steps when a Garda came over and put his hand up and said: 'You can't park there.' So I said: 'I'm the new junior Minister in Justice' and he said: 'Oh, I'll keep and eye on your car for you, Minister.'

"I went in and met the secretary in Sean Doherty's old office, and basically took on the job of law reform, which was non-existent in the Department in those days. Ironically, I spent a lot of time working on divorce. I brought in William Duncan from Trinity to help me. We were starting from square one. There was nothing done. Jim Mitchell, the Minister for Justice was upstairs. I often wondered why I could never get in to see him but having been in the Cabinet myself later I realised why. You spend most of your time hurrying around. I tried to grab Jim but he was always rushing and racing."

The first FitzGerald Coalition lasted only eight months. Because Fine Gael and Labour were relying on the support of independents from day one, they were always going to be in a precarious position. The Government's first act was to introduce a draconian mini-budget, which the Minister for Finance, John Bruton, argued was necessary because of the profligacy of Fianna Fáil. Nearly all independent economists supported the Bruton approach but the Government strategy of increased indirect taxation and spending cuts caused huge difficulties for the Labour Party, particularly its Ministers.

In an early blow to O'Leary's leadership, the Administrative Council declared that the Labour Ministers, by agreeing to the mini-budget, had exceeded the mandate they had received from the special conference.

Within Government, Labour Ministers argued against Fine Gael's plans for income tax cuts and, given the financial constraints facing the Government, the cuts were soon abandoned. Barry Desmond annoyed Fine Gael Ministers by publicly calling for the tax reform package to be postponed and he was also the moving spirit behind a decision of the Government not to provide any more funding for Knock airport.

As the Government wrestled with economic problems, its commitment to law reform took a back seat, but Spring was working away when disaster struck on 15 December. His State car, which was being driven by a Garda, crashed head-on into a car driven by an off-duty Garda a mile outside Nenagh on the road to Dublin. A passenger in the other car was killed and it took twenty minutes for firemen to cut Spring out of the wreckage. He was very badly injured and his back was broken in a number of places.

Although the Department of Justice issued a press release minimising his injuries, Spring was in a very bad way. "I spent weeks lying on my back or lying on my face, strapped down in a frame to keep my back in position.

"Luckily I can't remember most of the details. The nurses used to turn me over every hour on the frame which meant I'd be lying down and they would flip me over and take off the top, on which I would have been lying for the previous hour. But because I had a broken arm and a broken leg, as well as the back, they couldn't put my arm into the frame. Invariably they forgot to lift it when turning me and I'd go: 'Where's my arm?' The pain was terrible but I think they kept me well doped up at the time. I was meeting people for a long time afterwards who were saying: 'You were in bad shape when I visited you in hospital.' I'd say: 'Did you visit? I can't remember.'

"I'll never forget visiting Dick Spring in hospital," says Barry Desmond. "One of my sons has arthritis and has had two hip replacements so I have some experience of seeing people laid up. But when I visited Dick after the accident I was shocked. I honestly didn't think he would have the raw courage to stand up and walk again."

Spring's mother recalls the shock of the crash. "It nearly finished me. I was in hospital in Tralee myself with a slight coronary problem and Dick came in to see me the night before. I was worried about him travelling on icy roads but he said: 'The roads are fine, don't worry.' The following morning I heard on the radio that there was ice around

Portlaoise and I travelled every step of the road with him in my mind. Later in the morning, Arthur came in and said: 'The boy has had a skid.' He was driving Kristi up to the hospital in Nenagh and after he left the nurses told me there had been a bit of an accident."

Because of her heart condition, the family wouldn't allow his mother to travel to see Dick in hospital and she wasn't sure how bad he was until he came home. "I went out to see him in the house. He was in bed and looked emaciated but it wasn't until he got out of bed that I realised how bad he was. He was bent over and he could only shuffle about. It was hard to keep back the tears."

Recovery was slow and it left Spring with a permanent stoop and constant pain in his shattered back. His backbone was held together by four large metal pins for over a year. "I got out of hospital anyway and I was down in Kerry. People had heard that I was slightly injured and they used to come in to see me. I was in such bad shape they had to bring a bed downstairs.

"We had just moved into a new house, no carpets down or anything, and we had to borrow rugs and stuff. I used to see people's faces and you'd know from their faces that they were absolutely shocked. I had lost weight, about two stone, I was as pale as a ghost and had to be lifted out of bed. Here I was. I had been comfortably running ten miles a day, just finishing rugby in good form, a healthy athlete and all of a sudden you realise you are not running any more. You may not play any sport any more. The trauma was only beginning to set in. Food meant nothing. For somebody who had been leading a very healthy, active and demanding life, I couldn't get enough to do. I always enjoyed work and all of a sudden felt like a spare part. And we had a young child. Aaron was only six months or so at the time and I couldn't even lift the kid. And he wanted to make his presence felt as well. My poor Kristi was often torn between the two of us. The two of us were like babies, quite honestly." During that time he found it almost impossible to sleep at night. Even after the pins were removed, he suffered a lot which accounted for his often morose expression. To this day he suffers pain, has to survive on little sleep at times and swims every day to relieve the strain on his back. That constant suffering has been a feature of Spring's life but it is something about which he never makes a comment in public or in private.

Two years later, when he was a Minister, he received a settlement from the State of £170,000 for his injuries. As an ordinary citizen he could have fought for and probably received a lot more, but because he was a Government Minister he accepted the State's initial offer. Still, the settlement provided him with a degree of financial security to cushion him against the precarious business of politics.

As Spring lay in hospital, the Government almost came apart in the run-up to the budget of January 1982. Labour Ministers demanded and got agreement to a 25 per cent increase in social welfare payments but the down side of the agreement was the abolition of food subsidies. A week before the budget, O'Leary rang FitzGerald in the middle of the night to say that he couldn't agree to this. Labour Ministers boycotted the next Cabinet meeting until they got a compromise which allowed for the continuation of most of the subsidies.

The resultant revenue gap was plugged by a decision to impose VAT of 18 per cent on clothing and footwear. It was that very decision which brought the Government tumbling down on budget day. A further irony, given his bitter hostility to Labour participation in coalition, was that Noel Browne, now an independent socialist TD, was persuaded to vote with the Government though Jim Kemmy and Sean Dublin Bay Loftus voted against. The budget was beaten and Labour was plunged into an election under O'Leary's leadership.

One incident took place that night which was to have long-term repercussions. Dick Spring was still very ill as he recovered in hospital from his crash injuries. However, Fianna Fáil, on the orders of Charles Haughey, refused to allow him a pair for the budget, which would have allowed him to stay out of the Dáil, and he was brought into the chamber on a stretcher. He was in considerable pain and it took him a long time to forgive Haughey for inflicting the ordeal on him.

"That incident left a very deep scar which wasn't expressed for a considerable time by me," Spring said a few years later in an interview with Sean O'Rourke in *The Irish Press*. "The chances are he many not have known what my personal situation was," added Spring. That could well have been true because the extent of Spring's injuries was not widely known at the time. Nonetheless, Haughey's insistence on dragging him into the Dáil in the circumstances was something he never forgot.

Spring recalls a nightmare plane journey in a Cessna from Kerry to Dublin and then a car journey to the Dáil where he spent the afternoon lying on a couch in Joe Bermingham's ground-floor office because he wasn't able to make it to his own office upstairs. As it happened, he then had to face a general election.

"So, then, it was the election and maybe that's what I needed to recover. All of a sudden, I forgot about my stomach pains and my problem with not eating. The story about me had now changed. Firstly it was that I had been slightly injured. Jim Mitchell had put out a statement that it was a minor accident – you always minimise these things. But then, because I wasn't seen for two or three weeks in North Kerry, the word was out that I was never going to walk again and that I was in bad shape. I couldn't stand or walk or do anything.

"Now the lads said: 'You had better come out and be seen on the platform.' I remember distinctly trying to get on to a trailer at the back of a tractor in Ballyheigue. It was like a plank and the boys just had to put me up and push me back. I had to stand there with a stick and speak. It was really a case of: 'Look, I am alive, I am walking; there's no wheelchair.' Whatever it was – the sympathy factor? – the vote went up."

Despite the grim circumstances of the election, Labour didn't do too badly. The party's share of the vote slipped to just over 9 per cent but it held on to fifteen seats. Dick Spring was unable to campaign as he was returned to hospital after the Dáil vote. However, his family and the Labour organisation pulled out all the stops. Kristi threw herself into the campaign along with the rest of the Spring family and he romped home comfortably with 8,278 first preferences, an increase of over 2,500 votes on the election of the previous June.

On a national level, Fine Gael lost three seats and Fianna Fáil gained three, which still left nobody with an overall majority. However, the odds were in favour of Fianna Fáil who managed to win the support of the four Workers' Party TDs and independent socialist Tony Gregory to get Charles Haughey re-elected as Taoiseach. Before the Dáil met, Fianna Fáil entered its convulsive phase with the first of the three heaves against Haughey's leadership in the space of a year. Haughey saw off the challenge but it demonstrated how volatile the political situation had become.

On the Labour side, the Administrative Council decided, shortly before the Dáil was due to meet, that the party should rule out coalition. The move caused intense bitterness in the party. The Council was split right down the middle and Michael D. Higgins gave his casting vote against another coalition with Fine Gael. O'Leary was furious with the decision and from that moment he decided to try to wrest control of the party and key decision-making away from the left wing.

The Haughey Government which took office in March 1982 lasted only a little longer than the first FitzGerald Government. Its minority status made its position very precarious from the outset. Things began to look increasingly rocky in the summer and autumn of 1982, when the Government entered its "GUBU" phase. There was controversy surrounding the Minister for Justice, Sean Doherty. Then came the incredible saga of Malcolm McArthur being discovered in the Attorney General's apartment. It was downhill all the way after that. In October, Haughey had to fight off the second attempt on his leadership within the space of a year and Des O'Malley and Martin O'Donoghue resigned from the Government.

Michael O'Leary decided to prepare for a general election by getting Labour to rethink its policy on the fundamental issue of coalition. He had no confidence in the existing Labour strategy, which left the decision on whether or not to enter Government to a delegate conference after an election. This policy had been adopted during the leadership of Frank Cluskey as a way of solving Labour's annual battles on the coalition issue and it had taken the decision on coalition out of the hands of the elected TDs and given it to a delegate conference.

O'Leary wanted to get decision-making power back for the elected TDs. Critically, he also wanted the freedom to enter a pre-election pact with another party, believing that Labour would do much better electorally if it were in a position to tell the voters at the beginning of an election campaign what it would do when the results were in, rather than waiting until after it.

The issue was put to the test at Labour's annual conference in Galway on the last weekend of October. Passions ran high from the outset. Party chairman Michael D. Higgins opened the conference with a ringing denunciation of coalition and outright opposition to his party leader's proposal. "We have to move beyond compassion and protection and take steps to build the real alternative to our present society – a socialist society," he said, arguing against any coalition with Fine Gael. "If this party will not stand firm for socialism, it will find that there are others who will or who will be perceived to do so."

Maeve Kennedy, writing in *The Irish Times* the following morning, 23 October, recorded that Dick Spring sat through Michael D.'s speech with his head propped on his hands, alongside other anxious-looking TDs. "The most worrying sound to their ears must have been, not the small, thin passionate voice of Michael D. but the constant deep rumble of support for him from the hall."

The issue was decided on the second day of the conference after a long and passionate debate. Dick Spring was unambiguously on O'Leary's side. In fact, he was one of the TDs most committed to the party leader's line. He was probably closer to O'Leary at that time than any other member of the parliamentary party and was frequently in the leader's company that weekend. Urging the conference to support O'Leary's resolution, he rejected the claim made by many speakers that coalition was to blame for falling support. He said that in the June 1981 election he had got 5,685 votes but in the election of February 1982, following the collapse of the coalition, he had increased it to over eight thousand.

In his own keynote speech to conference, O'Leary made a strong appeal for support. "I ask you to reject those approaches to the coalition issue which would effectively align us against participation in Government or would confine us to external support. I ask you also to reject the resolution which seeks, in effect, to take no decision tonight but to wait for yet another conference."

O'Leary managed to make it over the first hurdle. He fought off the left amid a confusing jumble of votes on anti-coalition motions and won a narrow victory by 657 votes to 523. Michael D. Higgins and Mervyn Taylor were the only two TDs to support the outright anti-coalition motion. However, on the question of allowing the parliamentary party and the Administrative Council to make the decisions on coalition and election strategy, O'Leary suffered a humiliating rebuff. The spearhead of the attack came from his old enemy, Frank Cluskey, who proposed an amendment to the leader's motion. Instead of leaving the decision to the elected TDs and the Administrative Council, the Cluskey amendment reserved the decision to a special post-election delegate conference.

Barry Desmond threw his influential weight behind Cluskey, arguing that a special conference, with full information before it about the results of any negotiations, was the best forum to make a decision on coalition. When the vote was taken, the Cluskey amendment was carried by 671 votes to 498. Spring and the Kerry delegates backed O'Leary to the end but their disciplined bloc vote was swamped in the tide running against the party leader. It was not just the left who were jubilant at his defeat. Senior figures like Cluskey and Desmond had demonstrated that they were unhappy with him as well.

None of them, however, anticipated O'Leary's next move. When the conference was over he proceeded to follow the logic of his position to its conclusion. In a move which astounded his enemies as well as his allies and rocked the Labour Party to its foundations, he resigned from the leadership and from the party.

In a statement issued four days later he said: "I have reluctantly concluded that I cannot contest the next general election guided by an electoral strategy in which I have no confidence. This is the most difficult and the most painful decision I have made in my public career. I leave the Labour Party with no bitterness, holding the lifelong friendships I have made. I wish the party well and hope to see it emerge as a strong force within our political system. It is important for the future of our political system. It is important for the future of our democracy that the Labour Party should grow stronger and I believe that, given time, this may occur. The challenge confronting our country is greater than at any time since independence. In the national interest, for all our sakes, there must be a change of Government at the next election. I intend to do everything in my power to bring about that change."

The shock in the Labour ranks was palpable, particularly as an immediate general election was widely anticipated. Dick Spring was as surprised as anybody else by the announcement, despite the fact that there were rumours flying around Leinster House that he might follow O'Leary's example. "It's unfortunate that Michael O'Leary has made this decision. He has made a tremendous contribution to the party over the years, especially during his period as Minister for Labour. I am sure his decision was not easily made," was Spring's response, but he made it clear that he had no intention of following suit.

"The internecine strife and the bitterness in Labour was terrible," says Spring, with the benefit of a decade to look back on those events. "We had reached the worst point heading up to the Galway conference. Micko had lost it to a large extent. He even went missing during the

East Galway by-election. Coming up to the conference, I think he decided to have one last shot at it, and that was the Galway strategy. I backed him there. Frank Cluskey and Barry Desmond, without telling anybody, tried to hedge their bets.

"O'Leary tried for his ultimate gamble. Things had become so contrary for him. Parliamentary party meetings were totally unsatisfactory, and it had got to the stage where there just wasn't any possible way he could pull it back together. It was so divided; the parliamentary party and the AC were just nightmare stuff during the previous Government and it was still that way. So at least he did the right thing. We tend not to forgive him. Of course he should have stayed in the party after resigning as leader but that wasn't his style. He was always a man for going to the extreme and he threw us into chaos."

At the time, the party chairman and leader of the left, Michael D. Higgins, said he was shocked and astounded, adding that he found the manner of the announcement disturbing. Ruairi Quinn was more blunt and summed up the feeling of many in the party when he said: "We need this like a hole in the head."

UNEXPECTED ELEVATION

THE SUDDEN DEPARTURE of O'Leary left Labour in a dreadful dilemma. The country was in the middle of a political crisis caused by the erosion of support for the Fianna Fáil minority Government. It was beset by problems following the publication of its programme *The Way Forward* which outlined a whole series of severe public spending cuts. With one Fianna Fáil TD, Bill Loughnane, dying suddenly and another, Jim Gibbons, critically ill, the Workers' Party and Tony Gregory, who had kept Charles Haughey in power, decided his Government was doomed and they prepared to abandon him.

It was in this atmosphere of crisis that the Labour Party TDs met to select a new leader. O'Leary resigned on a Thursday. The new leader was selected the following Tuesday and a general election was called two days later. It was a baptism of fire if ever there was one.

For the first day or so after O'Leary resigned, Dick Spring didn't figure in the media as a possible successor. Ruairi Quinn recalls being at a branch meeting when Spring's name was first mentioned and somebody remarked that the bookies were giving odds of ten to one on Spring. "I turned to Dermot Lacey, who was handling our election debt and I said: 'Put £100 on Spring and we'll clear our campaign debts.' Unfortunately, by the time he went to the bookies' they had changed their odds."

The initial focus of attention was on former leader Frank Cluskey, deputy leader Barry Desmond, and on long-serving Wicklow TD Liam Kavanagh. It was the decision of both Cluskey and Kavanagh not to go for the leadership that catapulted Spring into the frame. Cluskey thought about it very seriously but decided that, with his own Dáil seat in such a risky position, he couldn't take the chance of trying to lead the party again. Kavanagh simply decided that he wouldn't be suitable for the job, though he made it clear that he saw himself as a Minister in any coalition Government.

Of the leading TDs from the mainstream of the party, only Barry Desmond threw his hat into the ring. Desmond had been one of the most prominent Labour figures for well over a decade but had been passed over for office in the Cosgrave Coalition and had been given merely a junior Ministry by O'Leary in 1981. An extremely able and courageous politician who was never afraid to take a stand on an issue that concerned him, Desmond had, by those very qualities, alienated many of his colleagues.

A TD for Dun Laoghaire since 1969, he held his seat against the odds on a number of occasions. He stood firmly in the mainstream of the party and was never afraid to take on left-wing opponents within and conservative opponents outside, regardless of popularity. Desmond's abrasive style did not endear him to the left and the positive relish he took in confrontation also frightened off potential supporters. They might secretly have agreed with him as he excoriated the left-wingers on the Administrative Council, particularly Michael D. Higgins, but they were not sure about the wisdom of such tactics in a party leader. Cluskey, once he had made up his mind not to run himself, agreed to nominate Desmond for the post.

Party chairman Michael D. Higgins also entered the race to carry the torch for the left. Former Labour TD John Horgan provides the following description of Michael D. Higgins: "The most prominent – and permanent – opponent of coalition and the most staunch advocate of further policy development within the party as a means of wooing the electorate has been Michael D. Higgins. His position in the party has been as chairman for a number of years now, but it would also probably be true to say that it is also, partly, that of a mascot. At the party's annual conference, where he will be rapturously applauded even by people who would be slow to vote for him in a contest, he makes the most of his chairman's address. The fact that his accent is a curious amalgam of phonemes from Clare, Galway, Dublin and academia in general is not a drawback. If anything, it seems to add to the fascination of his verbal flourishes as, sweating lightly under the arc-lights, he seems practically to levitate with the passion of his indictment of all that is wrong with Irish society."

With these two candidates of decidedly opposing views lining up for a battle, Labour TDs cast around for an alternative and the spotlight fell on Dick Spring. He was largely an unknown quantity but he was young, he came from a traditional Labour background, held a safe seat (or so everybody assumed) and he was clearly sensible and moderate in his views. Liam Kavanagh and Ruairi Quinn pushed Spring to run but he was initially reluctant because of his back problems which still left him in severe pain. However, with enough powerful backing to guarantee him the job, Spring didn't resist for too long.

When the fourteen Labour TDs gathered to make the decision on 1 November 1982, three candidates were nominated. Barry Desmond was proposed by Frank Cluskey, Michael D. Higgins was nominated by Mervyn Taylor and Dick Spring was proposed by Michael Moynihan from South Kerry and seconded by Liam Kavanagh. The TDs discussed the issue before putting it to a vote and every single one gave their views on the leadership question. With a clear majority of TDs around the table expressing their support for Spring, the drift became obvious. There was an adjournment while Frank Cluskey and Barry Desmond went to another room to confer, and when they came back Desmond announced that he was retiring from the contest.

"I was in no way upset at not becoming leader," says Desmond, looking back. "I know I would have found it difficult to accept the huge constraints which leadership imposes. There are times when one should let fly and I have never pulled back. As deputy leader I could continue to be very up-front with my views, both internally in the Labour Party and externally."

There was some pressure put on Michael D. to do likewise but he refused and the issue was put to a vote which went twelve to two in Spring's favour. Only Michael D. himself and Mervyn Taylor opposed Spring who, at the age of thirty-two, became the youngest party leader since William Norton took over Labour at the same age in 1932.

"The leadership came about ten years earlier than I planned it," says Spring. "I think people started manoeuvring for position. There weren't too many really. Barry Desmond was trying to set himself up. Michael D. was trying to set himself up. And I think the middle-ground people, like Toddy O'Sullivan, Liam Kavanagh and Michael Moynihan, in particular, decided they would go for somebody new and young. It all happened very fast.

"I had planned to be leader. I had actually put a bet on in my Trinity days that I was going to lead the party and I collected it too. A long time later but I got my £50 from quite a successful businessman. That was an ambitious bet back around 1972. But I would have thought, in terms of political planning, that one would have wanted to be around the place and to have had front-bench, if not governmental, experience for some time before even aspiring to the leadership.

"So, in that context, I would have said it would need about ten years to build oneself up for it as a politician of standing. Ironically, I had to do it the other way around. I had to spend four years in Government and wait until 1987 to get a chance to establish myself as party leader. Ideally, if you become a leader of a party, you probably need the opportunity of opposition, to get space and time. It all happened so fast at a time when the party was so absolutely disorganised."

It was an enormous challenge for the young leader. The party he took over in November 1982, was one in steep decline, deeply demoralised, racked by division. Of the fourteen TDs ten represented rural constituencies and the party was clearly in deep trouble in the capital city. O'Leary, who had joined Fine Gael the day Spring took over as Labour leader, had now gone the way of most other bright hopes of the 1960s like Conor Cruise O'Brien, David Thornley, Justin Keating and John Horgan.

Still, Spring put the best face on it at a press conference immediately after his election. Labour, he said, had a major role to play in redressing the economic and social difficulties facing the nation. He conceded that the party had allowed itself to be run down and its organisation weakened but he still claimed there was hope for the future. At the time few could share his optimism.

"Apart from the political side of it, there were all the worries about the physical side. Strictly speaking, I wasn't ready for it, politically or organisationally. I was thrown in at the deep end. In fact, I remember distinctly I had never been interviewed by Brian Farrell. I had never been on *Today Tonight* – or *Seven Days* as it was in those days – before I became leader, so that was really plunging in at the deep end. It's hard to believe in retrospect. I recall, after the first press conference as leader, eating economics for about two hours before going to meet Brian Farrell, who asked me all about politics."

Two days after he became Labour leader, the country was plunged into the expected general election when Fianna Fáil were beaten in the Dáil on a confidence motion. With many people now writing Labour off, Spring was up against it from the beginning but he fought a skilful election campaign. His political inexperience was not a handicap to the voters who welcomed him as a new face.

He had a number of balancing acts to perform during the campaign. "I had the curious situation of trying to appeal to the voters of Castleisland and all they wanted was a mains drainage scheme while the BBC were trying to follow me to find out what I was about. And you were conscious of wanting to avoid sending out to the world the signal that the issue in the election was a drainage scheme or whatever."

He also showed political courage on the abortion issue. During the first election of 1982, Haughey and FitzGerald had agreed to a request from the Pro-Life campaign to hold a referendum on a constitutional amendment to prohibit abortion. The wording for this amendment was produced by the Haughey Government as the second election of 1982 got underway. FitzGerald agreed to accept the wording but Spring said no and refused to be budged from his position. It was a courageous act for a novice political leader and his refusal to be bullied into it showed shrewd political judgement.

"On the abortion amendment, I have always felt strongly about the privacy of the individual. And I got an awful lot of hassle. But I brought in good advice. I had John Rogers and Dermot Gleeson advising me and my own brother was giving me medical advice. We spent about three days identifying the weaknesses in the Pro-Life amendment, all of which came to be exposed in time."

During the campaign he undertook a 1,600-mile tour of the country with the twin objectives of trying to win Labour seats and revitalise an organisation shocked by O'Leary's departure. He was never under any illusion about the difficult choices that would await him if Labour held the balance of power after the election. During the campaign, he told Sean MacConnell of *The Irish Press*, who accompanied him on his election tour, that the bottom line for his party in any coalition deal would be capital tax on the rich, reform of the PAYE system and no spending cuts at the expense of the poor. "To be honest with you, I have a completely open mind on the whole coalition question. But if it is to be, those are some of the things I'll be asking for. This is not going to be a coalition like the last one between 1973 and 1977."

When the results of the second 1982 election, held on 24 November, were counted, Spring could feel proud of his performance. He confounded the prophets of doom, some of them in his own party, who had predicted annihilation in the wake of the O'Leary resignation. Labour pushed up its national share of the vote to almost 9.5 per cent and the party gained two extra seats. With Fine Gael gaining seven, to bring its total to a record seventy deputies in the Dáil, just five short of Fianna Fáil, the way was open for another Fine Gael-Labour Coalition.

Spring's problem now was that, while his colleagues acknowledged he had saved Labour from disaster, he was pitchforked into a situation where he had to make critical decisions. One problem was that because of his youth and relative inexperience he didn't have any trusted friends or even close political allies in the parliamentary party. He began his career as a TD by being close to O'Leary, who was now a Fine Gael TD, excoriated as a traitor by most members of the Labour Party, and had succeeded to the leadership before he had time to build any power base of his own.

Faced with a situation where he had to make crucial choices for both the party and the country, Spring didn't feel he could seek out the party elders. Instead, he turned to two close friends, John Rogers and Joe Revington.

Rogers was then, and still is, Dick Spring's best friend and closest political advisor. When Spring was elected in 1981 and was immediately made a junior Minister with responsibility for Law Reform, he relied heavily on advice from his old TCD room-mate, who by that stage was a rising star of the bar. That support became even more important once he became party leader.

Writing about Rogers and Spring a few years later, journalist Peter Murtagh commented: "Both men have similar personalities. In public they can appear shy and reserved, almost austere, while in private they can be wry and witty. Mr Rogers is very tall, has dark features and, when he is pleased, a big wide smile."

Joe Revington was another long-time friend and his associations with Spring went even further back. A Kerry Protestant, Revington was from Spring's home town of Tralee and had campaigned for Dan Spring from 1969 onwards. He, too, had been to Trinity and had been involved in student politics. A realist in the rural Labour tradition, Revington kept an eye on the constituency and was more *au fait* with the internal workings of the party than Rogers.

The third important figure in the Spring entourage at this stage was Pat Magner. A working-class Labour activist from Cork, who had been a hard-line left-winger in his early days, Magner was appointed national organiser of the party by Michael O'Leary. Known within the Labour party for his meticulous organisational abilities, his wit and his down-to-earth charm, Magner had moved very much to the centre of the party by the time O'Leary appointed him to the job. Spring got to know Magner during O'Leary's tenure, and having to face into an immediate general election, kept him on as a vital part of his own team.

Apart from these three individuals, Spring relied on his parents for advice and support during and after the election of November 1982. Dan and Anna had a fund of political experience between them and Dick consulted them about local and national issues. It was his own family and his close friends that Spring called on at this critical stage, a pattern that was to continue right through his leadership, to the intense irritation of the left.

Both his family and advisors were agreed that he should begin talks on the formation of a coalition with Garret FitzGerald. Negotiations began a week after the election and a fortnight before the opening of the new Dáil. "The level of disorganisation in the party at that time was appalling. It was the world's worst. There was no back-up; there was nothing in terms of organisation. We tried to put a team together, round up the usual suspects, people like William Scally, and start negotiating," recalls Spring.

"I suppose it was almost a formality in terms of starting negotiations. There were no options. There was the Haughey scene and there was no point talking to Fianna Fáil so I started talks with Garret FitzGerald in a convent in Eglington Road. John Rogers organised it and we got away with it for a long time, actually. We had to leave it on one occasion. The nuns had something on and we had to find alternative accommodation, so we took over the McCullough household in Dartmouth Square for a day."

In the unlikely surroundings of the Good Shepherd Convent at Eglington Road in Donnybrook, the talks went well. With the nuns supplying the negotiators with tea and coffee, Spring and FitzGerald carried out their discussions in front of a big open fire and under the gaze of the Infant of Prague. The Labour and Fine Gael leaders barely knew each other and had to develop a relationship in the course of the negotiations.

"Although Dick and I knew each other only slightly at that stage we soon established a rapport, based on our common commitment to social democratic values and to integrity in public life," FitzGerald recorded in his autobiography.

While the two leaders certainly shared many values, they also had some serious differences. Labour wanted big increases in capital taxation, a wealth tax and a property tax and rejected Fine Gael proposals to eliminate the budget deficit over four years. Spring also insisted on the indexation of social welfare payments during the lifetime of the Government and sought the establishment of a National Development Corporation with £500 million in capital to initiate industrial projects.

"In the negotiations there were one or two difficulties. We had to bring Frank Cluskey in a few times. I remember one day in particular, Frank had a go at Alan Dukes, who was there as a technical expert with Garret. With Frank it was politics, not facts and figures. It worked out all right. There was one other sticky moment when Garret was going off abroad to some meeting of the Christian Democrats and the talks were going nowhere at that time. So I said: 'Look, if you want to form a Government, you had better stay on the island,' so he did."

Fine Gael's priorities were a little different from Labour's but they assumed a deal would be put together. The party wanted to tackle the budgetary crisis as a priority and were opposed to capital taxation. There was no disagreement on increasing social welfare, although Fine Gael didn't want to be tied to indexation.

The two leaders hammered out a programme for Government without too much difficulty. Garret himself saw no problem with concessions to Labour, such as the introduction of a residential property tax, but others on the Fine Gael team were unhappy with it. In fact, FitzGerald records that an income-related property tax was an idea of his own on which he had worked during 1982 with his daughter-in-law, Eithne Fitzgerald, who was then a Labour councillor and who is now junior Minister in the Tánaiste's office.

Despite FitzGerald's support for it during the negotiations, the property tax was criticised by some Fine Gael TDs as representing an unacceptable element of Labour ideology. John Kelly spoke for them when he said the proposal was "neither rational nor capable of being fairly implemented". Stephen O'Byrnes, in his book on Garret FitzGerald's Fine Gael, *Hiding Behind the Face*, writes that the property tax was seen as "simply screwing Fine Gael supporters" and a "blunt concession to socialism". It was symptomatic of the problems that would arise between the two parties in Government. Fine Gael TDs had so little idea of what their own leader was at that they often blamed Labour in the wrong.

There was, however, agreement in the programme on extra capital taxation and a commitment to minimising the impact of any spending cuts on the less well-off. While Garret got the elimination of Government borrowing stated as an aspiration in the agreed programme, no concrete steps towards the achievement of the objective were outlined.

Most of the negotiation was carried on directly between the two leaders, with the advisors in the wings. Rogers, Magner and Revington met Spring each morning for breakfast in Rogers's flat to plan their strategy. Deputy leader Barry Desmond and former leader Frank Cluskey also took part in the talks from time to time but were not centrally involved and intervened only when invited by Spring.

Garret FitzGerald relied on his long-time friend and political ally, James Dooge, and also Gemma Hussey and Alan Dukes. Even though he had been Minister for Finance in the first FitzGerald Government, John Bruton was not consulted by Garret in the course of the talks and he learned with surprise and anger of Alan Dukes's role when he read about it in the newspapers.

The negotiations began on 1 December and went on for more than a week. A Labour delegate conference was planned for 12 December in Limerick and the programme had to be ready by then.

Spring was under no illusion about the fact that he would have to take on the very substantial anti-coalition faction in the Labour Party, led by prominent figures like party chairman, Michael D. Higgins, who had just lost his Dáil seat. Dublin TD, Mervyn Taylor, was another leading anti-coalitionist and there was deep hostility to going into Government again from many members of the party organisation in Dublin.

The selection of Limerick as a venue was regarded as a ploy by Spring to ensure that the rural constituencies would be well-represented. Spring, however, was in a relatively strong position, having performed well in the election after being catapulted suddenly into the leadership.

After the coalition deal was agreed, however, he felt exhausted and needed somebody to write him a rousing speech for the Limerick conference. He asked Pat Magner's advice and was given an inspired choice. Fergus Finlay was a young personnel officer with the Cork company, Ridge Tool Ireland Ltd. He had formerly been a union official with the Local Government and Public Services Union and was involved in Labour politics. Magner had involved him in the party and in June 1981, when it appeared that Michael O'Leary might be in trouble in his Dublin constituency, Finlay had produced a mock newspaper with the headline: "O'Leary is more popular than Charlie Haughey." Magner paid a few newsboys in Dublin Central to insert the production into the Sunday newspapers.

Now he suggested Finlay's name to Spring and the Labour leader asked for a draft speech. Magner rang Finlay and gave him the outlines of what Spring wanted to say. Finlay stayed up all night and produced a speech that fitted the bill exactly. Up to that point he hadn't known Dick Spring, but when the Government was formed he was appointed assistant Government press secretary and became a pivotal aide to the Labour leader, forming an inner circle along with Rogers and Magner.

The special delegate conference in Limerick's Savoy Hotel was closed to the media to allow delegates to speak their minds freely. After a day of impassioned debate, the programme for Government was ratified by 846 votes to 522 but it was no easy ride for Spring.

"There were clear lines of division – the coalitionists and the anti-coalitionists and ne'er the twain should meet. Conference reflected that. It was fairly vicious stuff and a lot of it was very personalised. You were just assumed guilty by the other side and the unfortunate aspect of it was that we won that conference by around eight hundred and something to five hundred and something. The margin was tight enough, and once the conference was over four or five hundred people, active members of the party, were campaigning against coalition," says Spring.

On the Fine Gael side, the decision on the programme was taken by the party's TDs. They were happier about it than were the Labour delegates, with John Kelly being the only voice of opposition. "In today's conditions, my feeling is that the Labour element is likely to make the Government's task more difficult. There are certain measures, which might be desirable, dealing with the general finances of the State, and the relationship between private enterprise and the State, which Labour cannot accept," Kelly declared with prescience.

SQUABBLING PARTNERS

DICK SPRING AT THE AGE OF THIRTY-TWO, with just eighteen months' experience as a TD and just one month as party leader, was now Tánaiste. It had been an extraordinary rise in the political world and would have been a daunting prospect for anybody, let alone someone of his limited political experience. He joked that he had gone from being a barman in New York to being Tánaiste all in the space of a couple of years. The fact that his three Labour Cabinet colleagues, Frank Cluskey, Barry Desmond and Liam Kavanagh, had a wealth of political experience served only to point up Spring's lack of it.

He was a little overawed by his rapid rise to political eminence. Within the Labour party he was conscious of his lack of experience compared with people like Frank Cluskey, Barry Desmond, Liam Kavanagh and parliamentary party chairman Joe Bermingham. However, he did have the invaluable political experience of his parents to fall back on, as well as that of his close-knit set of advisors.

Within Government he was conscious of the intellectual capabilities of FitzGerald and Dukes and had the feeling, probably mistaken, that they regarded him as an intellectual lightweight. While he was certainly no economist, and still isn't, Spring had the advantage of a basic political grounding on his way to winning and holding the family seat in Kerry. That was the kind of invaluable political experience which would stand to him in the end. Spring was deeply insulted when, only a few weeks after he took office, Peter Barry described him as "a sheep in sheep's clothing".

He was never quick to forgive insults. There is a prickly side to his nature which expresses itself in a dry humour which can quickly become barbed if the occasion demands.

"Dick is touchy, particularly if he feels somebody is trying to look down on him in any way. He is a middle-class person from a working-class background. That is the secret of his strengths and weaknesses," says one person who knows him well.

His touchiness exists side by side with a wry charm and a disarming modesty. Which side of him people see depends on how he gets along with them. "Dick makes up his mind about people and that is that. If he decides you are a gobshite, then he will treat you as such and make no attempt to hide his feelings. That's just the way he is," says a person who had regular dealings with him over the past decade.

From the beginning, however, Taoiseach Garret FitzGerald was impressed by Spring. "I had been heartened by my experience of negotiating the formation of the Government with Dick Spring, and I believed that at a personal level he and I could work well together. It was clear to me that he was a serious politician. We shared many of the same values; my own instinctive sympathy with the younger generation, derived from my years as a university teacher and from what I had learnt from my own children, would, I believed, help me to overcome the age gap between Dick and myself, although it might take some time for him to feel entirely comfortable with someone so much older." That assessment was made years later but it appears to reflect FitzGerald's genuine affection for Spring particularly in the early stages of Government.

Spring acknowledges that his rapport with FitzGerald was good in spite of the difficulties they faced. "Our own personal relationship was very good and I must say, in all fairness, that we had a good working relationship. We tried to work together to avoid problems. I suppose one of the difficulties from my point of view was that my constituency is almost as far away as you can get in Ireland and the demands of the constituency were enormous."

Barry Desmond says that Spring adapted very well to his responsibilities. "It was quite an extraordinary performance from a man who was a generation younger than Garret. Yet he had more basic political cop-on than Garret, in the same way as Peter Barry had. Dick and Peter were excellent chairmen of Cabinet when Garret was away. Dick could dispose of an agenda in a cryptic way and there was no prolonged, argumentative debate. Essentially Dick is a doer rather than a talker and is not very happy making speeches. He reminds me of his father in that respect."

The other Labour members in Cabinet responded to their position in different ways. Liam Kavanagh never said much but was regarded as a wise owl with a cool head and a shrewd judgement of what would or wouldn't be politically acceptable. His contribution on the major issues before Cabinet was minimal but he provided some solid advice. Frank Cluskey never settled down in Government. He engaged in frequent and furious rows with Fine Gael Ministers, particularly John Bruton, and never established a relationship based on trust with Garret FitzGerald.

Barry Desmond, on the other hand, adjusted to Government as if he had been born for the job. Although he immersed himself in his own departments, he also took an interest in wider Government business and was ready to challenge Department of Finance memoranda at any and every opportunity. "Dick Spring was at least as lost as myself, I think, in the maze of figures; Barry Desmond was extremely impressive," Gemma Hussey recorded after just a month in office.

Desmond had the two biggest spending departments in the State, Health and Social Welfare. As a Labour Minister he tried to protect the budgets of both while implementing necessary reforms. The elimination of anomalies in social welfare, which meant that people on short time could earn more than those who worked a full week, and his rationalisation of the health service embroiled Desmond in bitter internal Labour rows, while he was also engaged in Cabinet wrangles to protect his departments from further cuts.

In the Cabinet room, Garret sat in middle of the table with the Cabinet Secretary, Dermot Nally, on his left. Initially, Spring sat on Nally's left but both he and FitzGerald found the arrangement unsatisfactory for exchanges between Taoiseach and Tánaiste. Accordingly, after a few weeks in office, the seating arrangements around the Cabinet table were changed and Spring sat opposite FitzGerald, beside the Minister for Finance, Alan Dukes. The Taoiseach was flanked, according to tradition, by the Cabinet Secretary and the Attorney General, Peter Sutherland.

The Fine Gael-Labour Coalition faced immediate problems. The budget led to a public clash between Dick Spring and Alan Dukes which has gone down in the folklore of both parties as an example of how unworkable the Coalition was from the beginning. The dispute was seen then and later as a straight fight between Labour and Fine Gael and appeared to justify John Kelly's prediction about their fundamental incompatibility.

In fact, the Taoiseach sided with the Tánaiste against his own Minister for Finance, so the ultimate responsibility for the budgetary strategy of 1983 rested with FitzGerald. In the Fine Gael mythology, the incident demonstrated that Labour was unfit to take the tough decisions but, according to FitzGerald's own account, he had come around to the same position as Spring even before the Labour leader went public on his differences with Alan Dukes.

What happened was that on 9 January 1983, less than a month after taking office, the new Minister for Finance, Alan Dukes, went on radio to say that the budget deficit for the year would have to be cut from the £900 million in Fianna Fáil's proposed estimates to £750 million.

Dukes faced an immediate public challenge on the matter from Spring, who was in Dr Steevens's Hospital at the time for a very painful operation to get four metal pins removed from his back. His economic advisor, Willie Scally, went to Spring and told him that he must take an instant stand against unilateral pronouncements by Ministers in advance of Government decisions. Spring agreed completely. He issued a statement saying there was no agreement between the two parties in Government on the size of the deficit and he phoned Garret FitzGerald to inform him of his action and to make known his anger.

However, Spring found that he was pushing an open door, because FitzGerald had already come to the conclusion that Department of Finance officials were being too alarmist. "They seemed to feel that unless the current deficit were reduced to a figure close to £750 million in 1983, external confidence in our economy might wither, and our ability to borrow this sum, plus our capital needs, might thus be prejudiced. Alan Dukes, pitchforked into the Finance portfolio in the most adverse circumstances conceivable, was in no position to challenge this rather apocalyptic view of his officials," writes FitzGerald in his autobiography.

The Taoiseach then took the extraordinary decision to cross-check his own Finance Department's forecasts with none other than Henry Kissinger, who was running a consultancy service in New York. FitzGerald rang Kissinger and asked him to check in the New York financial markets to establish what the reaction would be to an Irish current budget deficit of £900 million rather than £750 million.

On 10 January, the day after Dukes's radio interview, Kissinger rang back to say the expectation in New York was that the Irish Government would be going for a current budget deficit of about £900 million, which would leave the exchequer borrowing requirement for the year at 12 per cent of GNP. "This conversation, which seemed to confirm my suspicion that Finance had been overstating its case, provided me with good grounds for rejecting its demand for a £750 million current deficit. The Department, which presumably had not previously had its advice challenged by a cross-check of this kind, was, not surprisingly, furious. Within hours, Alan Dukes – under pressure from his advisors, I assumed – came out publicly in favour of a £750 million deficit," records FitzGerald.

In fact, Dukes had made his statement the day before Garret records that he heard from Kissinger, so it does not appear to have been a peevish response by Finance to being by-passed for advice as FitzGerald imagines. However, the Dukes statement in a Sunday radio interview prompted the immediate hostile public reaction from Spring and a phone call to FitzGerald. The Taoiseach visited his Tánaiste in hospital to discuss the issue and it was considered by the Cabinet two days later.

A statement issued after the Cabinet meeting said: "There has been concern on the part of the Taoiseach, the Tánaiste and a number of Ministers of both parties that the figure of £750 million, which the Minister for Finance has mentioned as a target to aim at, should be taken as reflecting a Government decision on a matter that is still under review." Dukes was then forced to abandon his plans and ultimately come up with a budget which contained the higher current deficit target of £900 million.

The incident was probably the critical moment in the lifetime of the FitzGerald Coalition. It meant that the Government effectively settled in its first month in office for a policy of containment with regard to the public finances. The real task of confronting Exchequer borrowing was put off for four years with dire consequences for both Government parties but particularly, in the long term, for Fine Gael.

In Fine Gael eyes the incident has achieved the status of a millstone which Labour hung around the Government's neck but, as FitzGerald's account makes clear, the responsibility rested equally with both parties in Government. Whether the Government could have done anything else, apart from fudge the issue in January 1983, is open to question. FitzGerald had clearly no more desire than Spring to cut borrowing still further and even if both had agreed to go for the lower figure the Government could possibly have collapsed due to the defection of Labour deputies.

The subsequent Social Welfare Bill, which contained cutbacks in the pay-related social welfare provisions, showed just how frail the Coalition was. Labour TD, Michael Bell, voted against the Bill, while Frank Prendergast eventually abstained after threatening to oppose it. Spring's position was clearly vulnerable, even within the agreed borrowing targets. "Deputy Bell and Senator Christie Kirwan were offside within a month of going into Government," he says. "There were some fierce doses of the wobbles at an early stage. Parliamentary party meetings were going on for hours and hours and there was fierce wracking of consciences by people in relation to aspects of the Social Welfare Bill, or whatever. So ultimately it was difficult. That was the politics of it and, of course, I think there were people who were disgruntled because they hadn't been appointed to Government."

The kind of cuts being recommended by Finance would, in the long term, have been better for the national economy, and might ultimately have benefited the two parties in Government if their partnership were to prove capable of enduring. But, as the Labour unease showed, there was no guarantee at all of that.

Spring takes the view that the Government just couldn't have survived the strains. "I don't think the Government could have lasted if we had gone for those type of Fine Gael decisions. There is also the fact that everybody argues in theory in favour of making tough decisions and cutting public expenditure. I have never yet heard anybody arguing against cutting public expenditure until they sit around the table and see what is going to be cut. The PDs talk about cuts but they are very slow to identify actually where they are going to make them."

There was another incident in April when, during a tax protest in Dublin, Dukes addressed a business gathering and said that tax relief would have to wait until the national finances were balanced. He also warned that subsidies on food, housing, agriculture and to semi-State companies would have to be reviewed and that the public would have to pay for health and education services which had been free.

Labour responded angrily and Spring had an urgent meeting with FitzGerald to tell the Taoiseach that the timing and tone of Dukes's remarks were totally unacceptable. Later, the Tánaiste made it clear publicly that Dukes's proposals were not on. "The Labour Party stands for high public expenditure, effectively allocated in the interests of equality and employment recovery," he declared.

Late in 1983, as the estimates of Government spending for the following year were being prepared, there was another clash between the Government parties. FitzGerald, in a speech in Carlow, and in a radio interview later, outlined the grim economic situation and said there would have to be spending cuts of £500 million the following year and that semi-State companies would have to be shut down if they were uneconomic.

A row that threatened to bring down the Government was the upshot. A furious Spring spoke to his Cabinet colleagues and decided to boycott the next Cabinet meeting on Friday, 30 September. The effect of the boycott was spoiled somewhat because Barry Desmond and Liam Kavanagh were out of the country and Spring couldn't get hold of Cluskey in time to tell him not to attend. Cluskey was in the Cabinet room and the meeting had just begun when the message was brought to him. He left the room and went to join Spring in the Custom House from where the Labour leader rang FitzGerald and told him Labour were going to pull out of Government.

Garret immediately asked Spring to meet him to discuss the situation. Spring told the Taoiseach there was no way that Labour would accept spending cuts of half-a-billion pounds. After considerable deliberation, FitzGerald agreed there would be no more public references to the estimates, apart from a speech by Spring in Millstreet, Co. Cork, that night. On the basis of that assurance the Labour Ministers decided to attend the Cabinet meeting.

Gemma Hussey wrote in her diary for 1 October. "Garret arrived rather late; apparently there was a big problem about his broadcast last Sunday where he talked about £500 million in cuts, which apparently sent the Labour Party backbenchers bananas. Anyway Dick and Garret had a good meeting and an agreement was reached that there would be no more statements off the cuff about figures like that.

That didn't leave all of us happy. I thought the whole point of such broadcasts was to prepare the people for the difficulties ahead."

A garbled leak of Labour's boycott hit the newspapers but it was to the effect that Cluskey had walked out of Cabinet in opposition to spending cuts. This put Spring back under pressure from his own supporters who got the impression that Cluskey was leading the Labour fight in Cabinet.

In any case, Spring delivered a speech in which he made it clear that Labour was not accepting Garret's line. The elimination of the deficit was subject to "prevailing economic conditions" and a balance had to be struck between spending cuts and borrowing. "But in doing this the Government must consider where the cuts will fall," he said. "Will they be on staff, on services, on benefits and what will be the implications of those cuts?"

In *Hiding Behind a Face*, Stephen O'Byrnes says that the incident and Spring's response constituted a blunt put-down for Fine Gael. "The implications were clear. Fine Gael was in Government on the sufferance of the Labour Party. The Labour Party did not accept Fine Gael's economic policy and was therefore vetoing it. FitzGerald had a choice: to pursue fiscal rectitude or to keep power. He and his colleagues chose the latter option."

As if the economic problems were not bad enough, the Government and the country were convulsed for the Coalition's first six months by the abortion issue. FitzGerald's ill-judged commitment in Opposition to hold a referendum was made in April 1981 but he had also accepted the Fianna Fáil wording which was produced as the election campaign got underway. Now in Government, he was told by his Attorney General, Peter Sutherland, that the wording was unsafe and he opted for a change.

The issue split Fine Gael. A number of conservative TDs insisted that FitzGerald stick to his original commitment. They voted against their own Government and supported Fianna Fáil to ensure such an outcome.

Spring's courageous stance during the referendum campaign took some of the pressure off Labour. But there were still deep divisions in the party and it was decided to have a free vote on the issue when it came before the Dáil. Labour TDs ended up voting three ways. Some voted against both amendments, others supported the new Fine Gael wording and still others backed the Fianna Fáil wording. Spring, as a member of the Government, felt obliged to support the revised Fine Gael wording and backed it along with Barry Desmond, Liam Kavanagh, Seamus Pattison and Michael Moynihan.

As well as the political pressure of being party leader and Tánaiste at such a young age, Spring also had to endure the enormous personal pressure which the weight of work and responsibility put on him and his family. When he took over as leader, he was the father of a young son and his wife Kristi gave birth to another son and daughter while he was in Government. He still remembers the shock of ministerial responsibility, even though he is back on the same treadmill again.

"One thing about going into Government, as I told some of the most-recently appointed Ministers, is that the moment you become a Minister your life changes fundamentally. You can't even prepare yourself for it. It is just a totally dramatic change in terms of the pressure, in terms of the responsibilities, in terms of the amount of work and in terms of the fact that you become separate and different.

"There is a huge volume of work. I got into a pattern which in retrospect was absolutely crazy. After getting home to Tralee late on Friday night after a long week, I used to start my clinics in Kerry on a Saturday morning. The long political week in Dublin was very demanding but it was made worse by the fact that the party was in such bad shape that I had to start rebuilding it, or attempting to rebuild it. You would go to a meeting in Parnell Square of a Dublin constituency which was anti-coalition and all they did was shout and roar at you: 'Why are you in Government with Fine Gael?' And that was very soul-destroying.

"And on a Friday night you would try to attend a function in Mullingar, Wexford or Galway or God knows where and you'd arrive home at two or three in the morning. You were starting your clinic at half-past eight. Some Saturdays my clinics went on until eleven p.m. And, meanwhile, if there was a problem in Dublin, they were on the 'phone looking for you in the backroom of a cold pub in Listowel or Knocknagoshel. You'd get these awful flashes through your mind. You'd be in the backroom of a pub at half-past ten on a Saturday night and a big black coat on you to keep you warm, and while you were waiting for the next client it would be going through your mind: What am I doing here? My family are at home!

"On Sundays you were so totally exhausted that your kids would be jumping on the bed and wondering if you were dead or alive. You were normal for about three or four hours in the afternoon and by the time the kids went to bed you were opening your files again to get ready to start work on Monday morning. Then you'd try to get a bit of work done in Kerry on a Monday if you hadn't to be in Dublin that day.

"Then when you set out you spend around four hours in a car – and I've great memories of what cars can do to you! – and then you arrive in Dublin. If you don't have to go up on Monday you try to be in Dublin at nine o'clock on Tuesday morning. That means leaving Kerry at five or five-thirty and for three months of the year that's taking your life into your hands with frost and ice. Then you are supposed to run a day of departmental business, attend a Government meeting, turn up for Dáil business. And then at half-past nine at night they are wondering why you look tired on television. You're dead at that hour of the day!

"The pressure on family life is unreal and that is a problem, as I found this week [March 1993] when my son fell off his skateboard and fractured his arm in three places and Daddy's not around, you know. That's the awful price one pays."

Spring concedes that by the time the FitzGerald Coalition came to an end he was looking forward to a rest. "I don't think I had any feelings coming out of Government. I was exhausted because of the sheer physical and mental demands. Sooner or later somebody is going to have to stand up and say it can't be done. The actual demands that people are putting on themselves are unreal – a working day from seven-thirty in the morning to eleven at night. The important thing is to try to have your break time. It is very difficult though. I am doing this five days a week and then I have to do a day in Kerry and that leaves just a day. And, God, if you can't give one day to your family, you can forget about it."

FEELING THE COLD

ON THE POLITICAL FRONT, DICK SPRING and his colleagues were under enormous pressure in 1983. The row over the first budget and the difficulties in framing it, followed by the intractable abortion referendum, was the worst possible way to start. There were long periods when the two parties worked together with a common purpose but they were always up against it, battling one storm after another.

The interminable Cabinet meetings that went on under FitzGerald's chairmanship didn't help matters at times but the Taoiseach tried to make up for this by gathering his entire Cabinet in Barrettstown Castle now and again during the lifetime of the Government for weekend brain-storming sessions. He believed these meetings had a positive psychological effect on his Ministers in helping them to understand each other's problems.

"At Government level there was tension, especially between Dick Spring on the one hand and Alan Dukes and John Bruton on the other. Although for the most part this tension was institutional rather than personal, both Dick and John, as distinct from Alan, had short fuses, and this occasionally led to fireworks at the Cabinet table," wrote FitzGerald. He added, gilding the lily somewhat, that the clashes were tempered by mutual respect felt for each other by Spring on the one hand and Bruton and Dukes on the other. Still, FitzGerald records, the more relaxed atmosphere of Barrettstown and a post-Cabinet drinks session from time to time in Sean Barrett's office helped to keep things on an even keel.

Overall, Spring recalls, relations between the two sets of Ministers were not too bad. "We were trying to get on with the business of Government and to do the best possible in terms of personal relations. The other thing, I suppose – and now I am much more experienced at doing it – is that you have got to try to keep your political relations separate from your personal relations. It's politics, and every individual politician has a particular perspective and you just deal with things politically."

Barry Desmond concurs with the view that relations between the two sets of Ministers around the Cabinet table were generally good. "People worked well together. For instance, I regarded Pat Cooney as one of the best members of that Government. He had an extraordinarily sharp intelligence and was very often on the Labour side of the argument whether the issue was social welfare, teachers' pay or Dublin Gas. Of course, he was on the other side from us on issues like divorce and family planning but he was an acknowledged conservative. He had genuinely-held views and was never in any way offensive."

The Government was held together by the close relationship between FitzGerald and Spring and on many issues the Taoiseach was disposed to ally himself with the Labour Ministers. This irked many Fine Gael Cabinet members who believed they were being undermined by it. Spring regularly breakfasted with FitzGerald, either at his house on Palmerston Road or in the University Club on St. Stephen's Green. According to Gemma Hussey, there were elements of a father-son relationship between the two men. Although her assessment of the Tánaiste was written a few years later and was clearly coloured by the various clashes in Government, it reflects how Spring was seen by many in Fine Gael during the lifetime of that Government. She wrote: "Dick was quiet, almost brooding. He was capable of sharp and witty comments, but these were mostly delivered in informal sessions. All the time we were in Government I was conscious of two things: the affection and respect in which the Taoiseach and Tánaiste held each other, the almost fatherly concern of Garret for Dick, and the terrific burden Dick carried of acute worry about the malcontents on his back-benches who always threatened revolt when the heat of public hostility rose. The combination of his back problems, the crisis in public finances and the consequent strains in the Labour Party gave Dick a bad-tempered, often sulky demeanour which irritated many of us in Fine Gael (particularly people like myself who felt beleaguered by huge public hostility and felt we were the ones who were carrying the can for the whole Government). With hindsight I feel more benevolent towards him, but at the time it was difficult. And all the time Fianna Fáil sought to destabilise the Labour Party over every minor expenditure cut. Dick and Garret sorted out a great many potentially explosive items before they ever came to Cabinet, quite often in Garret's basement sitting room in Palmerston Road."

As Ministers got to know each other better, relations within the Cabinet improved. In particular, despite their bitter clashes in the early days round the Cabinet table, Spring and Alan Dukes, Minister for Finance, developed a good working rapport, largely perhaps because they were both inexperienced young politicians who had been catapulted to office on their first day in the Dáil in 1981 and they were close enough in age and background. While some other Fine Gael Ministers seethed with anger at the drift in economic policy, Dukes sought to ensure that difficulties like this would not bring the Government down.

With John Bruton at Industry, Spring's relations were very different. From the beginning the two grated on each other's nerves and they took opposite sides on almost every serious argument that cropped up in Cabinet. They had a basic ideological difference to begin with. Spring may not have been a radical enough socialist in the eyes of some of his own more left-wing members but he approached issues from a Labour perspective which Bruton fundamentally rejected. Bruton is by no means a dogmatically right-wing politician but he was in tune with the international mood of the early 1980s which was trying to roll back the power of the State. Naturally, Spring was on the other side of the argument but so were FitzGerald and Dukes, for that matter.

There was more to it than a simple left-right divide, though. A fundamental clash of personalities was at the root of their problems. Spring is cautious, slow to commit himself and not given to off-the-cuff direct statements. He has a quick sense of dry humour which friends accept as funny but opponents often regard as unduly sarcastic. By contrast, Bruton is impatient, direct and prone to throw himself into arguments without having worked out all the consequences. In his dealings with Spring, he expressed impatience again and again at the failure to come to decisions he regarded as necessary.

"What John couldn't take in his dealings with Dick was that, while he [Dick] was usually pleasant enough in a face-to-face meeting, he would never stick by an agreement. A deal would be made but then when the issue came to a full Cabinet meeting Dick would pull back from it as if it had never been made," said one close ally of Bruton's.

The Labour perspective on the relationship is very different. "Bruton and some of the others in Fine Gael could never appreciate the kind of difficult position Dick was in with our own supporters and it didn't seem to matter to them," said a Labour advisor from that period. "They also gave the impression that they wanted all the pain of tough decisions to be inflicted on our constituency. They were not prepared to concede on things like a wealth tax, which would have affected their own supporters, so we had to fight to protect our own, particularly those on social welfare," he added.

The clash between Spring and Bruton was based on a number of factors. Social background, ideology and the huge difference in personality militated against the development of mutual understanding. Spring is candid about this. "I think I was prejudiced about John Bruton from the time he was a junior Minister in the Department of Education. My father used to say things about him. 'That fellow, Oh, no!' My father was an old-style politician who would assume that if you wanted to do something for people in terms of, say, a bus route in North Kerry, you should do it. If people were being inconvenienced and there wasn't any great hassle you should bloody well do it. I don't think the response was great or that there was any real understanding of the problem."

The ideological differences between Bruton and the Labour Party crystallised during the first year in Government over the future of Dublin Gas. It was Frank Cluskey, rather than Spring, who did most of the fighting on Labour's behalf on this particular issue. Bruton, who was Minister for Industry and Energy, came up with a plan for refinancing the near-bankrupt Dublin Gas. The package amounted to £126 million in bank loans, State grants and cheap natural gas. Cluskey, the Minister for Trade Commerce and Tourism and the Labour leader between 1977 and 1981, was adamantly opposed to such State investment in a private company.

Cluskey believed the deal would create a pot of gold for the private owners of Dublin Gas and he advocated nationalisation of the company instead. "The relations between Frank and Bruton were just dynamite," says Spring. "It was explosive from start to finish. Frank Cluskey and John Bruton did not share the same world, either in background or philosophy. Frank found it very difficult from that point of view. I am not saying that John did not find it equally difficult.

"The Dublin Gas clash was just looming for months and months and months. Now I have to say that I don't think Frank Cluskey enjoyed being in the Cabinet. He wasn't one for long meetings and our meetings were very long. That wasn't his style, wasn't his forte."

There were fierce tussles with Bruton in which Cluskey was eventually out-voted at Cabinet. Spring and the other Labour Ministers backed up their colleague but they were not as passionately convinced as he was that there was something sinister in the deal. Following a pattern which was not unusual in that Government, some Fine Gael Ministers like Pat Cooney actually voted with Labour. However, when the decision was made, Cluskey promptly resigned.

The resignation came as a severe blow to Spring and undermined his confidence in himself as Labour leader for some time. Cluskey had scuppered Michael O'Leary just a year earlier and Spring naturally feared that he might form an alliance with the left wing of the party and cause similar problems again. The atmosphere in Government was tense at this stage as Gemma Hussey reveals in her diary for Monday, 12 December.

"Depressing to find over the weekend that some Cabinet member had apparently leaked the precise voting figures on Dublin Gas question. Very depressing that this should happen after all the indignation expressed about leaks – it would make you sick. Garret believes that Dick faces a possible re-shaping of the Administrative Council at their March conference which may lead to a Labour conference decision to pull out of Government. Frank Cluskey has obviously set the wheels in motion of God knows what, and now we can only hope that Dick can stop it and control it."

In the reshuffle that followed Cluskey's resignation, Spring moved from Environment to Energy, which was detached from Industry and Commerce. He did so because he felt the workload at Environment did not give him enough time to fulfil his role as Labour leader. Liam Kavanagh took over Environment and Ruairi Quinn came into the Cabinet at Labour. Initially Spring offered the Cabinet vacancy to Mervyn Taylor, the leading left-wing TD in the parliamentary party.

Taylor appeared interested and he was briefed by the Cabinet Secretary, Dermot Nally, about the duties of a Minister and given a copy of the Government Procedure Instructions. The next day, however, he went back to Spring to say he couldn't take the job because of heavy business commitments – he was a partner in the busy law firm of Taylor and Buchalter. He also said that in the light of the briefing on Cabinet procedures he felt there would be a possible conflict of interest with his legal practice.

Taylor's refusal to join the Cabinet caused added problems all round. Spring was disappointed as he had hoped to neutralise Cluskey by appointing Taylor. His refusal to become a Minister left the leading left-wing TD in the party free to continue sniping at the Government, possibly in alliance with Cluskey. There was also a suspicion in Ministers' minds that Taylor declined the job because he felt the Government was going to collapse and he didn't want to be contaminated. Ruairi Quinn admits that he was incensed at being initially passed over in favour of Taylor. He was also disappointed to end up at the Department of Labour, rather than in Environment where he had enjoyed his stint as a junior Minister to Spring.

On the Fine Gael side, Bruton was deeply annoyed at losing Energy and he had a furious battle with FitzGerald to try to hold the Department. He regarded the switch as a vote of no confidence in his handling of the Dublin Gas issue but Spring insisted on taking it, however, and the Taoiseach agreed. It was another major blow to Bruton just a year after FitzGerald had passed him over and given the Finance portfolio to Dukes.

The whole affair destabilised the Government for a time and put Spring and the other Labour Ministers very much on the defensive. The Labour leader felt himself very weakened and feared the Cluskey departure would undermine his moral authority in the party. The resignation was widely perceived as not only the result of a row on a single policy issue but as a product of unhappiness at the general thrust of Government policy. This was not strictly true as Cluskey in Government had agreed to the shape of the following year's spending estimates, which had almost all been agreed by that stage.

However, when Ministers came to draw up the 1984 budget, there was a degree of uneasiness in Labour about the political consequences of what they were doing. Following the public row between FitzGerald and Spring the previous autumn over the Book of Estimates, a lot of work had been done to prepare a budget which would begin to cut into the deficit in a significant way. One of the measures aimed at reducing public spending was a cut in the cost of food subsidies from £94 million to £64 million. Labour had been preparing the ground for this and Donal Nevin, secretary of the Irish Congress of Trade Unions (ICTU), had even delivered a helpful speech calling for direct help for people in need, rather than food subsidies which benefited rich and poor alike.

After a lot of work in the early days of the New Year, the budget was finally approved by the Cabinet on Friday, 20 January. It was due to be printed over the weekend and to come back to the Cabinet for the last time on the following Tuesday, the day before the budget was to be announced. This was regarded as a mere formality.

It was far from a formality, though. After the Cabinet meeting, Spring attempted to make sure senior colleagues like Mervyn Taylor and Joe Bermingham were on-side. He discussed the cuts in food subsidies with them and how they would be regarded by the rank-and-file party members. The reaction of the two TDs and other senior Labour figures was totally hostile and they told him they could not accept the budget as proposed. In a panic, the Labour leader contacted the Taoiseach to try to avert a crisis in his party.

Over the weekend, FitzGerald, Spring and Dukes met at the Taoiseach's house and began redrafting key sections of the budget. The food subsidies were retained and other taxation measures had to be devised in order to compensate for the lost revenue. By that stage, the budget had gone to Cahills the printers, and it had to be recalled. In fact, it was too late to do anything about some sections which had already been printed, so the final version appeared minus one page which was dropped in the last frantic effort to redraft the document.

When the Cabinet met on the day before the budget, most Fine Gael Ministers were stunned to discover that fundamental changes had taken place over the weekend. Bruton, who might have been expected to be the strongest objector to the affair, was out of the country on Government business and didn't hear about the incident until later. Most Fine Gael Ministers were furious but there was nothing they could do. They were shocked that the budget they had agreed to had been rewritten at Labour's behest. They viewed the whole episode as a clear breach of normal Government procedure and the constitutional concept of Cabinet responsibility.

"We should all have resigned then and there," one Fine Gael Minister says, looking back on his years in Government. "It was the only thing to do in the circumstances. Trust had been broken on two fronts. Firstly, the budget that emerged was not the one agreed by the Cabinet and, secondly, the secrecy of the Cabinet table had been breached and outsiders consulted on what should be in the budget. I don't blame Spring so much as Garret. After all, Spring was only fighting his own corner as best he could, but Garret let us down and we should not have stood for it."

Garret makes no reference to this incident in his autobiography, but in the minds of many Fine Gael Ministers it was one of the key moments in the lifetime of the Government. Of course, nobody quit and the Government continued on, but at the price of paralysis on the economic front. The effect of putting off the elimination of food subsidies rebounded on both parties because, in the summer, they were panicked into corrective budgetary action by a Department of Finance miscalculation that spending and revenue targets were away out of line.

Just before Ministers departed for the August holiday weekend of 1984 and their annual summer holidays, the Government was rushed into a decision by Finance. The cuts in food subsidies planned for the budget in January were recycled and announced to journalists by the head of the Government Information Service, Joe Jennings, on a Friday evening, 20 July. Most members of the Government headed off on holidays that evening and were not available for comment when the weekend media splashed the story. Only Dick Spring was around to defend the cuts and the Labour leader took a pasting for his troubles. He had to endure widespread criticism from all quarters, particularly his own left wing.

"Appalling flak going on about the food subsidies," Gemma Hussey recorded in her diary. "The hysteria from Michael D. Higgins, Joe Higgins of the Labour left, John Carroll, the housewives, you name it, as well as Fianna Fáil's Michael O'Kennedy being extremely rude on radio. The media are totally gone off mad; the whole thing is pointed straight at the Labour Party. Dick Spring was on the radio yesterday evening. He was extremely strong in support of the Government and determined-sounding about the country."

The irony of the situation was that if Spring had allowed Dukes to proceed as planned in the January budget he would not have been placed in such an unenviable position. On the other hand, if a few Labour backbenchers had rebelled on the budget the Government might not have been around by the August bank holiday. The episode – from the row on the budget in January and the victory of the Labour Ministers in their rejection of cuts in food subsidies at that stage to the final implementation of the cuts in August – illustrated the dilemma facing Spring and his Ministers. Although they fought valiant battles in Cabinet against Fine Gael and regularly came off better, the wider public was not and could not be aware of what they were doing. By contrast when the watered-down cuts finally emerged Spring was under fire from his own supporters for not fighting hard enough to prevent them. It was a situation that led to increasing frustration in Labour and, for that matter, in Fine Gael, and there was no way out for anybody unless they wanted to bring down the Government.

FitzGerald records how, despite the sense of camaraderie and warmth he felt existed between members of the Government, there was also an underlying tension that wouldn't ever go away. "The Labour Ministers clearly feared that at some point a misjudgment on the Fine Gael side might push them over the brink, making it impossible for them to remain in Government while retaining authority within their own divided and unnerved party. At the same time, among Fine Gael Ministers there was a persistent concern that the problems faced by Labour Ministers might at some point precipitate a split. There was, moreover, frequently irritation and at times alarm at the leaks by Labour Ministers' aides to the press, which seemed to be designed to keep their more restless TDs and non parliamentary left wing happy. The apparent implication of these leaks – that only the constant vigilance of the Labour Ministers saved the country from savage cuts in public services – was particularly galling for Fine Gael Ministers."

As the Coalition partners tottered from one crisis to the next, Fianna Fáil was making hay on the Opposition benches. Every proposed financial cut and every failure to provide more resources for education, health and social welfare was lambasted. Spring still recalls the Fianna Fáil style of Opposition with annoyance. "We had Haughey in Opposition at his worst. Every day of the week he was attacking us for not spending money on local authority houses, for not spending it on the health services. That put more and more pressure on our people. At health board and council level they were making it very difficult for us at every opportunity. Haughey was just dreadful. He did absolutely nothing constructive. He made no attempt whatsoever."

THE ENEMY WITHIN

DICK SPRING FOUND IT GALLING that many Fine Gael Ministers appeared to have no appreciation of how difficult things often were for him during those Coalition years. His battles in Cabinet were mirrored by even more spiteful tussles within his own party organisation, where he had to fight every inch of the way to keep his left wing from pulling the plug on the Government.

"They were quite vicious and they let me know from the very start that they weren't going to support the Government," says Spring. "So you were up against that straight away which made life very difficult. At every AC meeting a motion would go down against the Government, no matter what you did. You were fighting a rearguard action all the time."

Spring had to face a range of enemies on the Administrative Council of the party, all of whom were determined to wreck the Coalition and bring him down if they could. His lack of experience in party matters was sometimes shown up at the monthly AC meetings. Occasionally he was goaded into giving his tormentors a verbal tongue-lashing which only confirmed their suspicion of him as a supercilious, Trinity-educated rugby player, out of touch with the party.

The left was very strong on the AC throughout most of the 1980s. In Spring's early years as leader, the Trotskyite Militant Tendency had three people on the thirty-person executive and through deals with more orthodox left-wing delegates was able to protect its position within the party. A group called the Liaison of the Left co-ordinated the anti-leadership activity on the AC and it received the backing of Brendan Halligan, the former party guru and architect of the 1973 Coalition, who temporarily became the champion of the left.

Halligan was opposed to coalition because he believed Labour would inevitably suffer at the polls as a consequence of the tough decisions he knew were economically necessary. At this stage, the party was playing musical chairs with the two European Parliament posts won in 1979 and Halligan had taken over one of the vacant positions in Strasbourg. He was able to avail of the back-up facilities provided by the post to promote the Liaison of the Left and its anti-Government policies.

Spring was deeply irritated by Halligan and couldn't help showing it. His anger boiled over on one occasion when Halligan, who had used his left-wing influence to get a nomination, pulled out of the European elections in 1984, saying Labour wouldn't win even one seat. He performed this embarrassing withdrawal at a public meeting in Dublin designed to promote Labour's Euro-election campaign. After the meeting, a furious Spring was asked by the reporters present what he thought of Halligan's remarks. "Brendan's a bollocks and you can quote me on that," was Spring's response.

It was a rare public lapse by Spring but it indicated the pressure he was under at the time. Before the lifetime of the FitzGerald Government was over, Spring and Halligan mended their fences and the Tánaiste made the former general secretary Chairman of Bord na Móna. Halligan did such a good job in the post that he was reappointed by the subsequent Fianna Fáil Government. But that was all in the future as the left plotted to torpedo Spring in the early years of his leadership. Tensions ran so high on the AC that the pro- and anti-leadership factions even had an informal pairing arrangement for meetings.

"Things were so bad you couldn't even go to the toilet without doing a head count first to make sure there was still a majority in the room for Spring. Otherwise you might come back to find that the left had taken over," says one Spring supporter.

A combination of factors – constant battles within the Cabinet, unending rows on the AC and a steady decline in popularity and party morale – even put Spring's leadership under threat.

Looking back, Barry Desmond has no illusions about the difficult position his leader was in. "The loyal majority for Dick in the party in the mid-1980s was very fragile. There was an extraordinary internal coalition of ambitious individuals who had no clear alternative strategy but who were prepared to use the problems he faced as a member of the Government as a weapon to try to destroy him."

A key member of the organisation who backed Spring through those difficult times agrees. "I know it's difficult to imagine it now but Spring wasn't that far away from suffering the same fate as Alan Dukes. He was really on the ropes within a year or two of taking over and there were plenty of people in the party who thought that he wouldn't survive it. It's amazing to think that it is the same guy, with the same strengths and weaknesses, who brought us to glory last November."

What encouraged Spring's left-wing critics was that the public mood turned against the Labour leader with increasing ferocity during his term of office. Spring was convinced that elements within RTE, favourable to the Workers' Party, were using the State broadcasting service to fan the mood of hostility towards him. He regularly complained to the station and on one occasion went to the Broadcasting Complaints Commission and won a case in which he claimed a programme was biased against Labour.

Spring was Tánaiste for less than a year when he received the first warning of the public animosity developing against his party. The Dublin Central by-election of November 1983 provided a salutary shock for Labour and a morale-boosting triumph for Fianna Fáil at a critical time in the early life of the Fine Gael-Labour Coalition.

Labour's candidate was ITGWU official Jimmy Somers. Fianna Fáil ran a former TD, Tom Leonard, while Mary Banotti had her first outing for Fine Gael. The constituency was the one which Michael O'Leary had represented for Labour from 1965 until a year before, but when the votes were counted in 1983 the scale of the party's decline was evident for all to see. Not only had the party's candidate failed to make an impact but he ended up in fifth place behind Fianna Fáil, Fine Gael, the Workers' Party and Sinn Féin.

Some of his critics within Labour blamed Spring for the fiasco. As Minister for the Environment he had introduced legislation to allow local authorities to introduce their own charges. This was necessary to keep basic services going in many counties and to protect the employment of council workers. However, Fianna Fáil and the Workers' Party made hay with the issue, particularly as demands for water charges came dropping through the letter-boxes of Dublin Central during the campaign. It was another example of Labour's dilemma about how to reconcile the aspirations of its supporters with the responsibility for taking decisions in Government.

In the six months following the Dublin Central by-election, Spring found the going steadily tougher. Morale in the party was sinking; he had to face his first annual conference in April 1984 and the European elections in June of that year. A profile of him written by Maeve Kennedy for *The Irish Times* just before the conference captures the downbeat nature of his image at that time and his own self-doubts after less than a year-and-a-half in Government. Nothing provides a better illustration of the fickleness of politics than the fact that the same man brought the party to its greatest victory less than a decade later.

"Dick Spring photographs abysmally and in the age of the image that's more of a problem than it might seem. Turn a camera on him and the long jaw looks sullen, the eyes under the frowning forehead and the mop of old-fashioned curly hair look shifty, the mouth is hidden entirely under the droopy moustache. The fact that he's so often photographed lurking just behind the Taoiseach's left shoulder doesn't help either. Would you buy a partly-used joint programme of Government from this man?" she wrote.

"I have a very major personal dilemma – to prove myself as Labour Party leader and to establish myself as a Minister," Spring confessed. "They can be difficult to reconcile." And as for establishing himself as Tánaiste, he remarked: "That's a strange office – I don't think I'll even comment on that."

In that and other interviews during his first term in Government, he spoke sadly of the toll taken on his personal life by all the responsibilities. His wife and young children lived, then as now, in Tralee while the business of national politics is conducted in Dublin. "If I can't somehow accommodate my family life better, I'll just have to reconsider the whole thing," he said.

Kennedy chided Spring in that profile for being too buttoned down, for keeping his irreverent thoughts to himself and she summed up the general mood at the time by predicting a bleak future for him. "It is inconceivable that he could ever become a hate-figure on the scale of Michael O'Leary. What's much more likely is a slow decline from the wild optimism of his election into a grey half-articulated blur of disillusionment and discontent, mirroring Labour's own decline."

Spring's first conference as leader a few days later seemed to confirm that gloomy prognosis. It was the first conference since O'Leary had been so spectacularly overturned. The left were geared up for an assault and made no secret of the fact that Spring was their target. The pretext was a move to change the standing orders of the conference to allow the whole question of coalition to be debated. After the internecine conflicts of the 1970s over coalition the party had accepted a rule that the issue should be debated only every three years. The left attempted to get around this by moving a motion at the beginning of the conference to suspend standing orders, thus allowing the coalition issue on to the agenda.

This first test of his party leadership gave Spring a terrible fright. The vote was taken on the Friday night of the conference, at the RDS in Dublin, before many of the rural delegates and the famous Kerry buses had arrived. After a short impassioned debate the party leader just managed to squeeze through by 363 votes to 324. The man who almost sank Spring that night was the party chairman, Michael D. Higgins, who at that time was a senator. He delivered his usual emotional appeal to the ordinary delegates, entrancing them with his oratory as he denounced coalition with "the redneck fundamentalists" of Fine Gael. In interviews around this time he also dubbed many of his Labour parliamentary colleagues as "rednecks" and made it clear that he regarded Spring as one of that species.

"There's a certain fever that precedes The Challenge, and it grabbed you by the ears last night, even outside the hall," wrote Mary Maher in the following morning's *Irish Times*. "First symptom of rising temperature, the Ringsend ESB workers; about 50 of them with artful placards and vocal messages of impending redundancy for Dick Spring, whose car was attempting to inch slowly past them."

Such was Spring's alarm at nearly being caught on the hop that only one annual conference has been held in Dublin since that weekend in 1984. He never again trusted his fate to the Friday night Dublin delegates who came within an ace of upsetting the apple-cart so early in his leadership career. Of course, it wasn't the last, or even the biggest, shock he got at a conference, but it was a very damaging blow at a vulnerable time for him.

In an attempt to find some point of contact with the widespread anti-coalition mood in the party, Spring used his leader's address to tell the delegates of the difficulties between the two parties in Government as well as their achievements in office. He paid tribute to his Fine Gael colleagues while leaving the delegates under no illusion about the wide divergence of views on some key issues. By far the most sustained applause was reserved for his bow in the direction of

THE ENEMY WITHIN   127

the anti-coalitionists. "I led this party into Government in the belief that it was in the country's imperative interests to do so. If at any time I feel that the country's or the party's interests would be better served by an alternative arrangement, I am perfectly capable of leading us out again." That remark brought the house down and it was the only one from his hour-long address which did so.

The April conference was designed as a launching pad for the European elections in June but it wasn't the time for successful Labour campaigns. The 1979 result, which had given Labour four Euro seats, had been something of a freak of proportional representation. The system which had over-compensated the party in 1979 went the other way in 1984 and Labour lost all four seats. The biggest shock was Frank Cluskey's failure to win a seat in Dublin and the loss of Eileen Desmond's seat in Munster and Justin Keating's failure to hold Leinster did not augur well for the party's future prospects and provided the anti-coalitionists with more ammunition to attack Spring and his Labour ministerial colleagues.

The food subsidies debacle a little over a month later put Spring under even more pressure. Far from rallying around their leader, many Labour members joined in the chorus of protest against the Government's decision. Party branches passed motions condemning the Government's action at a time when Spring and his fellow Labour Ministers were caught up in the preparation of the Government's new national economic plan, entitled *Building on Reality.*

This document, which temporarily revived the Government's fortunes, was published in October 1984, but only after protracted struggles in Cabinet between Fine Gael and Labour Ministers. One of these struggles involved fierce resistance by the Labour Ministers to a proposal that social welfare increases should be decoupled from the consumer price index. Spring went public on the issue in a speech to a meeting of Labour activists in Cork, saying Labour wouldn't stand for the move.

If he expected applause for his stand, Spring was bitterly disappointed. Instead he was subjected to a bitterly hostile reception from his Cork members on a range of issues, particularly the food subsidies. "I vividly remember that meeting in the Imperial Hotel in Cork because Dick was excoriated by the people there," recalls one of the people who travelled down from Dublin with him that night. "It went on for hours and somebody ultimately proposed a motion of no confidence in Spring and the Government. The chairman was about to put it to the floor around midnight and it would have been carried overwhelmingly.

"Spring's bacon was saved by Pat Magner who took the microphone and told the hostile crowd that there was no provision for the passing of any resolution at the meeting. Eventually they left after midnight without a vote being taken." After a bruising night, Spring had to stay up until three a.m. to meet a number of deputations who were waiting for him. It was part of the drudgery of being a Minister. The height of absurdity was reached when it transpired that one of the delegations from West Cork wanted to complain about the introduction of DIY artificial insemination of cattle with foreign semen.

While there was some easing in the pressure after the launching of *Building on Reality*, it didn't go away and the left planned another ambush on Spring at the 1985 annual conference in Cork. That conference opened with another attempt to suspend standing orders to get coalition discussed. The leadership fought off the challenge by just fourteen votes. On the Saturday night, after the leader's speech, there was another attack by the left. Michael D. Higgins and Mervyn Taylor again threw their support behind the combined forces of the left and the Militant Tendency who were demanding a renegotiation of the national plan, *Building on Reality*.

The vote was taken around ten p.m. when many of the rural delegates had adjourned for a pint in the pubs around the City Hall. On a show of hands, party chairman, Michael D. Higgins, adjudged that the motion had been carried but Spring supporters demanded that tellers be appointed and the votes recounted. This gave time for some of his supporters to be rounded up. When the vote was called again, Spring kept his hand in the air to indicate to his supporters, who were pouring into the back of the hall, what way they should vote. He won by just eleven votes out of more than a thousand.

According to Sean O'Rourke in *The Irish Press*, Spring was saved only by the large Kerry delegation who stayed in the hall to back their leader. As it was, delegates voted for another motion to condemn *Building on Reality* because of its effect on public service pay, despite a plea from Spring for them not to do so.

In his keynote address, Spring adapted to modern technology by reading his speech from an autocue invisible to television viewers at home. His style, however, was still a little hesitant and he fluffed some of his best lines. Even more ominously, the only sustained burst of applause during his address was when he made a complimentary reference to Michael D. Higgins. This won a standing ovation from a majority of delegates, which added further to the ire of the Labour Ministers on the platform.

One critical decision, which had the support of left and right, was the establishment of a special commission to examine Labour Party electoral strategy for the future. This commission was given twelve months to report and it afforded Spring a breather of sorts from the rows over coalition.

The conference was bruising enough but worse was to happen in June 1985 when the postponed local elections were finally held. Labour was under pressure on two fronts right through the campaign. Fianna Fáil mounted a huge effort to destabilise the Coalition by winning control of as many local authorities as possible. The party promised to abolish local charges and mobilised every interest group it could against the Government.

On the left, the Workers' Party also saw the local elections as a major opportunity and attacked Labour's base, particularly in the capital, concentrating its fire on the local charges which had been introduced by Spring when he was Minister for the Environment and which were supported by Labour councillors.

At that time nothing could go right for Labour. At one stage during the campaign, Fergus Finlay arranged a publicity stunt in which a giant banner with the message "Labour Is Working for You", in seven-foot-high letters, would be attached to a small plane and flown over Dublin. The media were invited along for a photocall to watch. Dick Spring, the Labour Lord Mayor of Dublin Michael O'Halloran, and the chairperson of the county council Bernie Malone, were among the Labour dignitaries. However, instead of a publicity stunt it turned into a disaster. For a start, permission to fly the banner over the city was withdrawn because of low cloud; then the plane had difficulty making the connection with the banner for a photo opportunity and when it finally did things got even worse.

Gene Kerrigan wrote a wickedly funny piece about the incident in *Magill*. "The hook caught in the rope, there was an almighty commotion as the metal uprights went flying, the banner rose a few feet and schwock something snapped and the banner came down. Dick looked at 'Labour is Working for You' fluttering down to earth and said. 'Put on a brave smile, everyone, and walk away.'"

It was the story of that election campaign for Labour.

The opinion polls gave the party only around 5 per cent in the run-up to polling day and while it did a little better than that, winning 7.9 per cent of the national vote, it was still a major disappointment for the party.

The local elections confirmed the trend of by-elections and the European elections – the Labour vote appeared to be in terminal decline. The party lost seats all over the country but particularly in Dublin city where the scale of the defeat was humiliating. Labour's vote was cut in half from 18 per cent to 9 per cent and owing to appalling vote management it won only two of the forty-five seats on the Corporation. The Workers' Party, with the same percentage share of the vote, won six seats and put itself into a great position to take over the mantle of the leading left-wing party in Dublin.

Spring's reaction to the result showed how insecure he felt. He began by saying there was no question of his giving up the leadership of the party. "Some people have written off the Labour Party. That is their mistake. Labour is not going to go away," he declared. He was right, but at the time there were many people, including not a few in Labour, who had grave doubts about whether anything could be salvaged.

Spring's vulnerability at this stage also showed in his dealings with RTE. Two days before the local elections he wrote to the Director General to complain about two programmes, a *Today Tonight* special on the elections and the weekly *This Week* radio programme. Spring warned that "the clear absence of fairness in RTE's treatment of this party" might lead to a different attitude within the party on the need to protect and develop the station.

What annoyed Spring was not just the slant against Labour, as he saw it, but the bias towards the Workers' Party within the station. He finished his letter of complaint by writing: "I hope it adequately conveys my anger – and indeed my sense of betrayal – at the abandonment of fairness among at least an element within RTE where my party is concerned."

After the election debacle Labour's general secretary, Colm O Briain, resigned. A director of the Arts Council for eight years, he was appointed in 1982 shortly after Spring took office. He hardly knew the party leader and was closer to Labour's chairman, Michael D. Higgins. O Briain couldn't get along with Spring and each found the other impossible to work with. At one stage during his tenure, O Briain publicly referred to the problems in the party caused by "personal fiefdoms" and it appeared that he was referring directly to the party leader. His resignation and the fact that Spring made no effort to persuade him to change his mind came as no surprise.

The appointment of a replacement for O Briain demonstrated just how weak Spring was in the party at that stage. Not only could he not deliver the post to his own man but the interview panel set up to make the appointment chose the person from the three-man short-list most unacceptable to him. On the short-list were Spring's advisor, Fergus Finlay; Ray Kavanagh, from the mainstream of the party who had worked as director of elections for Ruairi Quinn, and Bernard Browne, an official of the Federated Workers' Union of Ireland (FWUI) who was on the left of the party. The advertisement for the job implied that the successful candidate would have to be a supporter of coalition, saying the post carried with it "a rare opportunity to be part of the Labour Party's participation in the Government of the country". Despite that, it was the left-winger, Browne, who got the job.

The fact that Spring was so weak he couldn't get either his first or second choice appointed to such a key party position was a public demonstration of his vulnerability and the question was raised again as to whether he might suffer the same fate as Michael O'Leary. Fortunately for Spring, Browne self-destructed before his appointment could be ratified by the AC. In an interview with Máirín de Burca in *The Sunday Tribune* he declared his outright opposition to coalition and simultaneously his name appeared on a list of "Trade Unionists for a United Ireland" who had come out against the Anglo-Irish Agreement. The matter was referred back to the interview board who refused to change their minds but Spring took his courage in his hands and asked the party officers to adjudicate.

Michael D. Higgins and Mervyn Taylor stuck by Browne but the others now agreed to Spring's wishes and Browne was not ratified in the post. Significantly, though, Spring didn't feel he had the authority to impose Fergus Finlay. The post went to Ray Kavanagh, who has since managed the task of running the party with quiet efficiency, remaining loyal to the party leader while keeping the respect of the broad mass of the party membership.

DISPUTE OVER ATTORNEY GENERAL

DESPITE THE STRESSES OF Government, Dick Spring and Garret FitzGerald remained on good terms through their first two years in office, but in the autumn of 1984 there was a disagreement which changed the nature of their relationship. The row didn't break the trust between them completely but it marked a fundamental change in the way they regarded each other and they were never again as close.

At issue was the question of who would replace Peter Sutherland as Attorney General. Dick Spring wanted his friend and advisor, John Rogers, for the job. Garret fought tooth and nail against this and the Labour leader came to suspect the Taoiseach of trying to dictate that Mary Robinson should be the Labour nominee.

The matter arose first in the summer of 1984 when the question of who should replace Dick Burke as the next EC Commissioner came up. Labour pressed the claims of Justin Keating, the former Labour Minister whose nomination as an EC Commissioner FitzGerald had himself supported back in the 1970s. This time around, however, the appointment would be a Fine Gael one. "Fine Gael, restive about what it saw – or at times imagined – to be a Labour Party tail persistently wagging the Coalition dog, was in no mood to concede this European appointment to a Labour nominee," stated FitzGerald.

Having considered various heavyweight candidates – including Alan Dukes – the Taoiseach decided he could not spare a senior Minister and anyway he didn't want the uncertainty of a by-election. On the advice of his wife, Joan, Garret FitzGerald decided that the Attorney General, Peter Sutherland, should be the Government's nominee. As the price of agreeing to a Fine Gael candidate, Spring insisted that

Labour should get the vacancy created at the Attorney General's post.

As Labour sources recall it, that was not a problem in the summer of 1984. It became one only in the autumn when Garret discovered that John Rogers rather than Mary Robinson was to be the Labour nominee. "Garret reneged," is how one Labour aide still bitterly remembers the affair. "There was a straightforward agreement that if Peter Sutherland got the EC Commissionership Labour would get the Attorney General's job. Garret didn't have any difficulty giving Labour the post; he was in a predicament only when he found out it wasn't going to be Mary Robinson." FitzGerald mixed in the same social circles as Robinson who was then a Labour senator. He admired her enormous talent and agreed with her on many social issues and it is probably no great surprise that he may have assumed she would be the Labour nominee.

Mrs. Robinson herself was very keen on the position and let her ambitions be known to Spring and the other Labour Ministers. However, they were agreed that she would not be suitable. "Mary has enormous ability but we just didn't regard her as a team player," says one of the Labour Ministers. "I still believe we were right because, while she has made a wonderful President, I am convinced she would have been a dreadful AG. She is too committed to a range of causes to provide the cold clinical advice that a Government needs on legal issues."

While Spring's colleagues were at one with him in rejecting the candidature of Robinson, they were taken aback at the proposal of his best friend, John Rogers, who was still a junior counsel at the time. Spring was adamant, though, and his colleagues didn't oppose his choice. He was growing more confident in his dealing with senior Labour people and felt it was time he had someone on the inside whom he could trust completely on both a personal and political level. FitzGerald couldn't disguise his surprise and shock when the name was put to him and he tried to talk Spring out of it.

FitzGerald records his version of the event in his autobiography: "To have my Attorney General chosen for me was something that I instinctively resisted, and Dick's choice, John Rogers, was not known to me, although I soon learnt that before moving to Labour he had been a member of the Fine Gael Youth Movement who apparently had approached me, with others, in 1969 in an attempt to persuade me to move against Liam Cosgrave."

Spring was angry at what he regarded as an attempt by FitzGerald to dictate who the Labour candidate should be and he stuck by his nomination of Rogers. "The whole thing soured relations between Dick and Garret. It wasn't because Garret wouldn't accept Dick's mate, but because Dick saw it as a clear case of Garret reneging on a commitment and he never forgave him for it," said one Labour source. Spring's fury was all the greater when he heard that Garret had consulted an eminent, and very elderly, Fine Gael lawyer about Rogers's reputation. All the lawyer could tell Garret was that he had only vaguely heard of the chap.

In the face of Fine Gael hostility, Spring refused to back down and he made it clear he would not support Sutherland's claims for the Commissionership unless Rogers got the Attorney General's post. "Dick became very stubborn about the new Attorney General to replace Peter Sutherland and I exploded, which Dick didn't like at all. That made Garret even more fed-up," recorded Gemma Hussey on 6 September. The following day, she wrote: "Cabinet meeting, high tension caused by Commissionership/Attorney General crux. Peter Sutherland up to ninety. I got very angry and told my Fine Gael colleagues that I couldn't wear any reneging on Peter. The whole thing is not looking good and makes me dislike Dick at the moment. I feel that Garret is too understanding and sympathetic to him. Behind and underneath it all Garret desperately wants to stay in Government."

It was not until December that the new Attorney General took up his post, to face an immediate onslaught from Fianna Fáil and some private bickering from Fine Gael. "The new Attorney General is John Rogers, a saturnine, tall fellow whose appointment has caused some uproar" wrote Gemma Hussey on 14 December, 1984, the day after the appointment had been made. Before he received his seal of office, Rogers, who was just thirty-four, had to become a senior counsel and was called to the inner bar. There was a great deal of criticism of this, although exactly the same thing had happened when John Kelly was appointed Attorney General in 1977, having been made a senior counsel on the same day.

When the matter came before the Dáil, Charles Haughey was scathing about the Rogers appointment. "We all know a Mr. John Rogers, junior counsel, but who is John Rogers, senior counsel?" he asked the House sarcastically. In an adjournment debate later the same day he went on at greater length. "Our national political life had been debased by the lengthy, semi-public and unprecedented wrangle which has taken place between Fine Gael and Labour over the appointment of the new Attorney General. It must raise serious doubts about the discharge of his constitutional responsibilities by the Taoiseach. The appointment of the Attorney General is reserved exclusively by the Constitution to the Taoiseach. It is certainly contrary to the spirit of the Constitution to have allowed anyone, a member of the Government or anyone else, to dictate to him who should be chosen for this fundamentally important constitutional office," said Haughey.

"The new Attorney General has never conducted a case in the High Court, still less the Supreme Court," said Haughey, adding: "The main qualification of the appointee is that he is a friend and advisor of the leader of the Labour Party." His attack was aimed at FitzGerald as much as at Rogers and Labour. "Is there no limit to the lengths the present leader of Fine Gael will go to hold on to office? Is there much point in being Taoiseach if you cannot even appoint your own Attorney General?"

Brian Lenihan was even more insulting. "It is proposed to appoint as Attorney General, to replace a Fine Gael Attorney General who is being transposed to Europe, an innocuous junior barrister who at the drop of a hat is being made a senior barrister in order to qualify for a job for which his only entitlement has been to write for the Tánaiste facetious scripts. This is the sort of corruption to which Irish public life has descended."

Despite the controversy and abuse which attended his appointment, John Rogers quickly established a high reputation for himself in his important post. A year later, following his successful intervention to ensure adequate compensation for the relatives of the Stardust victims, Haughey had the decency to make one of his very rare acknowledgements that he was wrong, and he stood up in the Dáil to praise Rogers. On the Fine Gael side, too, there was private acknowledgement that Rogers was well up to the job.

"John Rogers was a fine Attorney General," says one of the former Fine Gael Ministers who is no admirer of Dick Spring. "I have no hesitation in saying that Rogers was a better Attorney General than

Peter Sutherland. His advice was always clear and fair-minded and there was no question of it being influenced by political considerations."

However, within Labour itself there was also criticism of the Rogers appointment. There were some on the left whose attitude can be summed up by one critic who remarked: "Spring was prepared to wear the cuts in food subsidies but he was willing to put the Government at risk to get a job for his pal."

As Garret FitzGerald makes clear in his autobiography, there were plenty of things on which Fine Gael and Labour were in agreement but there were also continuous niggles which damaged the cohesion of the Government. The handling of Dublin Gas became public knowledge but there were a number of others. The future of Irish Steel and Clondalkin Paper Mills, the establishment of a National Development Corporation and an abortive Radio Bill were all instances of issues on which the two parties failed to get along.

On Irish Steel there was a fierce clash between Spring and Bruton. The Fine Gael Minister believed that, in view of the mounting losses at the State-owned steel plant, there was no option but to close it down. Spring was totally opposed to the idea, particularly in view of the closure of Ford's, Dunlop's and Verolme dockyards in Cork around the same time. One Labour advisor recalls a meeting in Spring's office in the Department of Energy where Bruton and the Tánaiste got stuck into each other. "I will never forget it. The walls shook with the shouting and roaring and the stamping of feet."

Eventually the two men agreed on a formula which provided for a cut of a third in the workforce but the company and the majority of the workers' jobs were saved. However, Spring was bitterly attacked by a local trade union official for allowing any jobs to be lost. "It was a good illustration of what went wrong for us in Government. We saved the company and most of the jobs but all our people could see was that some of the jobs had been lost. If only we could have had a video of Dick doing his stuff in Cabinet, but that is not the way Government works," said the Labour advisor.

There were other similar squabbles. Early in the life of the Government, Fine Gael proposed the idea of a daily charge of £12.50 for the use of public hospital beds in order to bale out the under-funded health service. Labour Ministers objected strongly and the idea was dropped.

Labour opposed a move by Alan Dukes to withdraw the customary social welfare Christmas bonus in 1985. Despite a real dogfight in Cabinet, the bonus was paid but Labour received no comfort from the public for their struggle.

The Radio Bill of 1985 represented another cause for tension between the two parties. Jim Mitchell got Cabinet agreement to the Bill which sought to introduce commercial and community-based local radio and to eliminate the pirate stations. Labour Ministers agreed to the plan but the party's backbench communications spokesman, Toddy O'Sullivan, objected. Along with Frank Cluskey, he had been briefed by the RTE unions and they decided to sabotage the Bill because it proposed to allow some form of commercial radio. Even though it had actually been introduced in the Dáil and debate had begun, the Bill had to be withdrawn at Labour's behest. This was a clear example of a futile ideological stance on Labour's part which made no political or commercial sense. A few years later, Fianna Fáil introduced commercial radio to the delight of the public.

The issue of a land tax, to bring in a realistic contribution from farmers, was one of the proposals Labour pressed for at Cabinet. The Labour Ministers regarded the tax yield from farmers as pitifully low, in comparison with the contribution of the PAYE sector, and they demanded a greater contribution both for equity's sake and also to prove that Fine Gael were prepared to take on some of their own supporters as Labour had done. When news of the plan broke, farmers' groups put heavy pressure on Fine Gael backbenchers and a number of them buckled and demanded that the Government back off. Eventually the Government did deliver on the proposal in a modified form but Fianna Fáil opposed the tax, as they opposed everything else the Government did, and it was abolished after 1987.

One issue which dogged relations for almost the entire period of that Government was the plan to establish a National Development Corporation (NDC). Labour pinned a lot of hopes on setting up this State agency whose job it would be to find areas where public money could be invested to create jobs. Fine Gael had actually made the NDC an election promise in 1982 but John Bruton regarded the venture as badly thought-out and woolly and could not see what investment opportunities it could possibly come up with. For Labour, however, the NDC remained something of a Holy Grail and Bruton's attempts to obstruct its creation only added to his unpopularity with Labour Ministers.

"John Bruton and Labour at odds again over the National Development Corporation," recorded Gemma Hussey on 26 January 1985. "I gave out hell at the beginning of Cabinet about it. Garret was conciliatory; it's really too awful that there should be another huge row after all our resolutions to preserve a united, decisive front."

After a great deal of squabbling, the NDC was finally established during the lifetime of the Government, but on a much smaller scale than Labour intended. Ultimately it was abolished by Des O'Malley during the lifetime of the Fianna Fáil-Progressive Democrat Coalition without ever having achieved the high hopes Labour had for it. The fate of the NDC was an illustration of Labour's limitations when it came to economic issues. The idea was an old socialist one which Labour brought forward at a time when socialist economics were going out of fashion all over the western world. The party was inclined to rely on old left-wing ideas which resulted in added bureaucracy and extra taxes without doing very much for the jobs crisis they were designed to tackle.

The party had better luck on the Family Planning Bill. Barry Desmond pressed very hard in Cabinet for changes in the law, as he was determined to provide for the widespread availability of contraceptives to everyone over the age of sixteen. Some Fine Gael Ministers refused to accept this limit and there was a considerable wrangle in Cabinet before the Bill emerged with an age limit of eighteen. This was not simply a straight Fine Gael-Labour battle and there were divisions within the two parties over it. Three Fine Gael TDs voted against the Bill but so did one Labour deputy, Sean Treacy. He was subsequently expelled from the party and remained an independent TD. He had the good fortune to hold the balance of power after 1987 and was elected Ceann Comhairle of the Dáil, retaining the position after the 1989 and 1992 elections.

On the economic front, the two parties tried to improve matters between them after the budget rows of 1983 and 1984 by putting together *Building on Reality*, designed to give them a clear programme for the second half of their term in Government. It was eventually published in the autumn of 1984 amid a great deal of fanfare. In the run-up to the publication there was a tussle between the two parties over the economic targets to be set and Spring issued a public warning at one stage about what he would and would not accept in terms of holding back social welfare increases.

The Fine Gael perspective illuminates how difficult Spring's task was just to keep going. "I hate having to govern with Labour," confided Gemma Hussey to her diary in April 1985, adding: "Maybe I'd be crucified worse with cuts if they weren't there – such schizophrenia. If only Dick had leadership and authority. Maybe he's too young."

As disputes raged between the Government partners, Fianna Fáil, now back in Opposition, fought tooth and nail against the compromise cuts that eventually emerged. Even though they were only a partial implementation of what Haughey himself had planned in the autumn of 1982, he maintained again and again that the reductions were unnecessary and slated the Government for its policies.

One thing Labour and Fine Gael could agree on and on which they could generally maintain a unified front against Fianna Fáil was Northern Ireland. That common purpose produced the biggest breakthrough in Anglo-Irish relations since the Treaty of 1922. The process began inauspiciously enough in 1983 when FitzGerald took up John Hume's idea of a Forum of all constitutional nationalist parties to chart the way forward. There were serious doubts in the Cabinet about the issue and FitzGerald had the support of only two of his Ministers when he first proposed the idea.

Frank Cluskey and Barry Desmond, on the Labour side, and Pat Cooney and John Bruton in Fine Gael expressed initial opposition to the creation of the Forum. FitzGerald, however, was determined to move on the issue but it was only when he insisted that the Cabinet swung behind him. There was a lot of tension in the Forum as the other parties sought to bring Fianna Fáil along with them in broadening the traditional nationalist position by looking for solutions involving joint authority in the governing of Northern Ireland. In one episode early on, Spring lashed into Haughey and to everybody's surprise the Fianna Fáil leader broke down. Things were quickly patched up, although, when the Forum Report was eventually produced, Haughey immediately denounced it.

The Report gave FitzGerald the opportunity to set off on the road to the successful conclusion of the Anglo-Irish Agreement. Spring regarded the negotiations as vitally important and was extremely proud to have taken part. While he may not have shared his father's strong traditional Nationalist views, he has always regarded the Northern problem as one of the key political issues.

"Dick's role in the Anglo-Irish talks was quite substantial but it was completely understated at the time," says one official involved in the talks. "During the summer of 1985 he was jetting backwards and forwards to London on a regular basis. Spring and Peter Barry, coming from a Munster Republican background, approached the talks from a very different perspective than Garret and were vital in getting the British to compromise. As on a lot of other issues dealt with by that Government, Dick's role was constructive but invisible to the public."

The road to the Anglo-Irish Agreement was a bumpy one. Margaret Thatcher in her famous "Out, Out, Out" response to the Forum Report in December 1984, put FitzGerald under terrible pressure. But he persevered in the endeavour and it resulted in the signing of the Hillsborough Agreement which gave the Irish Government a mechanism, through the Anglo-Irish Inter-Governmental Conference, for representing the views of the Nationalist community in Northern Ireland. It also provided for the establishment of a permanent Irish secretariat to the conference at Maryfield in Belfast. Spring and Barry went to Hillsborough with Garret FitzGerald to sign the Agreement with the British Government on 15 November 1985.

Haughey denounced the Agreement, claiming it was unconstitutional and a betrayal of nationalism. "I see this as a very sad day for Irish nationalism and I think there has been a very severe blow dealt to the concept of Irish unity. I think the position of constitutional Nationalists in Ireland has been severely undermined," he said on the day the Agreement was signed.

Spring, coming from Kerry where the Republican tradition was still relatively strong, had no qualms about his role in the Agreement and regarded it as one of his great achievements in Government.

SLOW DISINTEGRATION

AS CHRISTMAS 1985 APPROACHED, Dick Spring had been Tánaiste for three bruising years. After the signing of the Anglo-Irish Agreement, the Government suddenly benefited from a surge of popularity and for a few weeks it appeared as if the partners might be able to defy the prophets of doom. Their cause was helped by the fact that Charles Haughey did severe damage to Fianna Fáil with an intemperate denunciation of the Agreement.

When it came before the Dáil, Mary Harney, the Fianna Fáil TD for Dublin South-West and long-time supporter of Des O'Malley, voted with the Government and was expelled from the party almost immediately. Rumours soon spread that she and O'Malley planned to launch a new party.

A few days before Christmas, the new party, the Progressive Democrats, was launched by Des O'Malley, Mary Harney and Michael McDowell. In the mood of economic despondency which had gripped the country, the party was soon widely regarded as offering a ray of hope amid the darkness, and the public flocked to its banner.

Its emergence was to have a profound bearing on the future direction of Irish politics. The PDs offered an economic analysis of the country's problems which ran directly counter to Labour's. Their whole emphasis was on getting the State off the back of the citizen, slashing personal taxes and freeing the market to create jobs and opportunities. Labour Ministers and TDs were scathing in their criticism of the PDs but a surprisingly large segment of the electorate, disillusioned and despondent at the state of the nation, responded positively to it.

The PD bandwagon continued rolling through January of 1986, with Fianna Fáil TDs like Bobby Molloy and Pearse Wyse joining the party. Two Labour senators, Helena McAuliffe and Timmy Conway, also enlisted. Conway had been selected as Labour's Dáil candidate for Kildare in succession to Joe Bermingham. However, the AC added

Emmet Stagg to the ticket after he failed to win the nomination and Conway left in disillusionment.

The new party started off well ahead of Labour and just behind Fine Gael and with all the publicity surrounding the defections of Molloy and Wyse its star rose even higher. A series of opinion polls showed it continuing to gain ground until it passed out Fine Gael who hit a new low of 23 per cent. The news was even worse for Labour. The party got just 4 per cent in one of the polls and Spring's own satisfaction rating hovered around the 30 per cent mark, behind FitzGerald, Haughey and O'Malley. Things looked so bad that Frank Cluskey, in typical fashion, joked to a few colleagues: "Well, lads, we are now within the margin of error of existing at all."

The foundation of the PDs had a curious psychological effect on Fine Gael. While Fine Gael TDs realised that the new party was a threat to their vote base, they also believed it might provide the option of an alternative coalition partner to Labour and a much more congenial one in ideological terms. Labour Ministers bitterly resented the change of mood on the Fine Gael side. Having struggled to keep the Coalition afloat, against the wishes of many of their own supporters, they were indignant at the clear signals from Fine Gael that they regarded the PDs as a better long-term partner.

It was against this background that, early in 1986, Garret FitzGerald tried to give his Government an early boost by reshuffling the Cabinet for the run-in to a general election. In his autobiography, he says that he was particularly keen to move Alan Dukes from Finance and Barry Desmond from Health in order to minimise the political damage they were likely to suffer as a result of having to take tough decisions. For the same reason he decided to move Gemma Hussey from Education. The Taoiseach consulted Spring about his plan to move Desmond from Health and Social Welfare and the Tánaiste agreed with his analysis and the planned move.

The only problem was that Barry Desmond refused to budge and told the Taoiseach he would resign from Government rather than do so. He refused to accept FitzGerald's reasoning, taking the view that a move from Health would be a concession to all the interest groups, from the Fianna Fáil Opposition and the medical profession to the tobacco industry, who had been howling for his head. He told the Taoiseach that he would prefer to lose his Dáil seat in Dun Laoghaire, if that was the price that had to be paid, rather than abandon his portfolio in the face of his critics.

Spring, who had initially agreed with FitzGerald's decision to move Desmond, was now in a dilemma as well. He had no more success than the Taoiseach in persuading his deputy leader that a move would be good for him. The following day he went to the Taoiseach and said that he and the other Labour Ministers would have to resign from the Cabinet if Desmond were moved from Health.

Barry Desmond confirms that Spring and FitzGerald had decided to move him from Health and Social Welfare to Justice. "To be fair to both of them, they thought they were acting in my own best interests and believed the move was necessary to save my seat in Dun Laoghaire. That's the reason I didn't fall out with either of them over the issue. But I took the view that if I was moved it would be a clear signal to a number of forces that they had been able to force a change in the Government.

"In particular, the Independent group of newspapers had been involved in a vicious campaign against me. I was convinced it was because of my plans to curb tobacco advertising and I wasn't going to give in to them. There were also the Fine Gael hospital consultants who wanted me out because they thought I was standing in the way of more private medicine. Then there were Fine Gael deputies, and for that matter Labour deputies, who wanted me out because of the decisions I had taken to rationalise and improve the health service. In the face of all that, I would have preferred to lose my seat in Dun Laoghaire rather than move from Health," says Desmond. He is amused by the recollection that, because of the way he wrecked FitzGerald's initial plans, "a couple of Fine Gael Ministers on their way to the political abattoir survived in Cabinet because of my obduracy."

With Desmond adamant he would not accept a new Ministry, the Taoiseach was stymied and the Government plunged into crisis. FitzGerald had compounded the problem because, just before lunchtime on 12 February, he had informed his parliamentary party that he was conducting a Cabinet reshuffle before telling the individual Ministers of his plans which he had expected to announce in the Dáil at the start of business the following morning. The Taoiseach and the Tánaiste were up most of the night trying to sort out the situation. The Minister for Health stayed in his Leinster House office all night, along with the secretary of his Department, Liam Flanagan, resisting all attempts to persuade him to change his mind. Not surprisingly, word of the dilemma leaked out and was all over the media the following day.

When FitzGerald was unable to announce his new team to the Dáil on the morning of 13 February there was uproar, with Fianna Fáil claiming the Taoiseach had lost control of his Government. It was after the Dáil hullabaloo that Spring told FitzGerald he, too, would have to resign if Desmond was moved. "In fairness to Dick, once I refused he stood by me. In fact, if Garret was as tough as he should have been I would have been fired before it got to that stage," says Desmond. With the Labour Ministers threatening to pull out of Government, the Taoiseach prepared to try to carry on as a Fine Gael minority administration.

"Shattered by this totally unexpected consequence of my concern, and Dick's, for Barry Desmond's political future, and aware of the growing atmosphere of rumour outside, I sat down to prepare a Fine Gael alternative Government. However, within half-an-hour Dick Spring was back with the news that Barry Desmond would relinquish his Social Welfare portfolio if he could keep Health; he had always given most of his time to health matters," wrote FitzGerald.

Desmond remembers events a little differently. "I was the one who suggested the compromise that got Garret off the hook. I remember going in to his office on my own around 2.20 p.m., shortly before the balloon was due to go up, and telling him the only way I could see the whole thing being resolved was if I gave up Social Welfare but held on to Health. Garret had no trouble agreeing to that."

Clutching at this minor back-down by Desmond, FitzGerald recast the Cabinet shuffle. Desmond got his wish and remained in Health. Among the other changes, Gemma Hussey took over Social Welfare, rather than European Affairs; Alan Dukes moved to Justice and John Bruton to Finance. The announcement of the new Cabinet had been postponed from 10.30 a.m. to 3.45 p.m. and again from 3.45 p.m. to 4.45 p.m. TDs wondered whether the Government was in its death throes and by the time the crisis had been solved by those involved it had assumed greater and greater proportions in the public eye.

"At 4.30 p.m. a tense group of Ministers, hardly looking at each other, obviously shocked, assembled in the Cabinet room and Garret rattled out the list of junior Ministers. We rushed into the Dáil at 4.45 p.m. where he read out all of the changes and uproar ensued," wrote Gemma Hussey.

The botched Cabinet reshuffle further eroded the confidence of the Government and undermined some of the gains that had been made by the Anglo-Irish accord and by agreement on a budget for 1986. With the opinion polls showing a surge in support for the fledgling PDs and Fianna Fáil holding up well, both Fine Gael and Labour were on the ropes.

It was against this background, with the PDs appearing to run away with the liberal agenda, that the Government decided to move on the divorce issue. The subject had been brought before the Dáil in November 1985, through an initiative by former Labour leader and Fine Gael TD Michael O'Leary. He introduced a private member's bill to remove the constitutional ban on divorce. The move embarrassed Fine Gael and Labour, both of whom were committed to the introduction of divorce. However, when the O'Leary Bill was put to the Dáil, it received the support of only four TDs – the two Workers' Party deputies, Tony Gregory, and Liam Skelly of Fine Gael. Labour didn't support it but decided that if the Government would not act the party would bring in its own Divorce Bill.

Labour's bill was introduced at the end of February 1986. Garret FitzGerald was reluctant to commit Fine Gael at this stage because he wasn't sure the timing was right and he was involved in consultation with the leaders of all the major Churches on the matter. Fine Gael ended up by allowing a free vote on the issue. After a lot of discussion, just eleven Fine Gael TDs supported the Labour measure and it was defeated. Spring was the first leader of a major political party to pledge himself to changing the divorce law and that carried its own risks in a conservative constituency like North Kerry.

Just two months later, however, FitzGerald completed his discussions with the Church leaders and decided that the time was right to put the matter to the test. Pat Cooney, who was now Minister for Education, opposed the referendum in Cabinet and said he would have to resign rather than accept it. Eventually, a theological compromise was worked out to keep Cooney on board. It was agreed that the "parties in Government", rather than the Government as a collective entity, would announce their intention to hold a divorce referendum.

That left Cooney free to campaign against the measure.

Other senior Fine Gael figures had misgivings about the prospects of a referendum succeeding but the campaign was launched at the end of April 1986. Initially it looked as if FitzGerald's assessment was right and that it would be carried. The first opinion poll of the campaign showed that 57 per cent of the electorate were prepared to vote "Yes" and just 36 per cent "No" to a change in the Constitution to permit the introduction of divorce.

Fine Gael, Labour, the PDs and the Workers' Party campaigned, with varying intensity, for a "Yes" vote. Fianna Fáil was officially neutral and, while a small number of its TDs supported the "Yes" campaign, the majority of them spoke against divorce in the Dáil debate on the issue and much of the party organisation campaigned for a "No" vote. The Catholic Church also spoke out against divorce and, as the campaign wore on, it became evident that there was a big swing in public opinion to the "No" camp. That swing was not detected in published opinion polls until the day before the referendum when for the first time the "No" side edged ahead.

When the votes were counted the proposal to introduce divorce was rejected by a decisive majority, with 63.5 per cent voting "No" and 36.5 per cent supporting the move. It was a serious setback for both Government parties after three-and-a-half years in Government at a time when a general election was inevitably looming closer. It was FitzGerald rather than Spring who forfeited most in the public mind by the defeat. As a small party, Labour felt that it had nothing to lose by pushing Fine Gael into the divorce campaign but the damage to the overall image of the Government didn't help the party.

The Labour commission to examine electoral strategy was nearing the end of its deliberation in the summer of 1986. Delicately balanced between the different factions of the party, the commission had to make a crucial decision on whether Labour should rule out entering another coalition for the foreseeable future. Spring and his supporters desperately wanted to avoid a categoric anti-coalition report and the commission meetings dragged on through the summer as a power battle was worked out. During August, as the final report was being prepared, the commission met for a week-end session in Bellinter in Co. Meath. Spring was very much on the defensive. Leaks about an initial draft of the report suggested that it would come down heavily against entering coalition in the future. Ultimately, however, a compromise was worked out. This said that Labour wouldn't consider another coalition until the party won a minimum of twenty-five Dáil seats but, in what some people regarded as a let-out clause, the commission conceded that Labour could enter Government if a national emergency of some kind occurred.

Two days before the report was published in September 1986, Spring gave a television interview in which he suggested that the possibility of another coalition after the following election was not ruled out if certain minimum demands by the party were met. The left wing of the party reacted with fury to this interpretation of the report and Michael D. Higgins was among those who publicly disagreed with the leader. Spring immediately did a U-turn and issued a public statement saying he "looked forward to being the first Labour Party leader to recommend to the party that we don't participate in Government and that we pursue an independent role." Labour left-wingers followed this by welcoming the *volte face* and claiming the commission report as "a victory for the party's left wing".

These developments confirmed Fine Gael, already looking towards the PDs as a possible future partner, in their belief that there was no chance of a renewal of their coalition arrangement with Labour, whatever the results of the following election. For both parties in office the only remaining question was how they could minimise the inevitable losses.

At this stage, in September 1986, the Government was beginning to unravel. During August the former Labour leader, Frank Cluskey, and the former parliamentary party chairman, Joe Bermingham, threatened to vote against the Government when the Dáil resumed. On the Fine Gael side, a raft of TDs – Alice Glenn, Liam Skelly and Brendan McGahon – were also threatening to withdraw their support from the Government.

Spring's position was not very strong after the on-again, off-again attitude to coalition following the electoral commission report. The party's Dáil strength was already weakened with the loss of two TDs. Sean Treacy had departed in 1985 over contraception and was now a strong critic of the Government. Joe Bermingham left in disgust at the decision of the AC to add Emmet Stagg to the Labour ticket in Kildare. Bermingham still voted with the party in the Dáil but by the autumn of 1986 he was in a truculent mood and threatening, like Treacy, to vote against the Government on social welfare issues.

When the Dáil session began in October, there was one crisis after another. Changes in the social welfare code to give full equality to women resulted in financial losses to some categories of welfare families and Labour TDs demanded changes. The introduction of extradition caused another row, while Labour left-wingers also expressed opposition to the Single European Act. With another set of rows preoccupying Fine Gael TDs, public confidence in the Government eroded.

It was also clear from October onwards that Labour and Fine Gael would not be able to agree a budget. The fact that John Bruton was now Minister for Finance was one source of friction but it was not the main impediment to agreement. It was simply that the inherent contradictions in the Fine Gael-Labour arrangement were about to come to their logical conclusion. Government spending began to go seriously off target and by September an overrun of £180 million in Exchequer borrowing for the year was likely. This prompted a loss of confidence in the financial markets, and a 4 per cent hike in interest rates was required to stop massive sales of Government stock.

Garret FitzGerald records that, in order to steady the markets and restore confidence, he proposed that the Government should announce financial targets for the following year involving a cut in the Exchequer borrowing requirement below the 11.8 per cent target for 1986, which was going to be exceeded in any case. He also proposed that they should make it clear they were not going to increase taxes.

"The clear implication of any such announcement was that significant expenditure cuts would have to be effected; this naturally presented problems for our Labour partners. Nevertheless, the threat to interest rates in particular posed by the decline in confidence in financial circles was such that I felt it necessary on this occasion to do what I had never previously done: to press for a majority decision, despite the opposition of our four Labour Party colleagues."

The Labour Ministers didn't go public on their opposition to FitzGerald's plan but they put him on notice that when it came to taking decisions on the departmental estimates for 1987 their future participation in Government couldn't be guaranteed. From that point on, the Government was effectively dead but it staggered on until Christmas, surviving one crisis after another in the Dáil.

The Government survived only on the casting vote of the Ceann Comhairle on the social welfare changes resulting from women's equality, even after the package had been modified because of pressure from Labour backbenchers. The support of the PDs helped to carry the Single European Act more comfortably but the Extradition Act was carried only with the Ceann Comhairle's vote. The Labour Party nearly split on the Single European Act because there was huge opposition from the party's left-wingers. Spring made a Dáil speech emphasising that the Act posed no threat to Irish neutrality but the Labour AC voted for it by a majority of only two. If the vote at the AC had gone the other way Labour would have faced a split which would have brought the Government down in very unpromising circumstances. After a series of close shaves, the Dáil eventually adjourned for the Christmas break with the Government surviving, by one vote, a Fianna Fáil motion calling for its dissolution.

Meanwhile, Ministers knew that their days were numbered because of disagreements on the estimates and the budget for 1987. It was the first time that Labour Ministers were simply outvoted at Cabinet along party lines. While the Taoiseach and Fine Gael Ministers argued that cuts in spending were necessary, the Labour Ministers were more than a bit suspicious that the new hard line had come about because of the arrival of the PDs on the scene. Labour refused point-blank to accept significant cuts in health spending and without them the Fine Gael targets could not be met.

Throughout January 1987, there was continued speculation about the Government's collapse and the inevitable happened on 20 January when the Labour Ministers formally resigned from Government. The move had been well-rehearsed and both Labour and Fine Gael had their policy documents ready for the immediate general election which Garret FitzGerald called.

"We were lucky to get out in time, I suppose," says Spring. "It was inevitable for a number of months. There were three or four major roadblocks ahead in terms of budgetary matters. Garret knew they were there too and we did try to see if there was any way we could get over them. Both parties had a different constituency to address coming into an election."

Despite all the rows and difficulties over their years in Government, most Ministers had established warm personal relations and the break-up of the Government was a sad occasion, particularly as many of them realised they were unlikely ever to serve in Government together again.

"After Dick had handed me his own and his colleagues' formal resignations, we all shook hands with each other warmly and with considerable emotion; Gemma Hussey was embraced by several of our Labour colleagues," wrote FitzGerald a few years later.

Two days after the break-up Gemma Hussey wrote: "Our final Cabinet meeting was slightly strained and obviously very hard for Dick. We took a formal vote at noon and then Dick handed over his prepared letter of resignation. There was a session of slightly sad, slightly emotional handshakes (a warm embrace for me from Barry and Ruairi)."

After the election, when Fine Gael were still in office as a caretaker Government and before the Dáil met to elect a new Taoiseach, some of FitzGerald's colleagues suggested that there should be a dinner for the Government, including the former Labour Ministers. "I found I was entitled to hold such a function at my own expense in Barrettstown Castle and there on 3 March the Coalition Ministers of both parties, the former Attorney General, John Rogers, and the Chief Whip, Sean Barrett, celebrated until a late hour a Government in whose record we all took pride," records FitzGerald.

In fact, even at that stage Rogers wasn't a former Attorney General because he remained right until the end of FitzGerald's administration and did not resign along with the Labour Ministers. He stayed to emphasise that it was a political difference rather than any deeper distrust that had prompted the break-up, and this also showed how trusted he was at that stage by his Fine Gael colleagues.

"We broke up on reasonably amicable terms. There was a certain amount of respect around the place for what we tried to do," says Spring.

3

From Survival to Triumph

STARING INTO THE ABYSS

DICK SPRING CAME WITHIN A HAIR'S BREADTH of a political and personal disaster on the night of 18 February 1987. Just four votes stood between him and the loss of the Dáil seat held by a member of his family since 1943. The experience was a harrowing one for him, all the worse for being so unexpected, and it burned a deep scar into his soul.

"It is only in recent weeks that I heard Dick make a joke about the four votes for the first time and even then I wasn't sure if he really was joking," said a friend in early 1993. Spring with typically laconic humour remarks: "I think I had some difficulty in that election."

As the drama of the Kerry count unfolded on television the night of the count, the nation watched in fascination. Spring, leaning over a crush barrier in the early hours of the morning, gave every appearance of a man about to face the gallows. It was one of those rare moments which gave the public a glimpse of just how unpredictable politics can be.

At the start of the campaign, although many people were predicting a Labour annihilation, Spring was regarded as the holder of possibly the only safe Labour seat in the country with the next safest being that of Frank McLoughlin in Meath. In the event, McLoughlin lost his seat while Spring held on by his finger-tips.

Labour and Fine Gael were fighting an uphill battle from the moment Dick Spring and his three Labour ministerial colleagues walked out of Government on the previous month. Garret FitzGerald opted for a longer than usual four-week election campaign, in the hope that the extra time would put Fianna Fáil under intense scrutiny and that his party might get the room to stage a rally.

The very first opinion poll showed just how deep the problems were for the former Government partners. Labour attracted the support of just 5 per cent of the voters with Fine Gael on 23 per cent. At that stage Fianna Fáil looked set for a comfortable victory with 52 per cent support while the PDs were looking good on 15 per cent. Spring launched the Labour campaign on 31 January, saying that there should be a radical shift in the burden of taxation with the vested business interests and the large farmers being asked to pay more. He fell back on traditional Labour policies such as the introduction of a wealth tax and protection for those on social welfare.

While the media wrote off the Labour campaign from the start, some of the TDs who were regarded as most vulnerable began to recover their confidence once they began canvassing. Frank Cluskey, who was always in difficulty at election times, sensed a positive enough response after only a couple of days and was able to predict correctly that he would survive. Barry Desmond, too, quickly gained in confidence.

"When I went out on to the doorsteps with my wife Stella and the Labour Party canvassers, I quickly realised that I was going to make it. It was extremely heartening to realise that there was a quota for a politician who would stand up for what he believed in, even though I had been vilified by some sections of the media, particularly the Independent group," says Barry Desmond.

In Kerry North, where a quota is much harder to get because it is a three-seat constituency, Dick Spring began to get a little uneasy towards the end of the campaign. He had had to spend a fair bit of time outside the constituency on the national trail but he sensed during his time in the county that something might be going wrong. On the weekend before the vote, he suggested to some of his supporters that another leaflet drop into every house in the constituency might be necessary, but having being assured that everything was all right he didn't pursue it.

"The biggest surprise was that I canvassed and got a very polite reception. There was no hostility on a person-to-person basis but, at the same time, I think that my mother and myself were the only people who detected that we were fighting against the odds," says Spring.

On 18 February, the day of the count, Spring's worst fears were quickly confirmed. "The morning of the count I was trying to read books at six o'clock in the morning. Later a friend of ours arrived with a cake so that we would have something to celebrate with just at the same time as my brother Arthur arrived in with the figures and his chin was down around his knees.

"He said: 'I think we are in trouble.' I said: 'Come on, give me the figures.' 'Deenihan [Fine Gael] is going to poll 9,000 plus and you are going to be away down,' he said. So I said if that is the situation I hope Deenihan polls 10,000 plus; the higher he goes the better for us. Because whatever chance I have of getting transfers I wouldn't get them from Fianna Fáil; I'd get them from Fine Gael. I made a calculation about twelve o'clock that I was going to lose my seat by twenty-five votes, judging the nuances of PR and where the votes would go."

Donal Spring also remembers that morning vividly. "I went down to the count at nine o'clock and, after watching three boxes being opened, I knew we were in trouble." When the first count result was announced in the evening, Dick Spring's vote was 6,737, over 19 per cent of the poll, but in the tight Kerry North three-seater it didn't seem enough. Fine Gael's candidate, Jimmy Deenihan, had bucked the national trend and had come in with a whopping 10,087 votes on the first count and it didn't look as if there was room for two anti-Fianna Fáil TDs in North Kerry.

Dick went down to the count centre late in the evening still not knowing if he was going to make it or not. When it came to the last count, it looked all over for him. The battle for the final seat was between Spring and Tom McEllistrim of Fianna Fáil, whose family had represented the constituency since 1923. On the agonising sixth count, 925 surplus Fianna Fáil votes were distributed. Spring got enough of them to keep just five votes ahead of McEllistrim but the Fianna Fáil man demanded a recount.

The recount was the most nail-biting episode of that election and much of it went out live on television. "There were twenty-four disputed ballot papers in my pile," recalls Spring, "and when they were doing the final re-check on those the first one was ruled out, so my lead went down to four. I remember my sister Kay fainted, but she couldn't fall because the people were crowding around so much. But I won by four votes anyway." The agony of his predicament was written all over Spring's face as the final votes were counted.

"All I remember is being there all day, getting more and more weary as time went on," recalls Donal. "Finally it was all down to the spoiled votes. The margin in Dick's favour came down to two at one stage and went up to six at another. It was one of the tensest episodes in my life. If ever I felt for Dick I felt for him then. Kerry just didn't realise how hard he had worked for the county in Government."

It deeply hurt Dick Spring, too, that the people of Kerry didn't appear to appreciate the work he had done. "The biggest shock really was that I felt I had worked my butt off. I really had worked night and day. I had done an awful lot for North Kerry. But I suppose I was the one that got the blame."

The role of Fine Gael's Jimmy Deenihan in nearly unseating him still rankles with Spring. "I got absolutely no support from the Fine Gael senator in North Kerry, Jimmy Deenihan [while in Government]. No support – he wouldn't defend anything. He used to attack Alan Dukes for public expenditure cuts and all that sort of thing. He used to attack the Minister for Health as well. He was obviously very active on the ground. There was also the factor that I had taken the young vote in 1982 but he swept the young vote in 1987."

On the other hand, Spring pays tribute to his defeated Fianna Fáil opponent. "I have to say I was very impressed by Tom McEllistrim's dignity on the occasion. For a while during the night there was the threat of a High Court action; at least Fianna Fáil were considering it. So I went for a long walk with John Rogers on Banna Beach and we discussed the nuances of such an action. Then Fianna Fáil said they had lost the game on the pitch and they weren't going to go to court. In fairness I have to hand it to Tom McEllistrim. After being in the Dáil for a long time, longer than ourselves, he was very magnanimous in the whole thing."

The result wasn't declared until nearly 5 a.m. and then the Springs went back to Dick's house. They opened a couple of bottles of whiskey and had a few drinks until the sun came up. "It was a beautiful frosty morning with a bright moon when we left the count centre," remembers John Foley, who covered the count for *The Independent* and who is now head of the Government Information Service. He went for a short sleep and met the Spring brothers, Arthur, Dick and Donal, after breakfast and they all went for a game of golf. (During breakfast, Dick's son Aaron, hearing all the talk about the four votes, asked who the four people were who had saved his father's seat.)

It was with an enormous sense of relief that the Spring brothers set out that winter's morning. "It was the first time in their lives that all three brothers went out together for a game of golf and they enjoyed it, even though we had been up all night," says Foley. When they finished playing they went back to the clubhouse in Tralee and Donal fell asleep on a bar stool, a pint of stout clutched firmly in his hand.

On a national level the Labour performance wasn't at all bad. The party held on to twelve seats, with just 6.4 per cent of the vote. Few commentators in the media or elsewhere had given Labour any chance of coming back with anything like so many seats and there had been a lot of speculation about the party's demise.

In a report on the election campaign to the AC, the general secretary, Ray Kavanagh, expressed satisfaction at the performance, pointing to the fact that while they had lost four of the seats held on the dissolution of the Dáil three new ones had been gained out of the nine targets. "We won seats in Galway West, Kildare and Wexford. The result in Kildare was particularly gratifying where the candidate achieved the second-highest Labour first preference vote in the country," wrote Kavanagh. But he added as a note of warning that with just 6.4 per cent of the vote the party could actually gain up to 3 per cent at the next election and still lose seats.

For the party and for Dick Spring the overall result was a great relief, even if the national share of the vote had fallen to its lowest point since 1933. From Spring's point of view he had not only saved his own seat but he didn't have to suffer the ignominy of leading the Labour Party into extinction as many had predicted in the run-up to the campaign.

However, the near loss of his own seat had a profound psychological effect on him and it took him a long time to recover from it. It wasn't simply the blow to his own self-esteem but the threat to the family honour which devastated him. On top of that, he needed to recover from the exhaustion of having served in a coalition Government under intense pressure for four years.

"He was so insulted, hurt and thick over the Kerry result that it was at least five years before he was able to laugh at it," says one member of the AC.

"When Dick left Government he was under intense physical, emotional and mental pressure," said a close friend. "He barely held on to his seat by the skin of his teeth. It was the most traumatic way possible to end four extremely tough years in Government and it certainly cured Dick of ever aiming at being in Government for its own sake."

For six months or more after that trauma, Spring virtually lay fallow. While he led the party in the Dáil there was, at that stage, little sign of the reputation he was to build later as the real leader of the Opposition. Alan Dukes had taken over as the new leader of Fine Gael and was trying to establish himself, while Des O'Malley, at the head of fourteen Progressive Democrat TDs, was cutting a dash in opposition to Charles Haughey's minority administration. The Workers' Party now had four TDs and they were providing loud opposition from the left to the spending cuts being implemented at the behest of Ray MacSharry at the Department of Finance.

Labour opposed the spending cuts which were attracting support in varying degrees from Fine Gael and the PDs. However, the performance was lacklustre even though the party had a more clearly-defined role in Opposition than either Fine Gael or the PDs who agreed to a large extent with Government policies. Labour ex-Ministers, in particular, were still recovering from the exhaustion of their term in Government. Spring adopted a low profile and in the summer of 1987 went with his family for a six-week holiday to Kristi's parents in the United States. There were even rumours that he would not come back, so exhausted was he by the strains of political life.

While Spring lay low, his enemies on the left of the party gathered themselves for another assault on his leadership. Michael D. Higgins had won his way back into the Dáil and Mervyn Taylor had held on to his seat, despite pressure from the Workers' Party. However, the main threat to Spring now came from newly-elected Kildare TD, Emmet Stagg, who had scored a very impressive victory in the election. Joe Bermingham, who had fought vigorously to prevent Stagg getting the Labour nomination, had long forecast that once Stagg had succeeded in ousting him in Kildare his next target would be Spring. He was proved right because, immediately he was elected to the Dáil, Stagg started to plot Spring's downfall.

Spring remembers the scene only too well. "We went into another period of tiredness and then the party decided they'd take over. Emmet came out to RTE on election night and told Barry Desmond to get off the panel, he was going on. So the whole thing started all over again. The office-holders were all tired and shattered and we faced our first conference totally unprepared. We just hadn't got ready for it."

"Emmet was a brash new TD in a hurry and he moved into a vacuum of leadership," says a Labour TD. "It wasn't just Dick who was out of it at that stage. Barry Desmond, Ruairi Quinn, Liam Kavanagh – they were all flat. By the time they woke up in the autumn of 1987, Emmet had virtually taken over the direction of the party."

Stagg achieved that by amazing organisational ability. If Spring could rely on the Kerry buses to provide him with the numbers at annual conference, Stagg determined to rival him with Kildare buses containing as many or even more delegates. Throughout the spring and summer of 1987, Stagg spearheaded a drive by the Labour left to mobilise every available delegate for the party's annual conference in Cork in September of that year. The conference had been postponed from November 1986 because of the impending election but it could be postponed no longer.

In the run-up to the conference it was the Labour left who made all the noise. Stagg led an assault to change the method of electing the party leader. Up to then, Labour TDs had always elected the leader and it is the standard method used by the major Dáil parties. But it did not meet with favour from left-wing militants because the TDs tended to be more conservative than the left would like. Instead, the left proposed that the leader should be elected by annual conference. The proposal was strongly resisted by Spring and there was every chance that if the motion was carried he would immediately be ousted from his position.

The Stagg faction was extremely well organised by the time conference came around. The Kildare TD struck a chord with many in the party when he said, in a memorable phrase, that Labour had to choose between being "a socialist party or the political wing of the St. Vincent de Paul".

Meanwhile Spring and his supporters continued to be gripped by lethargy. "Dick was warned time and time again that summer but he refused to prepare properly. He wouldn't organise the branches, he didn't fight for the hearts and minds of the delegates in advance of the conference," says one supporter.

Such was the mood in the party that little attempt was made to pay off the election debts and head office almost ceased to function. Without money even to buy paper for the photocopying machine, the head office staff had to go down the street to borrow paper from the Marine, Port and General Workers' Union. Envelopes and paper clips were recycled, such was the desperation.

Spring's mood going into that conference was captured by Joe Joyce in a profile in *The Irish Times* the morning conference started. Quoting a senior Fianna Fáil man who stopped Spring in a Dáil corridor and advised him to kick the Labour left in the testicles before they destroyed him, Joyce commented: "Spring is not the man to follow that advice. He doesn't have the gut political instinct to do it to them before they do it to him. And most of Labour's left is heading for Cork convinced that the boot is on their foot at long last. All week they've been telling each other a new and redder dawn is about to break over the Labour Party. Mervyn Taylor will defeat Ruairi Quinn for the chairmanship, Emmet Stagg will win the vice-chair and conference will wrest the election of leader from the parliamentary party. Spring is rattled, they say, boxed into a corner and may have no option but to resign."

Joyce's assessment was very close to being right. Mervyn Taylor did defeat Ruairi Quinn for the chairmanship and Stagg beat Spring supporter, Niamh Bhreathnach, for the vice-chair. It seemed as if the left would sweep all before it at the conference attended by over a thousand delegates in the Cork City Hall. There was even talk in the Spring family circle of Dick running for the European Parliament in 1989 as a way out of the embarrassment of having to step down as party leader.

Spring tried to placate the left by giving in on a number of points but they were in no mood for a deal. "We compromised on nearly everything you could compromise on, but it didn't matter," Spring remembers. "They wanted a victory, they just wanted blood. The big thing in our mind was that if you were beaten on the floor of conference it was a bit like Michael O'Leary – here we go. I mean where do you go after that? But we rallied and pulled up the shirt sleeves."

It was in the teeth of this adverse mood that Spring proved once and for all that he had what it takes to be a party leader. The debate on methods of choosing a leader took place on a motion from the Amalgamated Transport and General Workers' Union (ATGWU) that annual conference would select a leader after the following election. All the pent-up bile and bitterness between the different factions overflowed onto the conference floor. Barry Desmond and the trade union leader, Bill Attley, had a furious row and hurled insults across the floor over the record of the FitzGerald Coalition. The union leaders made it clear that their bloc vote was going onto the scales against the party leader as they too sought his scalp.

As the debate wore on and it became clear that the anti-leadership motion was likely to be carried, Dick Spring's own Rock Street branch in Tralee proposed a compromise motion which would allow the party to set up a commission to examine new forms of leadership election. This was unacceptable to the left who now scented blood and were not going to be deprived of it.

The debate was interrupted to allow Spring to deliver his televised leader's address. He had never shown himself to be a powerful speaker and his address that night was no exception. It was a well-argued defence of his record in Government and an appeal for unity in the years ahead but the delivery was hesitant. While he received the ritual applause at the end, it didn't appear as if he had done enough to save his own skin on the leadership issue.

Debate resumed later that night and as it built to a climax, with the clock moving on towards midnight, Spring intervened to try to turn the tide. With his jacket off, he marched to the podium in his shirt-sleeves, announced himself simply as "Dick Spring, Rock Street Branch" and delivered the best speech of his life. It was short but it was passionate, powerful and angry. He turned on his left-wing critics and told them to stop whingeing about élites in the party controlling the leadership. Instead they should get out and get more Labour TDs elected to the Dáil if they wanted to change things.

Spring also attacked the left for trying to change the leadership selection process without giving him time to consider the issue. "Give me the one courtesy I deserve on this change," he said, asking for support for his branch's amendment which would allow a commission to examine all aspects of the issue. It was not what he said but how he said it that grabbed his audience by the scruff of the neck.

"You see, the number of votes you were playing for were very few because the blocs were easy to determine. There were probably about two hundred people in that hall that you could sway and they were the ones we had to hit. They were the ones we were fighting for. Luckily some of them saw some hope in what I said. After that conference we decided we weren't ever going to be in that situation again," Spring recalled just before the 1993 conference. "In organising for conference this time there isn't the Spring bloc versus the Stagg bloc, but in those days it was strictly the building of the armies. If they were going to bring 200, I'd bring 206."

Writing about this episode a few years later Gerald Barry, political correspondent of *The Sunday Tribune*, maintained: "His determination was rock-like as he tore into his critics, defended himself, fought passionately for the kind of party he wanted Labour to be, a party of the left but not one encumbered by a hardline ideology and a puritanical abhorrence of power. It was quite a brilliant political performance and it was the birth of the new Dick Spring."

When the votes were called, the result was still so close that Spring, as at previous conferences, had to keep his hand in the air, delegate card aloft, long after his own vote was counted, so that his supporters would know what to do. Mervyn Taylor, Michael D. Higgins, Emmet Stagg and Toddy O'Sullivan all voted against him but he won the contest by 543 votes to 501. It was a tight enough margin, but considering the mood in the hall all day and the results of the various elections for officers, it represented an astonishing turn around.

In his final plea to the 1987 conference, Dick Spring didn't just turn the tide on one issue, he finally established himself a party leader of substance. Never again would the left threaten to overwhelm him. From the moment he threw caution to the wind and walked up to the microphone in his shirt sleeves, as the representative of the Rock Street branch, he had launched himself on an incredible journey which would bring his party astonishing triumphs.

WINNING THE PARTY

THE TURN AROUND IN SPRING'S FORTUNES didn't manifest itself immediately after the 1987 conference but he had done the essential groundwork just by surviving. The leader now had fire in his belly and he set about systematically establishing his control of the party. Because the left had been better organised for the Cork conference, they had taken the chairmanship and the vice-chair and were very strongly represented on the Administrative Council. It was a return to the position of the early 1980s with pairing arrangements between the different factions and constant battles at the monthly meetings.

Instead of remaining somewhat aloof as he had previously, Spring now began to organise his own supporters. There were meetings nearly every Wednesday night with a small group of his backers – Fergus Finlay, Brendan Howlin, Pat Upton and James Wynne. They planned in detail for the next party conference to make sure that Spring would have it his way. Branches were reorganised; constituencies which backed the leader got their delegate numbers up and detailed preparations were made to put the left finally in its place.

"It was a question of winning the party back for Dick. Emmet had brought a huge degree of organisation to the left and we had to respond in kind and match him organisationally," says one Spring supporter. Stagg had been building up his forces for two years and the battle to win back control of the party was not an easy one. Stagg had a full-time assistant, Michael Taft, who was distrusted by Spring supporters suspicious of his mysterious background. An American, Taft was utterly committed to the removal of Spring from the leadership and he and Stagg constituted a formidable team.

While one group dealt with the nuts-and-bolts issues of party organisation, another was established to look at the fundamental issue of Labour's economic philosophy. A small group composed of John Rogers, Willie Scally who had been Spring's economic advisor in Government, Brendan Lynch a stockbroker economist, Greg Sparks an accountant, and party activist Tim Burke, met regularly to consider where the party should be going.

The fundamental issue for the group was how Labour's approach to the economy should be modernised. They were determined to come up with a blueprint which would jettison many of the traditional socialist solutions and at the same time challenge the emerging right-wing economic consensus. "We had to demonstrate that we were prepared to change ourselves before our aspiration to change the country could be taken seriously by the voters," said one of those involved.

After nearly a year's deliberations the group produced a document which was submitted to the party's economic committee. After amendment by the committee it was ultimately circulated to party members under the title "Labour's Agenda" and received wide internal debate. Much of that debate centred on a proposal to introduce a national property tax, but the central thesis of the document was an unequivocal acceptance of the market economy, and abandonment of much of the socialist rhetoric of the sixties. Instead, there was an emphasis on the principles of liberty, equality and fraternity and on the economic policies which might bring those principles about in a free market economy.

Spring's first goal was to get control of the AC. This was difficult because of the way the left had dominated the voting at the Cork conference. The parliamentary party appoints six people to the body and Spring saw this as a way of reversing the left-wing majority and giving himself a slight edge. However, when Spring tried to make the six appointments he was confronted by furious opposition from Stagg. Not only did Stagg fight the issue internally, but he threatened to bring Spring to court.

Interestingly, in view of what was to happen only a few years later, Stagg's legal advisor in the attempt to gut Spring was none other than Mary Robinson. When the party leader offered a compromise method of election, whereby the twelve TDs could select their representatives on the AC, Robinson issued a legal challenge to it on the basis that it was not being done by strict proportional representation. The matter was on the point of going to court but it was ultimately settled without recourse to law but with a lot of bad feeling all around.

Spring got his way and again had a slight majority on the AC but it was a battle every inch of the way. The difference between the 1987 period and the early 1980s was that Spring was now taking on his enemies in a co-ordinated way. He decided once and for all to get the Trotskyite Militant Tendency out of the party. The 'Millies', as they were known, were led by another Kerryman, Joe Higgins. A courteous and charming man, Higgins was personally popular with a great many in the party, even with those who regarded his views as political lunacy. The Militants had powerful allies on the Labour left, including Michael D. Higgins, who actively protected them from attack. Nonetheless, Spring, encouraged by Neil Kinnock's attack on the Militants in Britain, moved to take them on. In another imitation of Kinnock, he adopted the red rose as the symbol of the party rather than the traditional Starry Plough, which had served since Labour's foundation in 1912.

There were frustrations for Spring along the way. On one occasion, the AC was ready to expel Joe Higgins and a number of other Militants, but one of the leadership supporters unaccountably switched sides out of personal sympathy for Higgins. The battle had to be left until another day. Eventually the AC voted to expel Higgins after he had been selected as a Labour Party candidate in Dublin West by the Militant-controlled organisation in the constituency. The AC expelled three Militant branches, including that of Higgins, and held a new selection convention but Higgins began a campaign to appeal the issue to the next annual conference.

With the Militants on the run, the rows with Labour left-wingers at the AC meetings continued. Spring proposed a motion to ban smoking at the meetings which tended to drag on for hours and hours. The move was directed against Stagg, who was a chain-smoker. Some of Spring's own people like Pat Magner, who is also a heavy smoker, had no choice but to support the ban as part of the psychological war against Stagg. At times the AC meetings threatened to degenerate from shouting matches into physical confrontation, and punch-ups were barely avoided on occasion.

In his capacity as vice-chairman of the party, Stagg was in a position to mobilise support throughout the organisation and he circulated letters and documents to every branch in the country. "Labour must build on our national success in leading the opposition to the right-wing consensus. We must take our radical programme directly into our communities. A new community politics can transform the relationship between Labour and the communities we live in," said Stagg in a newsletter distributed to every branch.

As he gradually organised himself to take on his internal opponents, Spring suffered a huge personal loss. In September 1988, his father, Dan, died. The numbers who turned up to pay their respects testified to the love and affection in which he had been held. *The Kerryman* reported that so many people came that the removal took a record five hours. It was the biggest funeral anyone could remember seeing in Tralee. Dan Spring's coffin was draped with the flags of the Labour Party and the ITGWU and with the colours of the Kerins O'Rahilly's and Kerry football teams.

In an appreciation in *The Evening Press*, Con Houlihan, who knew him well, wrote:

> "The secret of his success was simple: he had a marvellous
> personality – roguish but palpably honest – and his

*capacity for work would make a coolie seem under-em-
ployed.*

"For good measure he had in Anna a marvellous wife.

*"Dan had no time for the kind of socialists who are now
turning parts of Africa into a living hell. His concern was
for better wages, better working conditions, better care for
the old and infirm.*

*"The family home, No 1, Strand Rd, was an open house;
there you could experience a kind of casual democracy
in action.*

*"I doubt if Dan Spring ever made an enemy. I know he
made a myriad of friends.*

"God rest his big soul."

Anna Spring, too, recalls that Dan never made an enemy. She says
the enormous crowd at his funeral testified to the love the people of
Kerry had for him. She cites as typical of his personality a comment
he made, not long before he died and after they had spent some time
talking about their lives, the hardships, the long hours and the
ups-and-downs of politics. "Didn't we enjoy it?" he said simply.

Meanwhile, Dick Spring was coping with the tensions that were
coming to a head in the run-up to the annual conference of March
1989, which was held in Tralee. The very selection of Spring's home
town as the venue was enough to enrage the left. He was able to push
it through only when the left walked out of an AC meeting in late 1988
after yet another row, leaving only Joan Burton behind. Spring
pounced to propose Tralee and it was agreed by a decisive majority
in the absence of the left-wing representatives.

In January 1989 there was an unedifying clash between Spring and
Stagg, when Stagg arrived at party headquarters in Gardiner Place and
demanded access to party records which list branches and membership. The general secretary, Ray Kavanagh, refused to make the
material available whereupon the Kildare TD physically tried to get his
hands on it. Spring was alerted at Leinster House and rushed over to
Gardiner Place where he physically prevented the Kildare TD from
leaving the building with the party records and there was a lot of
pushing and shoving. The confrontation got so bad that one of the
Labour officials threatened to call the Gardaí. In the end, tempers
cooled and Stagg left the building empty-handed.

Another incident involving Spring in March 1989 showed the combative side of the Labour leader's temperament. In early March, he had an altercation with John Cooney who was then a journalist with *The Irish Times*. The two men had clashed a few years earlier during a Christmas dinner hosted by Spring as Tánaiste. On that occasion, Spring left the function in annoyance at Cooney's behaviour. This time words were exchanged after an argument earlier in the evening. Spring removed Cooney's glasses and slapped him on the face. Cooney later wrote a letter of apology to Spring over the incident which took place just a few days before the Tralee conference.

At that conference, Spring and the left formally confronted each other again. This time, the question of how the leader should be elected didn't pose a problem. The special commission set up to examine the matter had produced a report which opted for the direct election of the leader by the entire membership of the party, rather than by conference. Spring accepted the report, even though it marked a huge change in procedure for a major political party, and the left also accepted it as a *fait accompli*.

The conference was an undoubted triumph for Spring. The media hadn't caught up beforehand with Spring's carefully-prepared plans to recapture the organisation and in some quarters the conference was billed as Spring's "High Noon". John Waters, columnist for *The Irish Times*, went as far as to suggest that the party leader would be ousted, if not at the conference then not long afterwards, with either Stagg or Michael D. Higgins taking over the leadership.

The reality was that Spring by this stage had finally got the measure of all his internal enemies. The left was beaten comfortably on the major issues and the unions, seeing the way the wind was blowing, came back on-side. There were two crucial tests of strength. The first one was expulsion of the Militants and Spring pinned everything on winning. His margin of victory, by 757 votes to 518, was by no means overwhelming but once he had them out the hard left was seriously weakened. The second issue was the vice-chairmanship where Spring's ally Niamh Bhreathnach challenged Emmet Stagg. Even though she did not have nearly as high a profile in the party and was not even a county councillor at that stage, Bhreathnach easily beat the hero of the left and wrested the vice-chair from him.

The Tralee conference became known in the party as "The Bread and Roses" conference because of the entirely new format for the leader's speech devised by Fergus Finlay. The televised speech opened with a socialist anthem *Bread and Roses* and was interspersed with poetry and song for the hour. The left sniggered, many of the rank-and-file delegates were bemused, but the television audience was given the clear message that the Labour Party was changing and changing quite dramatically.

"There can be no doubt about it – this was an unqualified triumph for Dick Spring, an unparalleled conference success for any Labour leader in recent times," wrote Sean O'Rourke in *The Irish Press*. "In one week-end, he had dealt decisively with several issues and irritants and emerged with his authority immeasurably strengthened. Spring is now poised to become a more assertive leader of Labour and of the left, having left the ghosts of coalition behind him and won the faction fight which has absorbed much of his energies in the past year," added O'Rourke in a prescient assessment.

A surprise general election came a couple of months later when Charles Haughey ignored the Tallaght strategy which had seen Fine Gael underpinning his economic strategy. He called the election for June 1989 after a defeat on a health motion in the Dáil, hoping finally to win the long-sought after overall majority for Fianna Fáil.

The Labour campaign was efficient and the party highlighted the issue of health cuts which became central to the campaign. Charles Haughey went on radio to admit that he didn't know of the problems in the Health Service and his dreams of an overall majority crumbled. The Progressive Democrats suffered a surprising collapse and their number of seats was more than halved from fourteen to six. Fine Gael struggled to make gains and managed only an extra four seats.

Labour did well enough but failed to make the impression that might have been expected. Having spent most of his energies for the previous two years sorting out his own internal difficulties, Spring was unable to convince the electorate that his party had something to contribute on a national level. In fact, as the only party standing on an avowed policy of refusing to consider entering Government in any circumstances, Labour was not all that relevant to the campaign.

Still, it managed to increase its seats by three to fifteen and to gain an extra 3 per cent of the vote, bringing it up to just over 9 per cent. The party was back to the vote share it had been getting in the early

1980s but there were no signs of the remarkable breakthrough that lay just around the corner. In fact, there was one very ominous development in that the Workers' Party finally managed the kind of result it had been threatening all through the decade, winning seven seats and outpolling Labour in Dublin.

For a short time it appeared as if Spring, having finally managed to see off his enemies on the left inside the Labour Party, might be outflanked by his left-wing rivals outside it. The European elections added to the tide in the Workers' Party's favour. Their new leader, Proinsias De Rossa, came in ahead of Labour's Barry Desmond and, while both of them were elected, things did not look altogether rosy for Labour in Dublin. Campaigning on the slogan "A Breath of Fresh Air" and with an expensive poster campaign all over the capital, the Workers' Party pulled off its greatest triumph.

There was something peculiar in the success in Ireland of a Marxist party with a strongly pro-Moscow bias at the very time Marxism worldwide was in a state of collapse. The Berlin wall came down in 1989 and the Soviet system fell to pieces. It seemed for a time as if the Workers' Party would be immune from these events but ultimately the party had to try to confront the issues that arose and it split in the process.

De Rossa's success also turned out to be a double-edged sword. "A major weakness after 1989 with De Rossa was the dual mandate [being a Euro MP as well as a TD]. You can't do it. The idea of being a leader of a party and trying to be in Europe as well is not on, particularly given all the disdain that was around in relation to dual mandates," says Spring.

It wasn't until the aftermath of the 1989 election that Dick Spring suddenly struck a chord with the Irish electorate which was to make him by far the most popular political leader in the country. During the 1987-89 period he had been competent rather that brilliant in Opposition. There was plenty of competition on the Opposition benches for star status, as Alan Dukes, Des O'Malley and Proinsias De Rossa competed with Spring during the daily jousting sessions in the Dáil. Labour had made a reasonable impact but hadn't captured the public imagination. Fine Gael were involved in the Tallaght strategy which had public support but did little for the party. The Government was defeated on six occasions in the Dáil and five of those defeats were as a result of Labour motions.

When the Dáil met after the 1989 election, there was complete political stalemate. The Fine Gael leader, Alan Dukes, had offered to revolve the position of Taoiseach with Charles Haughey as part of a Fianna Fáil-Fine Gael Coalition deal but the notion had been rejected out of hand, as indeed Dukes expected it would be.

It was on 29 June, the day the new Dáil met for the first time, that Spring came into his own and established for himself the reputation as "the real leader of the Opposition". His opening came when the TDs, for the first time in the history of the State, failed to elect a Taoiseach on the resumption of the Dáil after an election. There was a general expectation that this would happen and Spring had consulted John Rogers about the exact constitutional position which would develop. Rogers advised Spring that Haughey would have to go to President Patrick Hillery and formally hand in his resignation as Taoiseach. He would then have to continue on in an acting capacity until the Dáil elected a replacement. Alan Dukes received similar advice from barrister Peter Shanley.

However, when all the nominees for Taoiseach were defeated in the Dáil, Haughey made no move to announce his intention to resign but simply proposed to adjourn the Dáil for a few days. Dukes agreed with Haughey's proposal for an adjournment and TDs were preparing to leave when Spring pounced and demanded that Haughey fulfil his constitutional duty by tendering his resignation.

"Let me seek some clarification from the Taoiseach. I would like clarification under Article 28.10 of the Constitution and would be very grateful if the Taoiseach would outline to the House the legal advice he has received in relation to that Article. As I see it, the Taoiseach has failed to retain the support of the majority of this House and the Article is quite specific that: *The Taoiseach shall resign from office upon ceasing to retain the support of a majority in Dáil Eireann.*" The Labour leader then asked if the Taoiseach would read from the advice given to him by the Attorney General, John Murray, on the issue.

Having initially agreed with Haughey, Dukes was then forced to backtrack and join in the chorus demanding Haughey's resignation. Spring continued to press his point and was backed up by Garret FitzGerald, who said that his recollection of the advice he had received in 1987 was that he had to resign as Taoiseach in similar circumstances.

Amid uproar, Haughey continued to seek an adjournment for a few days but Spring proposed that the House should adjourn for two hours until the Opposition could consider the legal advice being made available to the Taoiseach. The Ceann Comhairle took up Spring's suggestion and there was an adjournment for a little over two hours.

Haughey then held a meeting of his bemused Cabinet to consider the position. There was total confusion at this meeting, with the Attorney General still insisting there was no need to resign. Regardless of the legal niceties, Haughey's Ministers were now very worried about the impact on the public of the row and of Haughey's apparent desire to cling on to power at all costs. Eventually they persuaded the Taoiseach, against his better judgement, to go back into the Dáil and announce that he would go to Aras an Uachtaráin and formally hand in a letter of resignation to the President.

It was a humiliating climb-down by Haughey but he put the best face on it. "It is of critical importance that we not just legally uphold the Constitution but be seen to do so. Our people hold their Constitution to be sacrosanct. I would never wish even to appear to do otherwise than adhere strictly to the precepts of the Constitution. Accordingly, even though I have the right to take a reasonable amount of time to consider which of the alternative courses of action is best, I now propose to go to the President and to convey my resignation as Taoiseach to him," said Haughey.

The full story of that day is that Spring, knowing in advance that Haughey was not going to resign, was just waiting to pounce. Just over an hour before the Dáil met, Wexford Labour TD Brendan Howlin was walking along a Leinster House corridor when he bumped into the Government Press Secretary, P.J. Mara. After a bit of banter, Howlin joked about how Haughey would feel having to go to the President that evening. Mara told him that Haughey had no intention of going near the President to resign and that he would be carrying on as if nothing had happened until such time as the Dáil elected a new Taoiseach.

Howlin, who wasn't sure about the constitutional position, met Spring a few minutes later. John Rogers was in Spring's room at the time and when they heard about the conversation with Mara both of them said that Haughey would have to resign because that was what the Constitution demanded. They checked the Constitution again just to make sure and discussed how they would deal with Haughey's attempt to act as if nothing had happened. Forewarned was forearmed, and Spring was prepared for battle when he entered the Dáil chamber that day.

"It was the defining moment at which Dick became the leader of the Opposition. He became identified in the public mind as Haughey's bugbear and from then on his reputation grew and grew," says one advisor.

It was undoubtedly a notable coup for Spring and one which helped to establish a reputation for him as a first-class Dáil performer. It had the reverse effect on Alan Dukes. Even though the opinion polls after the general election showed him with a remarkably high rating, Dukes was marginalised by Spring on the first day of the twenty-sixth Dáil and he never recovered.

GUTTING CHARLIE

HAVING EARNED PLAUDITS FOR TRIPPING Haughey up on the first day of the twenty-sixth Dáil, Spring discovered the key to his political fortune. He emerged as Haughey's fiercest and most determined critic, and never looked back. Des O'Malley had enjoyed a similar role in the previous Dáil but he was now in Government, and Alan Dukes, for all his sharpness and intelligence, never struck an equally trenchant or incisive tone when he came up against the Fianna Fáil leader.

The more he attacked Haughey, the more popular Spring became. Haughey was such a controversial political figure that, while he attracted fanatical loyalty from many Fianna Fáil supporters, he also provoked feelings of deep suspicion and distrust among many other voters. Garret FitzGerald had capitalised on that polarisation for and against Haughey and Spring now managed the same trick, from a much smaller political base.

On the order of business in the Dáil he launched into Haughey whenever the opportunity arose and his speeches became tougher and more abrasive. Spring was greatly helped in this strategy by John Rogers and Fergus Finlay. Rogers, with his keen legal mind, was able to identify opportunities for Spring to create openings for himself in the Dáil on a range of issues, particularly legal ones, while Finlay wrote powerful and dramatic speeches for his leader which grabbed the headlines. This back-up team was of enormous importance to Spring but it would be a mistake to conclude, as some people have done, that Spring was little more than a puppet on a string.

"Dick has a tremendous instinct for what is important and a natural sense of political timing," says a senior Labour Party figure. "Sure, he did get fed a lot of stuff but he had to sort out the wheat from the chaff himself. For every ten ideas provided by Rogers and Finlay he used one or two, but he was the one on the floor of the House who made the crucial decisions about what would run and what wouldn't."

An example of how this operated was the controversy surrounding the re-appointment of the Ombudsman which developed into a major political storm at the end of 1989, when the Fianna Fáil-PD Coalition had been in office less than six months. Fergus Finlay was in Strasbourg in the middle of December and was lunching with Barry Desmond, who was now an MEP. During the meal, Desmond said that he had received a 'phone call from a very reliable source to tell him that the term of office of the Ombudsman, Michael Mills, (former political correspondent of *The Irish Press*) was about to expire. Instead of re-appointing him, the Government intended to make no announcement but to let the matter lapse. Haughey then planned to make former Labour Minister Eileen Desmond the new Ombudsman instead of Mills – and thus bring Labour on his side.

The crucial point was that if Mills were not re-appointed by the Dáil before the Christmas recess his term would automatically lapse and the House was now in its last week before the holidays. Immediately after lunch, Finlay rang Leinster House but couldn't contact Spring who was in the Dáil chamber. He then spoke to Spring's secretary, Sally Clarke, around 3.30 p.m. and asked her to get a note to the party leader before the Dáil order of business fifteen minutes later. The note simply told Spring to ask the Taoiseach if the order re-appointing the Ombudsman was going to be introduced that week. Spring got the note with "urgent, urgent" written on it and stood up to ask Haughey the question without knowing anything about the background.

Spring immediately knew by Haughey's evasive response that he was on to something and pursued the matter vigorously. The following day, armed with all the background information, he raised the issue again and put down a marker for the PDs. O'Malley then went to Haughey and the matter was sorted out, with Mills being re-appointed for another term. It was an example of the way things were to go during the lifetime of the Fianna Fáil-PD Coalition. Spring would aim unerringly at a weak point, putting the pressure on Haughey, and the PDs would then use their leverage to force the Taoiseach into an embarrassing U-turn.

As 1990 dawned, Spring was in a happier position than he had been ever since he took over as Labour leader. He had put the left to flight within the Labour Party and was gradually establishing his ascendancy on the Opposition side of the Dáil. He had also resisted the pressure from some of his own TDs to form a left-wing alliance with his old adversaries in the Workers' Party, whose confidence was beginning to be undermined by the collapse of communism.

"We started to rebuild both in the Dáil and in the party," says Spring. "We set out our masterplan, so to speak, consolidating the constituencies we held and negotiating with the Democratic Socialist Party. But the important thing was the constituencies – strengthening the ones we had, targeting the next division in which we were hoping to make gains and then organising in the third division ones, like the two Mayo constituencies. We put a lot of work into that and 1989 went well."

Then, early in January 1990, with the Dáil still in recess, Spring made a move that was to have remarkable consequences, not just for his own career but for Irish politics. He went on radio and said that Labour would be putting forward a candidate in the presidential election due to take place the following November. He added that, if necessary, he would run for the office himself in order to ensure there was a contest. Spring recalls the moment vividly:

"It was the fifth of January 1990, when I went out to Baile na nGall and said I was going to stand myself. I would have stood. People might have tried to stop me but we needed to have a contest for the office of the presidency. And the Labour Party had to stand up to the other parties to show we were prepared to do it, particularly after the way it had happened previously and especially since Fianna Fáil were just trying to set up Brian Lenihan to assume automatically the mantle of

President. There had to be a contest. Otherwise the office would have been totally demeaned as well."

Most people at the time presumed Spring had no intention of standing himself, but he insists that if the party had not found a suitable candidate he would have done so. "I suppose you have to have a streak of madness in you to get involved in politics anyway but I was determined that we were going to do it. The only way I could establish my *bona fides* was by saying I was prepared to do it myself. And one good thing was that the parliamentary party, from the time we discussed this back in October or November of 1989, accepted the strategy all the way. We didn't have the candidate agreed and names were emerging, but we were going to contest that election. The Labour Party ten years previously wouldn't have done that. They would have said: 'No, we don't want to get involved. We don't need another election.' They wanted to do it and it was part of the strategy to open up politics."

After a lot of internal debate about who the Labour candidate should be, Spring decided to sound out Mary Robinson about the Labour nomination. John Rogers went to her house on St. Valentine's Day, 1990, to see how she felt about it and the idea took off from there.

There were problems and risks in the move from the Labour point of view. Spring and Robinson had clashed in the past. Robinson was not a party member; she had resigned over the failure to consult the Unionists in the talks that led to the Anglo-Irish Agreement in 1985 and hadn't contested the Seanad elections in 1989. However, after considering the idea of running for the presidency, she became very enthusiastic about it but refused to rejoin Labour, preferring to run as an independent candidate with Labour support.

"At one stage, the talks broke down, with Spring insisting that he couldn't sell an independent candidate to his colleagues and Robinson insisting with equal force that she would never rejoin the party," wrote Emily O'Reilly in *Candidate*, her book about that election campaign. "An early meeting between the two ended with Robinson bidding Spring farewell and telling him, without rancour, that she wished whatever candidate he did choose the very best."

Confronted with Robinson's determination to go forward on her own terms, Spring backed down and agreed to propose her as Labour's nominee. At that stage, the Labour leader was running into a problem because some of the party's left-wingers, including Michael D. Higgins and Emmet Stagg, had approached Noel Browne to see if he would stand. Spring was totally opposed to nominating Browne, who had long been the icon of his left-wing opponents within the party. He felt that Browne's appeal would be too narrow and that he might say or do something embarrassing to Labour during the campaign. Nonetheless, the charismatic Browne was a very popular figure in the party and a groundswell of support for him was on the point of developing.

Once he had Robinson's agreement to run, Spring moved quickly to head off the Browne camp at the pass. There was a fierce row after a meeting of the Labour AC in early April when Spring informed the meeting of his invitation to Robinson to be the party's nominee and publicly presented her candidature as a *fait accompli*. Stagg immediately denounced Spring, saying he had been given no authority by the meeting to nominate Robinson. Spring was by now powerful enough in the parliamentary party and the AC to get his way, and a joint meeting of TDs and the AC produced a four-to-one majority for Robinson's nomination. However, the public row on the issue incensed Robinson, according to Emily O'Reilly.

"Mary was furious," O'Reilly quotes a member of her campaign staff as saying. "One of the reasons she had split from the Labour Party over the Anglo-Irish Agreement was because Spring had announced that the agreement had the unanimous support of the parliamentary Labour Party. Now here was the same story all over again. She felt that Michael D. Higgins and Emmet Stagg, in voicing objections to what Spring had done, were acting honourably but that the whole thing had been handled badly and she told Spring about this in no uncertain terms."

This was just the first of a series of rows that convulsed the Robinson campaign team throughout the entire presidential election campaign. Despite – or possibly because of – all the internal bickering, however, the campaign was an incredible success which brought Mary Robinson to the presidency and added enormously to Spring's reputation.

The campaign committee was chaired by Labour's deputy leader, Ruairi Quinn, and the other Labour members were Fergus Finlay, John Rogers and Ray Kavanagh. Mary Robinson's people on the committee were her husband, Nick, Bride Rosney and Peter MacMenamin. Ann Byrne and Ita McAuliffe of the Labour Party staff were also seconded to the campaign on a full-time basis, while others joined the meetings as their services were required.

Some of the rows at the campaign committee have now achieved legendary status in Labour circles.

"It was a committee which consisted of a number of powerful individuals, each of them committed to making a success of Mary's candidacy and each with their own very strong ideas about how it should be done. The mix was often explosive," wrote Fergus Finlay in his account of the campaign, *Mary Robinson – A President with a Purpose.* Some of the fiercest clashes were between Finlay himself and Bride Rosney, who was Robinson's closest confidant. "Those meetings were extremely difficult and it was very hard to avoid being sucked into one of the warring camps. I don't know how Ruairi Quinn kept his cool for most of the time," recalls one individual who took part.

Emily O'Reilly sums up the nub of the argument. "Tensions were running high between the Robinsons and the Labour Party with both sides keeping to their own private agendas – Labour's to keep a very public and definite link with the candidate and Bride Rosney's to sever that link as far as politically practicable in the public mind."

"There was the odd wobble, mind you," concedes Spring. "The *Hot Press* interview and whatever. I didn't get involved in the campaign squabbles. I was the court of appeal."

In July 1990, the new form of leadership election, over which there had been such controversy since 1987, took place with the entire party membership entitled to vote. A sign of just how strong Spring had become was that not only was there no candidate to oppose him but his deputy leader, Ruairi Quinn, was also returned unopposed.

Meanwhile, Spring was continuing to establish himself in the public mind through his Dáil performances. The House was recalled in an emergency session at the end of August to deal with the threatened collapse of the Goodman Group. Labour had initiated the criticism of Goodman's operations in early 1989 when Barry Desmond challenged the Fianna Fáil Government about it. The PDs had also been highly censorious of the way the Goodman companies had been given export credit insurance to Iraq.

Now, with the Gulf War in progress, the Iraqis stopped paying and the whole Goodman empire was threatened with collapse. A special Bill had to be rushed through the Dáil to allow the company to be put into the care of an examiner. Spring used the occasion further to enhance his reputation. What was remarkable about his contribution was not his attack on Goodman or on Fianna Fáil but the fact that he was in possession of confidential information which had been passed on to him by senior bankers.

It was an extraordinary position for a Labour leader and it indicated just how far he had gone to dominate the Opposition benches. Previously, the captains of industry would have gravitated naturally to Fine Gael with the inside story on such a matter, but Spring had established such a reputation for himself as leader of the Opposition that they came to him instead. During the debate, Spring called for a sworn judicial inquiry into Goodman's affairs. It was not the last that was to be heard on that particular issue.

Meanwhile, as the presidential election campaign moved into the autumn, the opinion polls showed Robinson well ahead of Fine Gael – who had very belatedly nominated Austin Currie – and beginning to close on the front runner, Brian Lenihan. From the beginning, Robinson was convinced she could win and her optimism gradually took hold of the campaign as Fine Gael were relegated to the category of also-rans.

Then, in the final run-in to polling day, the campaign was thrown into turmoil by the sensational revelation of the Jim Duffy tape. The tape, which was in the possession of *The Irish Times* was played to journalists at a press conference in Dublin, following days of speculation about who had phoned Aras an Uachtaráin on the night of 27 January 1982, when Garret FitzGerald's first budget had collapsed.

During the campaign, Lenihan had denied that he or other leading members of Fianna Fáil had tried to contact President Hillery on the night in question to attempt to persuade him not to dissolve the Dáil at FitzGerald's request. However, in a taped interview with Jim Duffy in May of 1990, he referred to a phone conversation he had had with the President on the night of 27 January 1982. He also said that Charles Haughey had tried to ring the President the same night.

The release of the Duffy tape caused a political sensation with a little over a week of the campaign to go. Lenihan compounded his problems by giving radio and television interviews in which he maintained that what he said on the Duffy tape was not the truth and that he had never rung the Aras.

He later explained in his book *For the Record* that he had been on heavy medication at the time of the Duffy interview, following his liver transplant operation a year earlier, and that accounted for his story to Duffy. However, he didn't provide that explanation at the critical juncture of the campaign and things began to fall around his ears.

The Fianna Fáil machine was thrown into turmoil and the Opposition parties moved in for the kill. Mary Robinson tried to steer clear of the tapes issue, as the polls showed her storming away ahead of Lenihan in the wake of the revelations. The focus was on whether the Government, of which Lenihan was a member, could survive. An Opposition motion of no confidence in the Government put it up to the PDs as to whether they could stay in power with Fianna Fáil.

During that debate, on 31 October 1990, when the Government was on the verge of collapse, Spring launched the fiercest attack on Haughey yet heard in Dáil Eireann:

"This debate is not about Brian Lenihan when it is all boiled down," he declared. "This debate, essentially, is about the evil spirit that controls one political party in this Republic, and it is about the way in which that spirit has begun to corrupt the entire political system in our country. This is a debate about greed for office, about disregard for truth and about contempt for political standards. It is a debate about the way in which a once-great party has been brought to its knees by the grasping acquisitiveness of its leader. It is ultimately a debate about the cancer that is eating away at our body politic and the virus which has caused that cancer, An Taoiseach, Charles J. Haughey."

Spring's denunciation of Haughey that day was the logical conclusion of the things he had been saying ever since the 1989 election, but his language was far from the ordinary, even by the standards of a bitter political debate. He compared Haughey with Josef Goebbels and Senator Joe McCarthy. "In the end, both these politicians destroyed themselves, but not before they had perverted the society in which they lived. And that is the danger we face here."

Spring was anticipating a general election as he spoke but when it came to the Dáil vote on the motion of confidence that evening the Fianna Fáil-PD Coalition survived. It did so only because Haughey sacked Brian Lenihan and that enabled the PDs to vote confidence in the administration. His dismissal put some fire back into Lenihan's campaign but by this stage Mary Robinson was unstoppable.

When the votes were counted on 9 November, Lenihan ended up

with 44 per cent of the vote, Robinson got 39 per cent and Currie got 17 per cent. Currie's transfers put Robinson well ahead of Lenihan on the second count and history was made. Fianna Fáil lost the presidency for the first time and Mary Robinson became the first woman President in the history of the State.

Still, nobody was quite sure what it meant for the Labour Party and for Dick Spring. Was there a new mood for change in the country or had Robinson won simply because the two big parties, Fianna Fáil and Fine Gael, had, in their different ways, made a total mess of it?

"The result was wonderful, despite the Aras Eight [the eight domestic staff removed from the president's residence], which gave us another dose of the wobbles," says Spring. "I couldn't have said it at the time because people would have thought I was exaggerating but I believed that politics would never be the same again after that."

That view was widely shared in the Labour Party. "We got the breaks. For a start, Fine Gael picked an unelectable candidate; then the Fianna Fáil candidate self-destructed," says one Labour strategist. "That said, there is still no doubt that Mary Robinson's election was the greatest victory we have ever had. Nothing else, not even the 1992 election result, comes anywhere near it."

There was no immediate indication, though, that Labour would be able to capitalise on the mood that brought the Robinson victory. The opinion polls showed the party still hovering between 9 per cent and 12 per cent of the vote – respectable enough figures given the party's near extinction a few years earlier, but hardly indicative of the breakthrough that was being widely talked about after the presidential election.

Fine Gael reacted to the humiliation of coming third by dumping their leader, Alan Dukes. It was easy to be wise after the event but only one member of the front bench, Jim O'Keeffe, had argued that the party should support Mary Robinson's independent candidature. Now that they had been so badly beaten, the party opted to change leaders and John Bruton was the unanimous choice of a parliamentary party desperate for a figure to challenge Spring's mastery on the Opposition benches. While Bruton brought a different style to Fine Gael's Dáil performance, he was no more successful than Dukes in competing with Spring for the mantle of the real leader of the Opposition.

Spring consolidated his position as the undisputed leader of the Labour Party at the 1991 conference, held in Killarney. A new party constitution and rules were approved by the conference and, in his leadership address, an increasingly confident Spring outlined the main objective as being to overtake Fine Gael as the second party in the State. The presidential election had shown that it could be done, but few took Spring seriously when he outlined his ambition to do the same at the following general election.

The Labour leader continued to pick opportunities for intervention and to flay Haughey whenever the chance arose. The Goodman issue erupted again in May 1991 following a *World in Action* report on Independent Television in Britain, and the Government eventually decided to hold the sworn judicial inquiry for which Spring had been pressing for so long.

The following month, Labour performed solidly in the local elections. The party's vote increased across the country and pushed up its number of seats from fifty-eight to ninty-one. While it was not a spectacular performance, significant gains were made in every county. The Dublin result was the most important of all because Labour pushed back the Workers' Party tide. It was a reversal of the trend which had been developing for more than a decade during which the Workers' Party had gradually eaten into the Labour vote.

Not only did Labour win back seats but its successful candidates were spread across all the Dáil constituencies in the city and county and, very significantly, a number of them were women. Labour figures like Niamh Bhreathnach, Joan Burton, Róisín Shortall, Pat Upton, Eamonn Walsh, Tommy Broughan, Derek McDowell and Joe Costello were all elected to a public body for the first time, joining councillors like Eithne Fitzgerald and Sean Kenny who had survived the dark days of the mid-1980s.

Labour was on the way back but how far could Spring take the party? Ruairi Quinn believes that the local election success, which had been carefully planned over a two-year period, was the key to future achievements. He was involved in the meticulous preparations for the local elections campaign in Dublin. Special workshops were run for managers and candidates and the lessons of the Robinson campaign were analysed in detail.

"The local elections of 1991 were the primaries for the general election. We found out which candidates were electable and which were not," says Ruairi Quinn. "I learned a lot from the successful approach to politics developed by Fine Gael, under the direction of Peter Prendergast, in the late seventies and early eighties. In 1979 we did well in the Euro elections but Fine Gael scored in the local elections and, in retrospect, it was clear their strategy was a much better long-term one. European elections simply consolidate existing politicians; local elections provide the base for the future."

An interesting sequel to the local elections in Dublin was that Labour had the choice of running the city through a deal with Fianna Fáil or a rainbow coalition of different parties, including Fine Gael, the Democratic Left and the Greens. Strangely, in view of what was to happen later on a national level, Labour spurned the chance of a deal with Fianna Fáil.

"There were some attractions in a Fianna Fáil-Labour alliance and John Stafford on their side was very anxious for it," says Ruairi Quinn. "It would have been easier to manage but there was no political support for it within the party. Also, people at national level felt it would have sent out all the wrong signals," says Quinn, who negotiated the Civic Alliance. Ironically, he emerged in 1992 as the strongest Labour proponent of the idea of a coalition deal with Fianna Fáil.

BOUND FOR GLORY

DICK SPRING BROUGHT LABOUR to an unimagined triumph in November 1992, when the hard work of years paid dividends in spectacular style. Strangely, in the light of what happened, the year began inauspiciously for the Labour leader and there were many who believed that his bubble was about to burst.

The year started off with the political drama surrounding the departure of Charles Haughey, who was finally taken out as leader of Fianna Fáil in a blaze of controversy and recrimination. While the PDs were the ones who put the gun to his head, his fate was sealed by his old friend, Sean Doherty. Haughey's other old allies, Padraig Flynn and Albert Reynolds, were waiting in the wings to take advantage of the situation.

When Reynolds became Taoiseach it looked for a few months as if the whole political atmosphere might be about to change. The new Taoiseach won huge satisfaction ratings in the polls and his political style was a total contrast to Haughey's. With his old adversary no longer there to kick around, it appeared that Spring might be losing his edge. On a personal level he got on with Reynolds and from the beginning treated him much differently than he had Haughey.

"There can be no doubt that the outgoing Government were stale and unimaginative and that Taoiseach Reynolds is now taking a fresh approach. I congratulate the Taoiseach. I believe that at least in terms of style he has made an encouraging start," Spring told the Dáil on the day Reynolds took office. "The incoming Government have a difficult and onerous task to carry out and they will need constructive support as well as vigilant criticism and constructive opposition. I pledge to the Taoiseach that they will certainly receive constructive opposition from the Labour Party."

Spring's attitude to Reynolds on his first day in office was a significant pointer to how politics would develop, even if its significance was obscured for a time by other events. Another highly significant statement in the same speech was contained in Spring's comments about the PDs.

"The Progressive Democrats have already exacted the highest price that can be paid for continuation in office. They have effectively presided over the removal of a Taoiseach and a Tánaiste; obviously, the only thing left is to destroy the Government themselves."

In the succeeding months, Spring's attitude to Reynolds continued benign. On his first day in office, the new Taoiseach was plunged into the abortion controversy which was to plague the Government until it collapsed, but while Spring frequently disagreed with Reynolds's approach he never treated him the way he had treated Haughey. There was a lot of speculation among politicians and in the media about whether Spring's more low-key style of opposition meant that his star was on the wane, now that Haughey wasn't there to provide the foil for him in the Dáil.

Another event took place early in the year whose impact on the

Labour Party was difficult to predict for a time. The Workers' Party had been in a state of crisis since its ideological guru, Eoghan Harris, left in 1990 having written a tract "The Necessity for Social Democracy", in an attempt to chart a new direction for the party. At the beginning of 1992 the Workers' Party split, with six of its seven TDs leaving to found a new party which was ultimately called the Democratic Left.

As this upheaval took place, there were rumours that Michael D. Higgins and Emmet Stagg were about to leave Labour to join forces with the new party. In the event, Michael D. stayed put and made it clear he had never had any intention of leaving, but Emmet Stagg formally resigned from the parliamentary party, saying he was not satisfied with Spring's anti-coalition credentials. It was widely expected that Stagg would join up with the six Democratic Left TDs but his flight from Labour was short-lived.

The bulk of the Kildare Labour organisation made it clear to Stagg that they had no intention of leaving the party. Faced with the daunting prospect of trying to build up a new constituency organisation from scratch and having to fight an official Labour candidate at the following election, Stagg quickly reconsidered his position. A few weeks after his resignation, he approached Labour's general secretary, Ray Kavanagh, and the national organiser, Pat Magner, in the bar in Leinster House. He told them that he wanted to get back into the parliamentary party. He added that, as a signal of his good intent, he had got rid of his aide, Michael Taft, and left instructions with the Superintendent of the Dáil that Taft was no longer to be admitted to the House.

Taft had long been a thorn in the side of the Labour establishment and the main organiser of Stagg's various attempts to unseat Spring. When Stagg told Kavanagh and Magner about his instructions barring Taft from Leinster House, Magner went to the Superintendent to check the story. When he had verified it, he went back to Stagg and said he would have a word with Spring on his behalf. Shortly thereafter, Stagg was readmitted to the Labour fold.

Stagg's humiliating climbdown was an indication of how effective Spring's control over the party had become. Not only was he strong enough not to be bothered by Stagg's resignation; he didn't feel in the least threatened by allowing him back into the parliamentary party. It marked a big change from 1987 when Stagg was almost powerful enough to force Spring out of the leadership.

The Maastricht referendum a few months later could have posed problems for Labour given the strain of anti-EC feeling in the party. But Spring had little difficulty in presenting a united front for a "Yes" vote, despite the Danish "No" vote and the reservations of many Labour people, including Spring himself, about a protocol in the Maastricht Treaty recognising Ireland's special constitutional provision on abortion.

After the Maastricht referendum, the Fianna Fáil-PD Coalition began to fall apart and, by the autumn of 1992, Labour was ready for an election. Fergus Finlay was convinced from the summer onwards that it was inevitable before the end of 1992 and while a number of senior figures like Ruairi Quinn disagreed, preparations were made accordingly.

The issue on which the Government collapsed was the evidence of Albert Reynolds to the Beef Tribunal. In June, when O'Malley appeared before the Tribunal, he was very critical of the way Reynolds had handled export credit insurance back in 1987-88 and described it as reckless. When it came to his turn to take the witness stand, Reynolds maintained that O'Malley had been dishonest in his evidence. The charge by the Taoiseach against the leader of his Coalition partner brought the Government crashing down in circumstances which rebounded badly on Reynolds.

In the Dáil confidence debate which preceded the election, Spring trenchantly denounced both Government parties. He was particularly scathing about Fianna Fáil and his tone was in marked contrast to the relatively tolerant attitude he had shown to Reynolds the previous February.

"I believe one political party in this House have gone so far down the road of blindness to standards and of blindness to the people they are supposed to represent that it is impossible to see how anyone could support them in the future without seeing them first undergo the most radical transformation," Spring told the Dáil in a speech that was to be quoted back in his face a few months later.

His condemnation of Fianna Fáil was vehement. "By their behaviour, time and time again they have cheapened and debased one of the highest callings there is, and dishonoured those who serve the public in political life." Warming to his theme, Spring denounced the PDs for serving in Government with Fianna Fáil. "It must surely be considered amazing that any party would consider coalescing with them."

The general election campaign which ensued was dominated by two developments: the demonisation of Albert Reynolds and the canonisation of Dick Spring. The media followed these two themes as if nothing else mattered right through the campaign. John Bruton and Fine Gael were virtually ignored; the PDs and the Democratic Left struggled for media space as all eyes focused on Reynolds's slide into the abyss and Spring's rise and rise to political fame and fortune.

Reynolds couldn't believe the collapse in his popularity once the campaign got underway. The simple fact of the matter was that he was blamed by the public for causing the general election, just as Haughey had been in 1989, and he suffered accordingly. He compounded his problems by using the word "crap" in a television interview on the first Sunday of the campaign and by giving a very poor radio interview a week later. Shocked by the avalanche of criticism which descended on him, Reynolds was badly rattled early in the campaign and never regained the initiative.

Spring, on the other hand, was able to project himself in the role he had carved out in the Dáil as the real leader of the Opposition. Yet there was very little serious analysis in the media of Labour policies or of what the party would do in the aftermath of the election. Labour's policy document entitled *Put Justice Back into Economics and Trust into Politics* met with a positive response. There was little criticism of Labour's plans to raise borrowing significantly to £1 billion in 1993 nor a deep examination of how the party would implement its campaign promises.

In fact the striking thing about the Labour manifesto was its similarity to the Fianna Fáil policy document. The only difference was in the media response. Fianna Fáil was lambasted for promising a whole range of public investment projects to create jobs while Labour's document was welcomed as a positive approach towards job creation.

There were, of course, some significant differences between the two documents. Labour's opposition to privatisation and its emphasis on ethics in politics did not feature in Fianna Fáil's document *We Can Make It Happen*, but there were few things in the two documents that were incompatible. An analysis of the party programmes in *The Sunday Press* found Fianna Fáil's and Labour's to be by far the most compatible but few made the logical deduction about what that meant for the future and Spring resolutely kept his options open.

At the beginning of the campaign, Labour expectations were relatively modest. "At the very start, I expected that we would get twenty-four seats at the outside," says Barry Desmond, the party's director of elections. "At that stage I would have regarded twenty-four or twenty-five seats as a great performance but I hadn't anticipated that there would be such a hostile reaction to Albert Reynolds's appearance before the Beef Tribunal. It was that performance that did Fianna Fáil such immense damage. There was a huge Reynolds factor in the campaign. I think Albert knows now what went wrong and has had to look into his soul and change his political attitudes."

Desmond also stresses the preparation for the campaign. "In terms of strategy the party got its act together as never before. We had, in every constituency, credible, young, competent and seasoned candidates." The seeds of success had been sown over a number of years as the party got its own house in order and then geared itself to win the support of the public.

This was another critical issue because the Labour parliamentary party had been a totally male outfit for nearly a decade. It was ironic that the party which espoused women's rights and which had sponsored the victory of Mary Robinson did not even have one woman TD. Now, a number of the women councillors like Niamh Bhreathnach, Joan Burton, Róisín Shortall and Breda Moynihan had been selected to contest the Dáil alongside an experienced campaigner like Eithne Fitzgerald.

"The mood going into the election was good," says Spring. "We had two good conferences. 1989 went well and the local elections and the presidential election obviously formed part of the masterplan. And I think we just got on top of the mood that was out there. It's all very simple, isn't it," he says with a smile.

"I think the presidential campaign was an anchor and had a huge bearing on the campaign. Also there was a good crop of young candidates. They were new and they were fresh. I think that had its own attraction. There were no major problems during the campaign, which was organised very effectively. I spent three days a week out of Kerry, working very hard with full media coverage. The only time I nearly got caught by RTE was sometime when there was a rainbow up in the sky and they wanted to get my picture in front of it but it vanished as we went around the corner."

What he doesn't refer to is his own domination of the 1992 election. But Barry Desmond does. "And, of course, there was the Spring factor," he says. "Spring himself had an enormous influence on the campaign. An avalanche of support developed for him as the public got to know him. He has a sane, sensible, steady, attractive personality and is not in hock to any ideological extreme. Of course," he adds, "under pressure Dick can explode now and again, but we all do that."

Ruairi Quinn says he was convinced from day one of the campaign that Labour would win a seat in every constituency in Dublin and that the party would end up with around thirty seats. Detailed preparations began in May 1992. A budget was agreed, a new standardised large-size poster for every constituency with photographs of the candidates was prepared, and a leader's tour was planned. A campaign committee was selected and went away for a weekend seminar in Donabate during the summer. Once the campaign itself started, Dick Spring, Ruairi Quinn and Brendan Howlin dropped off the team. "One of the key lessons I learned from the presidential election was that a candidate should not be involved in the running of a campaign," says Ruairi Quinn.

The first opinion poll was encouraging for Labour, giving the party 15 per cent of the vote. Before the election Labour had been getting ratings in the 12 per cent to 14 per cent range so the indications were that extra support was there to be picked up. It also showed Fianna Fáil beginning to slide but it did not anticipate the scale of the political earthquake that was about to happen.

By the end of the first week, the polls were giving Labour 17 per cent, and by the time the campaign moved into its final stages the party was on an extraordinary 22 per cent rating, by far the highest it had achieved in the history of polling in Ireland. Spring's own popularity also soared in the course of the campaign and he received ratings double those of the other party leaders. Reynolds and Fianna Fáil simply nose-dived in popularity as the campaign progressed while John Bruton and Fine Gael just didn't go anywhere.

The reason for the extraordinary surge in Labour support and Spring's popularity is due to a number of factors, some stretching back years. One key advisor believes that take-off came after one critical decision during the campaign. "I think Dick's suggestion early on that he should be Taoiseach, even on a rotating basis, was all-important. While the suggestion could have back-fired, nobody shot it down and it began to take off in the public mind. People thought about the idea of Spring as Taoiseach and they began to like it."

Spring and John Rogers had come to the conclusion that every contest since 1977 had been a presidential-style campaign. Elections had not been decided on policies but on who the voters wanted as Taoiseach – Jack, Charlie or Garret. As the contests had become increasingly gladiatorial and presidential in style, the leader of the Labour Party had been inevitably marginalised. This time around, Spring decided to put himself in the frame early on and the strategy worked beautifully. On a personality basis it became a competition between Albert and Dick, and Fine Gael leader John Bruton was pushed into comparative obscurity.

A key element of the Labour campaign was to get at Fine Gael and its leader and the notion of Spring for Taoiseach was another way of achieving that purpose as well. While Fine Gael naively believed Labour would make itself available for another coalition with them after the election, a vital part of the Labour strategy aimed at replacing Fine Gael as the second-largest party in the State. The muddled Fine Gael campaign provided Labour with the opportunity it was looking for and "Spring for Taoiseach" was a vital element of that strategy.

"You can't ignore the importance of the fact that, just as in the presidential election, both Fianna Fáil and Fine Gael made a balls of it. Albert destroyed himself by the way the election came about. Bruton just never clicked with the electorate as an alternative Taoiseach while Dick grabbed that position for himself. We must never forget, though, that a lot of our success was due to the fact that the others were so bad," said one Labour strategist.

At the very beginning, the question arose as to what could replace a Fianna Fáil-led Government. Bruton tried to create an alternative in the public mind by floating the idea of a rainbow coalition of Fine Gael, Labour and the PDs. He didn't seek the agreement of the other parties in advance to this notion and Spring responded coolly when asked by reporters for a reaction to it.

In fact, the Fine Gael proposal annoyed him deeply. "I think it was awful politics, very bad politics. One thing we were not going to be was to be taken for granted and that took us for granted. That was Fine Gael at their worst. It was resented by all shades of our party and it was not going to be the basis of how things would work."

After he had floated his own name as a possible Taoiseach, more and more people began to regard Spring's notion of a rotating Taoiseach as a realistic possibility in a rainbow arrangement.

However, he never tied himself down at any stage by saying what he would do after the election. While there was a widespread media presumption that he would join a rainbow coalition if the numbers were right, he never made any statement committing himself to it. Neither did he ever rule out coalition with Fianna Fáil, though he was never pressed on the matter.

"It was wisest to keep the options open because the election itself was very unpredictable. I wasn't beholden to anybody. I wasn't doing deals with anybody. We had been working on the objective of getting up to the thirty-seat mark. We said twenty-six but that would have been a stepping stone to where we wanted to go. I always felt very strongly that once Labour got thirty seats in Irish politics, you then have a third force. Obviously the question now is can we sustain that, consolidate that? Because if we do, politics has changed dramatically in this country, forever and a day."

Significantly, for most of the campaign, Fianna Fáil avoided any open attack on Labour. Reynolds, too, was keeping his options open as his chances of bringing Fianna Fáil to an overall majority evaporated. For most of the campaign, Labour faced virtually no criticism. In marked contrast with the campaigns of the past, when the party had been attacked from all sides, this time around they were left unscathed for the greater part of the campaign.

Fine Gael didn't criticise Labour because it wanted to keep its main potential rainbow coalition partner sweet. Fianna Fáil had a similar agenda, although it wasn't obvious at the time. At a senior level in the party, decisions were taken early on to go soft on Labour so that the possibility of a coalition deal would remain as a fall-back position after the election. With both Fianna Fáil and Fine Gael fighting with one hand tied behind their backs and the media more favourable than it had ever been, Labour continued to gobble up votes from the other main parties. Only Des O'Malley consistently had a go at Labour, targeting Michael D. Higgins in particular.

It wasn't until the last week-end of the campaign that Fianna Fáil changed tactics. Reports from all around the country confirmed the trend of the opinion polls – Fianna Fáil voters were deserting the party in droves and flocking to Labour. When pushed into the corner Fianna Fáil hit back with a series of newspaper advertisements designed to shake the Labour campaign. "Hard Labour" was the huge headline on the Fianna Fáil ad which showed a voter's feet tied to a ball and chain inscribed "Tax". "In 1987, Dick Spring walked out of a coalition Government that had doubled the national debt and brought the country to the brink of insolvency," ran the small print of the ad. "This Labour manifesto means: Higher spending, Higher borrowing – up to £1 billion next year. This means for you: Higher taxes, Higher mortgages."

By this stage of the campaign, the voters were past being influenced by Fianna Fáil ads and the Labour surge was unstoppable. The original target of twenty-five seats was clearly going to be exceeded, if the opinion polls were in any way accurate. But Labour strategists still insisted that they would be happy with twenty-five seats, the target set by the party's electoral commission as marking the decisive growth point.

The country went to the polls on 25 November and when the ballot boxes were opened the next morning, it quickly became clear that Labour was on the way to its best-ever electoral performance. For the first time ever, the party won a seat in every constituency in Dublin. That was hardly surprising, given the consistent poll results, nonetheless, it represented an enormous breakthrough. The really surprising results, however, came from outside Dublin. Declan Bree won the party's first-ever seat in Sligo; Willie Penrose won a seat in Westmeath and Pat Gallagher took a seat in Laois-Offaly. Results which astonished everybody was the victory of John Mulvihill, who took Joe Sherlock's seat in Cork East, and the success of Moosajee Bhamjee in Clare.

When the results were totted up, Labour had thirty-three seats and could have won about four more if they had run additional candidates. It was more than Spring had anticipated in his wildest dreams but the victory was his.

"From the beginning of the campaign, it was all Dick Spring. The feedback was incredible and even people who had been against him all their political lives within the Labour Party suddenly started calling themselves Dick Spring's candidates," said one of the headquarters staff. "The day Emmet Stagg contacted us and asked Spring to speak at a meeting in his constituency, we knew we were on to a winner."

A Labour analysis of opinion poll data showed just where the wave of support had come from. In regional terms the huge swing was in Dublin. In September the party was getting 13 per cent of the vote in the capital but this had more than doubled to 28 per cent in the final days of the campaign. In class terms the biggest jump was among the middle class voters, from 8 per cent before the campaign to 22 per cent just before polling. Working-class backing also rose to 22 per cent but from a much higher base.

Another significant trend was a massive Labour swing among women, who have been traditionally much less inclined to vote Labour than men. Here again, support more than doubled during the course of the campaign.

An analysis of the vote carried out by Lansdowne Market Research for *The Sunday Press* asked people how they had voted in 1989 compared with 1992. It found that almost a quarter of Labour voters in 1992 had come from Fianna Fáil, while 15 per cent had come from Fine Gael. Only 34 per cent of Labour voters had chosen the party at the previous election, so nearly as many ex-Fianna Fáil supporters as traditional Labour voters backed the party in 1992. The single most import reason given for switching to Labour was the desire for change.

If the Labour voters were much more middle class than in any previous election, so too were the newly-elected Labour TDs. Traditionally, Labour TDs tended to be trade union officials but this time around most of the new faces in Leinster House were professionals of one kind or another. College lecturers and teachers predominated but there was also a solicitor, a barrister and, of course, the psychiatrist, Dr Bamjee.

At the end of the day, it was Spring's election. The whole campaign hinged on his standing with the voters but that was the product of hard, painstaking work over a long number of years. At the victory celebration in the Riverside Centre at the end of the count, Spring paid a special tribute to Fergus Finlay, saying the victory could not have been won without him. Barry Desmond echoes this sentiment. "If there was a Spring factor in the election, there was also the Finlay factor. He has had a profound impact of quite extraordinary dimensions on Spring and the Labour Party. He is a man of immense intellectual capacity and a political power-house in his own right," says Desmond.

Smiling at the recollection of some of the stormier moments of the campaign, he adds: "While we would frequently shout and roar at each other, he has had in the 1980s as huge an impact on the party as Halligan had in the sixties and seventies or Luke Duffy in the Norton era. I have nothing but admiration for him and while, like many people of immense ability he is not short of intellectual arrogance, he has made a vital contribution to the history of the party."

POWER PLAY

IT WAS LATE ON THE NIGHT OF 13 DECEMBER that a group of Dick Spring's closest political allies and friends sat with him in a suite in the Berkeley Court Hotel in Dublin to advise him on one of the most important decisions of his life. At issue was the central question of whether Labour should go into Government with Fianna Fáil or pursue the option of a rainbow coalition. Earlier that evening, Spring had met Albert Reynolds in the luxurious penthouse suite of the hotel to see if there was a basis for negotiating with Fianna Fáil.

After the meeting, Spring retired to another suite reserved for a group of his friends and advisors and reported back on his conversation with Reynolds. Spring told them that Reynolds was anxious to do business, but the question was should Labour do business with him?

Ruairi Quinn asked his leader if he felt he could work with Reynolds and whether there was anything in the Beef Tribunal which contained a time-bomb with the potential to destroy the Government. Spring gave his view that, at worst, Reynolds would be found careless or incompetent but nothing more than that. Quinn, who strongly favoured a deal with Fianna Fáil, was happy at the response.

Apart from Spring and Quinn, the other people present were Barry Desmond, Brendan Howlin, John Rogers, Donal Spring, Fergus Finlay, Pat Magner, James Wrynne the party's financial secretary, and two economic advisors Willie Scally and Greg Sparks. Quinn and Howlin were the leading supporters of the Fianna Fáil option, while Desmond and Finlay still thought that, on balance, the rainbow might be on. After the pros and cons had been weighed up again and again, Spring asked the ten other people present to vote on the better option to pursue. Five people supported the Fianna Fáil option and five voted for a rainbow coalition as long as it involved the Democratic Left as well as the PDs.

"That's a great help," remarked Spring wryly, and the meeting broke up with the issue still in the hands of the party leader.

Since the election result two weeks earlier, all eyes had been on Labour because the party held the key to the formation of a Government. In the immediate aftermath of the election, Reynolds issued a statement saying that, in view of the result, it was up to the other parties to see if they could put a Government together. The prevailing view in the Fianna Fáil Cabinet was that some form of inter-party Government would emerge but not everybody believed the game was lost. Agriculture Minister Joe Walsh, who had been involved in the contacts which led to the formation of the previous coalition with the PDs, always believed there was a chance of a deal with Labour and, at the first Cabinet meeting after the election, he proposed that they should prepare a policy document so they would be ready for talks with Labour at any stage. He told his colleagues that one of the flaws in the approach to the PDs after the 1989 election was that Fianna Fáil had no policy document of its own but had to rely completely on the Civil Service while the PDs had a detailed shopping list of demands.

At that Cabinet meeting, a number of Ministers, including Seamus Brennan, David Andrews, Charlie McCreevy and Padraig Flynn, said Fianna Fáil should prepare for Opposition and not have any truck with Labour. Reynolds and some other Ministers, however, agreed with the view put forward by Walsh and the Cabinet approved the drawing up of a programme which would form the basis for negotiations with Labour. The task was given to the Taoiseach's advisor, Martin Mansergh, who trawled through every policy statement produced by Labour for over a decade and put together a document which he felt would be compatible with the positions adopted by both parties in the election campaign.

Ruairi Quinn, who was firmly of the view that a coalition with Fianna

Fáil was Labour's best option, was also making moves in the background. He had a meeting in the Mont Clare Hotel in Dublin with Brian
Lenihan to open a channel of communication between the parties.
Lenihan in his book *For the Record*, written after the presidential
election, had strongly advocated a Fianna Fáil-Labour Coalition.

"There was a shared understanding between Labour and Fianna Fáil
in the 1930s when de Valera was Taoiseach. That understanding must
be recast for modern times to ensure future stability in the political
system. It would be a stability based on the principled support of
people sharing similar social and national values," he wrote.

Another tentative exploration of the possibilities of a Fianna Fáil-
Labour deal came when Bertie Ahern, as Finance Minister, briefed all
the Opposition leaders on the country's financial situation. Ahern used
his meeting with Spring and Quinn to establish just what Labour's
bottom line was on a number of issues, including privatisation.

In the immediate aftermath of the election, however, the prevailing
view was that a rainbow coalition involving Labour, Fine Gael and the
PDs was the most likely development. Then something happened
which took the potential rainbow partners completely by surprise –
Labour opened up negotiations with the Democratic Left on a joint
programme and made it clear they would talk to nobody else until this
process was complete. The move was a warning to Fine Gael and the
PDs but they found it hard to believe. Both parties had ruled out going
into coalition with the Democratic Left during the election campaign
and they stuck to that position.

Dick Spring had never been an admirer of the Democratic Left, to
put in mildly, and had fiercely resisted all previous attempts by his
own left-wingers to bring the parties together. "If there is one person
Dick dislikes more than anybody else in the Dáil it is Proinsias De
Rossa," remarked an ex-Fine Gael Minister, puzzled by what was going
on. Another surprising aspect of the talks was that they came at a time
when the Democratic Left were at a low ebb having lost seats in the
election, although for a time it looked as if Eric Byrne would bring
their numbers up to five.

The Labour move to embrace the Democratic Left was a strategy
devised by Fergus Finlay, who hoped to put a bloc of nearly forty
left-wing TDs together so that they could negotiate with Fine Gael from
a position of strength. Such a bloc would have almost the same number

of seats as the second party in the State and would put Labour in the driving seat going in to Government.

On the Saturday after the election, Finlay rang Spring, who had returned home to Kerry, and pointed out that if Eric Byrne were to take the seat in Dublin South Central, as looked likely on that first weekend after polling day, then Labour, Fine Gael and the Democratic Left would have eighty-three seats between them.

"We don't need the PDs," Finlay told Spring and asked for permission to make contact with the Democratic Left.

The Labour leader approved the move and Finlay phoned Pat Rabbitte to arrange a meeting in the Braemor Rooms the following morning. When the two met, Finlay told Rabbitte that Labour wanted to be part of a centre-left Government including the Democratic Left party. He made it clear that Labour didn't want any truck with the PDs, but wanted first to work something out on the left so that they could go to Fine Gael in a strong position, with the left making up half the Government. Rabbitte was very interested and after he reported back to his party talks began.

Finlay was joined on the Labour side by Brendan Howlin, while Rabbitte was accompanied by Des Geraghty, the party's MEP. Labour initially presented the Democratic Left with a two-page document and were given back a much longer one in reply before negotiations began in earnest on a detailed policy agreement. Some people in both Labour and the Democratic Left outside the negotiating teams were highly suspicious of the motives of those involved. But their doubts were nothing compared with the apprehensions which developed in the other Opposition parties and in the media as the discussions dragged on and on, with no sign of Labour opening negotiations with the bigger players.

Well over a week went by before the Labour-Democratic Left agreement was reached and Fine Gael and the PDs began accusing Spring of not being interested in forming a Government at all. As well as the inclusion of the Democratic Left in any coalition, Spring was still sticking to his election campaign suggestion that the Taoiseach's job should be rotated between him and the Fine Gael leader in any rainbow coalition.

The first meeting of the greatly-expanded Labour parliamentary party took place in the appropriately upmarket Shelbourne Hotel. The vast majority of the TDs were delighted to be in the Dáil and were prepared to leave all crucial decisions about Government to Spring and his close advisors. "It was a love-in at the Shelbourne and the mood was akin to the old Barry McGuigan joke: 'Thank you very much, Mr Spring.' There was no serious analysis of our position at all," says one TD. Only Pat Upton, who had been close to Spring in the past, and left-wingers Joe Costello and Declan Bree, expressed some disquiet about Labour going into Government.

As the pressure on all parties mounted, Spring agreed to a meeting with John Bruton, but by the time the two men met a gulf of misunderstanding and suspicion was already well-developed between their two parties. Labour saw the handling of the talks with the Democratic Left as part of the process of persuading Fine Gael to treat them as equals in any Government. Fine Gael, on the other hand, regarded the Labour position as posturing and some of the party's TDs thought Spring was trying to avoid going into Government at all.

A full week after the election, when no moves had been made in Fine Gael's direction, John Bruton wrote to Spring asking if he would agree to a meeting to discuss the formation of a Fine Gael-Labour-PD Government.

"As you know, Fine Gael indicated before the election that it would be willing to take part in such a Government within certain parameters. These parameters include an agreed programme for Government, an agreed budgetary position for each of the five years and the distribution of power and responsibility within the Government in proportion to party strength," wrote Bruton in his letter.

Instead of providing the foundation for talks, the letter infuriated Spring who regarded it as pre-empting any negotiations on a number of issues. Labour issued a statement accusing the Fine Gael leader of arrogantly setting down preconditions for talks. Bruton tried again the next day with another letter expressing regret they had thus far not been able to meet in person. Fine Gael also put a press release accusing Labour of completely misrepresenting the contents of Bruton's first letter. "Public patience is being stretched to the limits by the sort of political game-playing we are now witnessing."

The public slanging didn't augur well for a rainbow Government. While contacts between the two parties were opened up through meetings between Senator Maurice Manning and Pat Magner, Spring and his key advisors, Rogers and Finlay, were determined that Fine Gael would have to acknowledge the scale of their party's rebuff by the electorate as part of the process of forming a Government with Labour. They were clearly hoping that Fine Gael would dump Bruton out of desperation for office but, far from obliging, Fine Gael TDs rallied around their leader through hostility to what they regarded as Labour arrogance.

Finally, a meeting between Spring and Bruton was arranged for Sunday, 3 December. It nearly didn't take place because on the day before, Barry Desmond, in the course of a radio interview, said that Spring would use the meeting "to put manners on John Bruton". Senior people in Fine Gael were infuriated at Desmond's comment and a number of his front-bench colleagues urged Bruton to cancel the meeting. After considering the matter for some time he decided to go ahead.

Looking back at that incident, Barry Desmond is contrite. "I very much regretted it and I still regret using that phrase," he says, but he adds that he did so in response to a comment on Rodney Rice's *Saturday View* programme by Nora Owen, who remarked that Dick Spring would make a fine Tánaiste and some Labour deputies would be fine Ministers. "That comment struck me as the height of Fine Gael arrogance. It got up my nose but I was foolish to respond in the way that I did. It just brought back into my mind all the pressures we had suffered between 1982 and 1987 and which I knew Dick was not going to stand again."

The meeting between Spring and Bruton took place in the Shelbourne Hotel on 6 December and in the immediate aftermath, it did indeed appear as if Spring had tried to live up to Barry Desmond's billing. When the two leaders appeared in front of the television cameras after the meeting, Bruton looked shattered.

In fact, according to both sides, the meeting was nothing like as dramatic as some people assumed. Spring wasn't personally abusive to Bruton. What happened was that Spring did most of the talking while Bruton listened and the Labour leader stayed on his feet most of the time while Bruton sat down. Spring told the Fine Gael leader that Labour were looking for a new type of relationship in Government which would reflect the different size of the parties in 1992 compared with 1982. At that time Fine Gael had seventy seats and Labour had sixteen. Now Fine Gael had forty-five and Labour had thirty-three.

The Labour leader also said that he wanted Bruton to acknowledged that mistakes had been made in the past and that any relationship this time around would be different. He also insisted that the Taoiseach's post would have to be rotated and that the Democratic Left would have to be part of any Government.

Bruton replied that he accepted the size of the two parties had changed and their altered relationship would be reflected in any Government arrangement. He was also prepared to acknowledge that mistakes had been made in the past and he recognised the need for a special role for the Labour leader and a special relationship in any Government that would emerge. Bruton ruled out the involvement of the Democratic Left in Government but on the question of rotating Taoiseach he said he would have to consult his front bench again.

Although the meeting between the two men did not degenerate into abuse, no basis for trust emerged during it. That was evident in media leaks which pointed out that Labour had paid for the room and that Spring had remained standing throughout the meeting while Bruton remained sitting down as if being lectured. Those newspaper reports added to Fine Gael's sense that their leader was being set up.

When Bruton reported back to the Fine Gael front bench they gave him their full support in rejecting the demand to rotate the Taoiseach's position. On the issue of the inclusion of the Democratic Left, some people favoured modifying the party's position stance but the majority continued to say no. This was a critical decision because, while Fine Gael couldn't have accepted both conditions, they might have made it much harder for Labour if they had accepted the Democratic Left as well as the PDs, while rejecting the rotating Taoiseach.

Early the following week, Spring and Bruton met again. This was a more amicable occasion and Bruton believed he had persuaded Spring to move from bilateral to tripartite talks, involving the PDs as well. At this stage there was a general expectation that negotiations between the three parties would go ahead but Labour pulled back from the brink just when the other parties clearly believed they had received a commitment to begin.

Fine Gael deputy leader, Peter Barry, who was being spoken about by some Labour sources as a possible compromise Taoiseach, responded angrily in an interview emphatically ruling out any possibility

of Bruton not being Taoiseach for the full term in a coalition arrange-
ment. He said that Labour should either open proper formal talks with
Fine Gael and the PDs or go into Government with Fianna Fáil.
Meanwhile, on 9 December, a Labour negotiating team of Ruairi Quinn,
Brendan Howlin and Mervyn Taylor met Fine Gael and the PDs, but
again they avoided giving a commitment to open tripartite discussions.
Instead Labour asked all other parties interested in negotiations to
come up with their policy positions.

It was at this stage, with impeccable timing, that Fianna Fáil struck.
The Government party had bided its time as suspicion and confusion
mounted between the other parties. Now when asked to come up with
a policy document, Fianna Fáil immediately presented Labour with the
fruits of Martin Mansergh's hard work over the previous week-and-a-
half. Labour were taken totally by surprise at the speed of the response
and at the content of the document which went a very long way to
meet their position on a whole range of issues. For instance, Fianna
Fáil's plans to privatise the ACC, the ICC and the Trustee banks were
dropped in favour of Labour's idea for the creation of a third banking
force by the State sector and a whole range of infrastructural projects
to create jobs were promised.

Labour was pushed further into a corner by Fine Gael and the PDs
when Spring finally offered the tripartite talks they had been waiting
for so long. Both parties refused to get involved at that stage, saying
they would await the outcome of the Fianna Fáil-Labour process. Some
people in Fine Gael were convinced that Spring's discussions with
Fianna Fáil would collapse and he would have to come back to them
in a weakened position. As Reynolds had firmly ruled out any
possibility of rotating the Taoiseach's position, the other parties
watched to see how Spring would deal with that, in view of his
insistence on it in his talks with them.

"It seems now that Labour have entered negotiations with Fianna
Fáil. We believe that it is not in the national interest for our party to
get involved in competing parallel negotiations. This process, we
believe, would signal a return to the auction politics which wreaked
such havoc with the public finances over a decade ago," said Bruton.

Labour's options had narrowed dramatically and unexpectedly.
Ruairi Quinn concedes as much. "The one miscalculation that we made
in the whole period after the election was that we felt we could keep

Fine Gael and the PDs in the air for some time longer. When we asked for the other parties to supply us with their policy positions on Thursday morning, we certainly never expected Fianna Fáil to come back with such a comprehensive policy document by that evening. As the Taoiseach was going to Edinburgh the following morning for the EC summit, we felt they wouldn't respond until Monday," says Ruairi Quinn.

"When Fianna Fáil came back at us so fast and so comprehensively, that effectively snared us and drew us away from Fine Gael and the PDs. The attitude of Peter Barry and Michael McDowell was also an effective incitement to do a deal with Fianna Fáil, because it was clear that we would have had to come crawling back if we couldn't put a deal together."

Spring had agreed to meet Reynolds on his return from the Edinburgh summit and when the Taoiseach arrived home with the promise of £8 billion in structural funds his hand was even stronger. That first meeting between Spring and Reynolds, to set the scene for talks, came the day before the Dáil met for the first time after the election on 14 December. At that first meeting of the Dáil, Reynolds, Bruton and Spring were all proposed and defeated for the Taoiseach's position by increasingly bigger margins. The failure of the Dáil to elect a Taoiseach had happened for the first time after the 1989 election but it now caused little excitement.

That night the Labour parliamentary party met to consider whether it should give Spring a mandate to open talks with Fianna Fáil. A few minutes before that meeting, Spring made his final contact with Fine Gael by ringing Bruton. The two men had a short conversation whose content has since become a matter for dispute. Spring referred to it at Labour's national conference in April 1993, during his leadership address.

"After a great deal of internal discussion, I telephoned the leader of Fine Gael on the night before the Dáil resumed, on the thirteenth of December. In that conversation (which was short) I told him that unless he was prepared to change his view and to agree to the inclusion of Democratic Left in negotiations, in order to achieve a more balanced structure, I would be unwilling to recommend taking negotiations with Fine Gael and the Progressive Democrats any further. "Even at that late stage, he refused to drop any of the pre-conditions he had tried to impose on negotiations. That was the moment the die was cast and every time I have to listen to Fine Gael carping and moaning, since I remember that moment when they had their chance and lost it."

Bruton has a very different memory of the conversation and, in a letter to the newspapers after the Labour conference, he insisted that Spring had got it wrong on two counts.

"Firstly, 13 December was a Sunday and I had no conversation of any kind with Mr. Spring on that day.

"Secondly, I did have a conversation with Mr. Spring on Monday the fourteenth at around 7 p.m. According to my notes of that conversation, Mr. Spring said he was about to go into a meeting of his parliamentary party. He asked if Fine Gael would agree to rotating the office of Taoiseach with him. I said we had decided we would not. At that point, Mr. Spring said he would 'have to do what he would have to do' (or words to that effect). At no point in this conversation did he ask about including the Democratic Left in negotiations.

"At this stage these events are of mainly academic interest. I do not understand why Mr. Spring devoted so much time to them in his address. As we have seen, Mr. Spring has since entered Government with Fianna Fáil, without obtaining either the office of the Taoiseach for himself or the involvement of the Democratic Left."

The differing accounts given by Spring and Bruton about this final conversation in their efforts to put a Government together reveal the depth of the mutual misunderstanding between Labour and Fine Gael at this point. Labour were convinced that Fine Gael and the PDs had already settled the parameters of an agreement and that they simply wanted Labour in there to make up the numbers. Fine Gael, on the other hand, became convinced that Spring was not interested in doing a deal with them in any circumstances.

So, on the night of 14 December, Spring went to his parliamentary party and told them he had just had a conversation with Bruton and that Fine Gael were not prepared to compromise on the question of the rotating Taoiseach. He asked for and received a mandate to open talks with Fianna Fáil. Some of the Labour TDs were very uneasy at this development, considering they had spent the entire election campaign lambasting Fianna Fáil.

John Ryan from North Tipperary expressed his uneasiness as did Seamus Pattison from Kilkenny. On the other hand, Michael Bell from

Louth expressed strong approval of doing a deal with Fianna Fáil. Most TDs were happy enough at the developments and were content to leave a decision to the leadership. With Spring in such total command of his party he was given the go-ahead to see if he could do a deal with Reynolds.

TÁNAISTE AGAIN

BY THE TIME THE NEGOTIATIONS with Fianna Fáil began on 16 December, the outcome was inevitable. Labour had made its choice and there was no going back to Fine Gael and the PDs if things went wrong. It was either do a deal with Fianna Fáil or opt out of the process of forming a Government altogether and see if by any chance Fianna Fáil and Fine Gael might be forced to some accommodation.

The Labour team for the talks was Ruairi Quinn, Brendan Howlin and Mervyn Taylor. On the Fianna Fáil side were Bertie Ahern, Noel Dempsey and Brian Cowen. The make-up of the negotiating teams helped to smooth the whole process. Both Quinn and Ahern had been Ministers for Labour. Despite facing each other across the floor of the Dáil as Minister and Opposition spokesman, they had developed a good relationship and trusted each other. Both were extremely anxious to do a deal.

Brendan Howlin and Noel Dempsey also knew each other quite well, being whips of their respective parties, and they had also established a level of mutual trust which helped the negotiations. The final members of each team, Mervyn Taylor and Brian Cowen, were not as comfortable as the others. While Taylor was reserved, Cowen emerged as the hard man of the talks. He played it tough right through, insisting on as much of Fianna Fáil policy as possible going into the joint programme and refusing to move on basic budgetary targets.

Ahern played his customary conciliatory role while Dempsey facilitated the talks by ensuring that the Labour team had access to any information they needed from the Department of Finance or other departments. The talks never ran into serious problems and, unlike the discussions between Fianna Fáil and the PDs in 1989, there was no great mutual suspicion between the teams or among members of the same team.

One reason for this was that, while Reynolds and Spring were waiting in the wings to deal with any problems that emerged, neither of them pulled the rug from under the feet of their negotiating teams to speed the process. One of the main problems for Fianna Fáil in 1989 was that Haughey negotiated directly with Des O'Malley without telling his own team what he was up to. This time around, there was unity on both sides and a healthy atmosphere around the table.

On the question of the spoils of office there was also an early understanding. Spring accepted that he would not get the Taoiseach's job on a rotating basis. Reynolds agreed to formalise the new partnership through the establishment of a special office for the Tánaiste which would have its own staff and budget. There was agreement that Labour would get six of the fifteen Cabinet posts but, surprisingly, Spring did not push for Finance but opted instead for Foreign Affairs. Fianna Fáil were fully expecting Labour to demand Finance and would have conceded it but the push never came.

Relations got off to such a good start that the Labour team and its advisors were issued with the special plastic security keys which enabled them to enter the Taoiseach's Department from Leinster House at will. Not only that, but Fergus Finlay was given the office inside the Department which had been occupied by Stephen O'Byrnes of the PDs, assistant Government press secretary in the previous coalition.

If the talks were amicable, they were also lengthy and it took a full four weeks from the first Spring-Reynolds meeting to the final acceptance of the deal by the Labour Party at a conference in the National Concert Hall in Dublin. It was during that period that the media consensus, which had been so supportive of Spring and the Labour Party, began to slip and the first hints of criticism began to emerge.

The length of the talks provided one ground for complaint. While the Christmas holiday inevitably slowed things down, the lengthy nature of the talks gave scope for Labour's critics in the other parties who now recognised the inevitability of the new arrangement. One major ground for criticism was the worsening currency crisis, which had not abated since the withdrawal of the British currency from the

EMS the previous September. Irish interest rates were pushed up higher and higher to cope with the pressure but things simply got worse. The absence of a permanent Government while such a serious crisis raged was used to justify critisms of the delay.

Spring also came in for criticism, particularly from Fine Gael, in late December for refusing to divulge the sources of his allegations to the Beef Tribunal about irregularities in the meat industry, especially since the Tribunal had been set up largely at his instigation to investigate his claims about the Goodman organisation. The State appealed the decision to the High Court which rejected the right of Spring and Democratic Left TD Pat Rabbitte to plead privilege but the Tribunal chairman, Mr. Justice Liam Hamilton, ultimately allowed the claim of privilege to stand on the basis of common law.

In the meantime, the Dáil met again on 22 December without electing a Taoiseach and again on 5 January with the same result. On that occasion, John Bruton used the opportunity of the Dáil debate to hammer away at Spring for being ready to do a deal with Fianna Fáil. He cited the Labour leader's speech on the dissolution of the Dáil in November.

"Deputy Spring did receive a mandate; he received a mandate for change. Now he proposes to give us that change by putting back in office the same Taoiseach, the same Ministers, the same political party against whom he spoke with such precious and high-flown rhetoric here in this house on 5 November last and for the previous five years," said Bruton.

During his Dáil speech, Des O'Malley made an obscure reference to the Taoiseach's access to documents. It transpired later than O'Malley had gone to Spring's office that very morning with a curious tale. He referred back to an approach Spring had made to him the previous October with a story going the rounds of the Bar Library that an attempt had be made by a State barrister, Gerry Danaher, to intimidate O'Malley's counsel, Adrian Hardiman, before his cross-examination of Charles Haughey and Albert Reynolds. The PD leader said that he now had further serious information to impart about other incidents and he wanted the Labour leader to be aware of them.

The central matter involved a claim that Fianna Fáil had access to privileged papers prepared by a member of his (O'Malley's) legal team at the Beef Tribunal, Gerard Hogan. O'Malley said that these documents had been photocopied and delivered to Fianna Fáil headquarters and subsequently made available to Gerry Danaher. He gave as the source of this information a Christmas Eve conversation in the bar of the Shelbourne Hotel between one of his barristers, Diarmaid McGuinness, and Danaher. McGuinness, apart from being O'Malley's barrister was a member of the Labour Party and well-known to Spring. O'Malley also mentioned a burglary at the Department of Industry and Commerce the previous November and the fact that notes about Hardiman's travelling arrangements to and from the Beef Tribunal were found in the possession of a suspected subversive by the Gardaí.

The Labour leader was taken aback by these allegations and immediately consulted his friend and legal advisor, John Rogers. Together with Rogers and Mervyn Taylor, another lawyer, he went to see Reynolds. The Taoiseach acted immediately by calling in the Attorney General, Harry Whelehan, and the Garda Commissioner and asked them to investigate the claims. Spring was reassured by the Taoiseach's quick response and some Labour people came to the conclusion that the timing of the revelations was a last-minute attempt by the PDs to scupper the formation of a Fianna Fáil-Labour Government. While the controversy continued for some time and eventually resulted in a Bar Council investigation into the various allegations, it quickly fizzled out as a political issue but it spurred the negotiators to move ahead as quickly as possible with the formation of a Government.

The Fianna Fáil and Labour *Programme for a Partnership Government, 1993-1997* was published two days later and immediately presented to two specially-convened meetings of the respective parliamentary parties. The fifty-eight-page document was handed to TDs of both parties only as they began their meetings but there was a wide welcome for it from both sides.

A small minority of Labour TDs either spoke against accepting the deal or had reservations. Pat Upton told the meeting he was opposed to going into Government at all as he believed it would damage the party. John Ryan again expressed his doubts about Fianna Fáil while Brian Fitzgerald from Meath was critical of the programme itself, saying it was too vague and aspirational. There was an enthusiastic welcome, however, from a clear majority of the party TDs.

The document accepted the budgetary constraints necessitated by the Maastricht Treaty. This was a major modification of Labour's position in the election campaign but Fianna Fáil refused to budge and it was also felt necessary to reassure the financial markets at a time when the currency was under such threat. The document placed a huge emphasis on job creation and the establishment of a National Economic and Social Forum to contribute to a national consensus on economic and social policy.

Another major theme was a chapter headed "Broadening our Democracy" which promised an Ethics in Government Bill, reform of the Oireachtas, a new committee system to do more of the work of legislation, State funding for political parties and longer sessions for the Dáil and Seanad. Labour had placed a great deal of emphasis on these issues in the election campaign and the document reflected this. In areas like health and social welfare Labour policies were included and the promise of a third banking force was also included.

On Northern Ireland there was a commitment to seek urgent resumption of the political dialogue but there was little on specifics and no reference to changes in Articles 2 and 3 of the Constitution. There was an undertaking to change the Constitution on divorce, to decriminalise homosexuality and to make condoms more easily available. There was also a pledge to spend £20 million immediately to cut hospital waiting lists as well as measures to improve the social welfare system.

Once the programme was accepted by both parties, the next step was a Labour national conference to give the final word to delegates from the party branches around the country. Arrangements were made to have the conference in the City Hall in Cork but Ruairi Quinn was among those who argued for the more salubrious surroundings of the National Concert Hall in Dublin. "If we have it in the Concert Hall the delegates will know they are in Government," he told colleagues.

Spring approached the conference confidently. After all the conferences down the years at which his leadership had been threatened again and again, he looked forward to greeting the Labour delegates as the hero who had delivered the party its thirty-three seats. "I don't just want a majority for coalition. This time around I want the benediction of the entire party for going into Government," he said.

The gathering in the National Concert Hall in January 1993 was very different from the conference at the Savoy Cinema in Limerick in December 1982, the last time he had brought Labour into Government.

Then he had to fight for permission to go into power and only did so on sufferance, with 40 per cent of his members voting against. This time, there was adulation all round for Spring's position. His old enemy, Emmet Stagg, actually seconded Spring's motion that the coalition deal be accepted and other old adversaries, like Michael D. Higgins and leading left-wing members of the Administrative Council, enthusiastically endorsed the deal. For old Labour hands it was like a blissful dream, the kind of conference they never believed they would see. At least 95 per cent of the delegates backed the coalition deal when the vote came at the end of the afternoon. How times had changed!

There is little doubt that things wouldn't have gone nearly as smoothly if Spring had been asking the delegates to approve a rainbow coalition, particularly as the PDs would have had to be involved. There was a huge groundswell within the Labour Party against any involvement in Government with the PDs, and while the deal with Fianna Fáil was unexpected, it generated greater support than any coalition deal in the history of the party.

Looking back on the events a few months later, Spring was convinced he had made the right decisions. "Had Fine Gael and the PDs been less hostile to the idea of allowing the Democratic Left in, despite reservations about having four parties in Government, the dynamic might have been there. Given that since the election the PDs have had no problem doing deals with the Democratic Left in the Seanad, their absolute hostility to them immediately after the election is just unbelievable. Personally I believe they [Democratic Left] were democratically elected and, in fairness to them, most of them are good performers in the Dáil, good strong politicians. I don't think Fine Gael or the PDs had the right to stand up and say they wouldn't be contaminated by the Democratic Left. That was far removed from the reality of the election.

"Fianna Fáil realised we had a programme that wasn't too far away from where they were at themselves. But to my dying day I will be convinced that if the PDs had another ten deputies they would have tried to do a deal with Fianna Fáil like a shot."

One wise move Spring made at his special conference was not to indicate in advance which Labour TDs would be appointed to Government posts. That kept all his TDs firmly on-side, although he had decided well in advance that he was going to bring in his former left-wing critics into the heart of the administration. His previous experience of a bitterly-divided party had persuaded him that the left would have to be included in key positions of power to protect the stability of the Government.

Barry Desmond, even though he concedes that he had serious misgivings about doing a deal with Fianna Fáil, says that the more he looks back at the post-election scene the more impossible the rainbow coalition option seems. "It is clear to me that the chemistry between Spring, Bruton and O'Malley would have made an explosive mix. Looked at coldly the reality is that it would have been a disaster and in my view the Government wouldn't have got beyond the first budget."

When the Dáil met on 12 January, Reynolds was elected Taoiseach with the biggest majority in the history of the State. Spring brought old adversaries Michael D. Higgins and Mervyn Taylor into the Cabinet and made Emmet Stagg, Joan Burton and Eithne Fitzgerald junior Ministers. On the other hand, old allies who had loyally backed him against the left, like Liam Kavanagh, Seamus Pattison, Pat Upton and Toddy O'Sullivan, were ignored. It was a bitter blow which hurt deeply but Spring was adhering to one of the oldest rules of politics. Successful leaders have to be prepared to sacrifice their friends to placate their enemies.

The full Labour team was Spring himself in Foreign Affairs, Ruairi Quinn in a new Department of Employment and Enterprise, Brendan Howlin in Health, Niamh Bhreathnach in Education, Michael D. Higgins in Arts, Culture and the Gaeltacht, and Mervyn Taylor in Equality and Law Reform. Three of these Departments, Employment and Enterprise, Arts, Culture and the Gaeltacht, and Equality and Law Reform were the product of the Programme for Government. They were devised in the first instance by Fergus Finlay, who was convinced of their potential and believed they would provide a clear signal that Labour was doing things differently this time around.

From the day the Government was elected and the names of the Labour Ministers announced, things began to get more difficult. In all previous coalitions, about half the parliamentary Labour Party had been office-holders of one kind or another so there was an inbuilt majority within the parliamentary party for the *status quo*. This time, a record number of Labour TDs, eleven in all, were office-holders but there was also a record number of backbenchers, twenty-two, who outnumbered their ministerial colleagues by two to one. With some of the twenty-two bitterly disappointed people who believed they had been let down by Spring and others dubious about the Fianna Fáil deal, there were forebodings of trouble.

Ruffled feathers were not assuaged by the appointment of Jim Kemmy as party chairman. Toddy O'Sullivan became chairman of the parliamentary party while the twenty-two backbenchers decided to form themselves into their own committee, with Liam Kavanagh as chairman, to maximise the pressure they would be able to bring on Labour Ministers.

The potential for serious conflict was immediately obvious as the new Government struggled to get a grip on the currency crisis and to prepare a budget. Political instability suddenly manifested itself within days of Labour going into Government. There were rancorous meetings of the parliamentary party while Jim Kemmy and other TDs gave interviews complaining at the direction of Government policy. At party meetings, Kemmy expressed his deep annoyance at the way his name and those of other people had been floated in the media as possible Ministers. He told colleagues he regarded this as part of an Orwellian disinformation campaign by certain people in the party.

The sudden instability in the wake of triumph raised all the old fears about Labour being unable to take the responsibility of being in Government. Fine Gael TDs nodded sagely and said they had seen it all before. Labour TDs were just not able to take the pressure of being in Government. On a number of big issues – the closure of Digital in Galway, the threat to the future of Aer Lingus, the proposed sale of the Government stake in Greencore and the appointment of Bernie Cahill as executive chairman – Labour backbenchers became restive.

Spring suddenly found himself under pressure at party meetings. Toddy O'Sullivan attacked him at one gathering. Jim Kemmy was still annoyed and became a feature of the nightly television news bulletins speaking on the plinth of Leinster House to Charlie Bird of RTE.

On top of this instability, stories began to appear in the papers about the appointments being made by various Labour Ministers. Niamh Bhreathnach chose her daughter as her Dáil secretary; Emmet Stagg installed his daughter in a similar post and gave a cousin the job of ministerial driver. Gerry O'Sullivan also selected his daughter as a Dáil secretary while Dick Spring's sister, Maeve, continued as his Dáil constituency secretary which she had been for the previous ten years. With the Dáil adjourned for a few weeks after the formation of Government while a budget was being prepared, the stories about the Labour appointments became headline news.

On top of that there were also stories about the sheer number of advisors Labour were bringing in to Government. In fact, there was nothing very remarkable about this and Labour had successfully used outside advisors since the Cosgrave Coalition days. This time, there was an added number because of the creation of a new post of programme manager in each Department, designed to ensure that the Programme for Government was implemented. Each Labour Minister brought in a programme manager as well as an advisor. With the appointment of relatives to minor posts, these moves gave Labour's opponents a stick to beat them with.

After basking in the glow of favourable publicity for so long, Spring and his Ministers seemed mesmerised at becoming the target for such heavy criticism and appeared unable or unwilling to respond.

The peak was reached when the Government had been less than two months in office. In *The Sunday Independent* on 28 February, there were, according to Fergus Finlay's reckoning, no less than fourteen stories critical of Labour and its leader. Typically, the most extreme piece was written by Eamonn Dunphy:"The Minister for Foreign Affairs should spend as much time as he can abroad. He is a disgrace to his county and his country and, to borrow a phrase from Brendan Behan, 'a bollocks of the highest order'."

Dunphy's piece was so totally over the top that, after it appeared, the tide began to turn back in Spring's favour. Even people critical of Labour's actions began to pull back in the belief that things had got out of hand. Spring himself, in an interview in *The Kerryman* and in a Dáil speech, helped to calm things down by admitting that mistakes had been made.

"We didn't handle it well. But also the media focused in on us. Fianna Fáil had been in Government and were going on in Government but all of a sudden we were the new guys. *The Independent* didn't want the Labour Party in Government and *The Irish Times* didn't want Fianna Fáil in Government so that didn't leave us with a great deal of media support. I said publicly that we handled it badly, but I am convinced that what we are doing in terms of advisors and managers is necessary for the administration of this country and I think that over a period of three or four years we will show that. I am only hoping now that we will get the opportunity of doing the work. We delivered on a massive amount in the first budget but because of the controversies, because I spent three weeks trying to explain and defend my sister who was appointed to the same job she had been appointed to ten years previously that passed unnoticed."

Still, all the controversies have had their effect and Spring's popularity has fallen back to normal levels in the opinion polls. Labour has also dropped from extraordinarily high post-election ratings but the party is still on, or slightly above, the 19 per cent it achieved in the general election. Criticism of the party will naturally continue and both political and media opponents won't let the party forget its mistakes.

After all the strictures Labour itself dished out in Opposition and all the promise of change which characterised its election campaign, Spring and his colleagues can hardly complain at being the butt of a few jibes. Typical enough of the kind of censure the party has faced, and will continue to face, was a column by anonymous *Irish Times* columnist, Drapier. Awarding mock school prizes during the 1993 Easter holidays he gave Spring the "Rotating Position Award for his changed views on Aer Lingus, Greencore, the Beef Tribunal, jobs for relatives, interpretative centres, Bernie Cahill, Albert Reynolds, Fianna Fáil."

However, the full fury of the initial media onslaught had stabilised by the time Labour's national conference came around on the weekend before Easter and the party's backbenchers had also calmed down. There were still serious tensions, particularly among former Spring supporters who felt disgruntled at being excluded from power. But as one backbencher put it: "The left has now become the right but it will take some time for the old right to turn itself into the new left."

In the days after the conference, Emmet Stagg reflected the change inside the Labour Party when a group of TDs in the Dáil bar asked him what it was like being on the platform in his new role as a Minister and supporter of Dick Spring. "I felt as if I had undergone a sex-change operation," he remarked.

At the conference Spring had virtually unanimous support and he was loudly applauded when he said he had no regrets about going into coalition with Fianna Fáil. He added that there were some things he did regret. "We have made mistakes since entering Government, mistakes for which I must take full responsibility," he told his delegates but they were in no mood to dwell on them. Instead they preferred to bask in the unaccustomed glow of success which Spring had brought.

In striking contrast with previous conferences when Labour were in Government, the delegates actually seemed proud to see their leading politicians arriving in State cars. Of course they were just eighty days in power at the time but the vast majority seemed prepared to believe Spring when he told them: "The best is yet to come."

FUTURE GOALS

DICK SPRING BROUGHT LABOUR to the highest point in its eighty-year history in November 1992. The big question now is whether he can build on that triumph and fulfil his ambition of making it the second largest party in the State or whether the political wheel of fortune will turn again at the next election.

There is no shortage of cynics, some of them in the Labour Party itself, who believe that there is nowhere to go but down, that after a term in office with Fianna Fáil the electorate will cast around for whatever alternative is on offer at the next election and desert Labour in droves.

The Irish electorate has certainly been in a volatile mood for the past two decades, with no outgoing Government retaining office since 1969. Fianna Fáil did remain in power in 1989 and 1992 but only because they agreed to share power with different partners on each occasion. That could be an ominous pointer for the future of the Fianna Fáil-Labour arrangement.

On the other hand, Spring is in the unprecedented position of having more than doubled his party's share of the vote. That is an extraordinary achievement, considering that the Fianna Fáil share has been slipping steadily over the past decade while Fine Gael's decline has been catastrophic. If those trends continue, Spring will be in a very strong position at least to consolidate Labour at a much higher base than it has ever had before.

It should be remembered that Spring has achieved success after ten years of hard slog and he won't be prepared to hand away his gains too easily. Having brought Labour close to the point of replacing Fine Gael as the second party in the State, he wants to press ahead and finish the job.

It is not as if the 1992 election came as a complete bolt from the blue. The presidential election of 1990 had already signposted the way and the party managed to repeat the formula in a general election. It will be a lot more difficult next time around, given that Labour will have to accept responsibility for the Government's performance, but everything will hinge on how the party does in power.

Over the past couple of years, Labour has tapped into a mood for change among a significant segment of the electorate and, if it can deliver on the promise, those new supporters might well stay with it. By getting its own act together, the party had put itself into a position, under Spring's leadership, to capitalise on the fundamental shifts which have been taking place in Irish society over the past few decades. In both 1990 and 1992, Labour was able to identify itself with the mood for change and may well have harnessed itself to an unstoppable force which will bring it to greater and greater success.

Spring's great achievement was to put Labour in a position to do this. His perceived weaknesses in the eyes of his own left-wingers turned out to be one of his greatest strengths. The very fact that he was never a dogmatic socialist proved in the end to be his trump card.

Spring has combined two apparently contradictory political impulses and turned that combination into a winning formula. The first impulse is a deep-seated commitment to the values represented by his father and other rural Labour TDs – a belief in the creation of a caring, compassionate society with steady improvements in the lives of poorer people through political action.

This rural Labour tradition was never socialist in the theoretical sense. It represented a practical and pragmatic approach to politics with the view that Labour should, if possible, be in Government to do the greatest good for the people it represented. This approach was scorned by left-wingers in the party and by the intellectuals who tended to follow socialist fads as they came and went, but it endured as one of the fundamental mainsprings of the Labour tradition and it provided the bulk of the party's TDs in the Dáil.

On top of this traditional Labour approach, Spring has grafted on a second impulse, which is in tune with the spirit of the times. It is a commitment to liberal, progressive values – a belief in the rights of the individual rather than the rights of the State or the big institutions. In some ways this commitment to liberalism runs counter to the rural Labour tradition, and on issues like divorce or abortion Spring's views are the complete opposite of those of his father and other rural Labour conservatives.

Yet Spring's success has been to hold the different strands together while identifying with the values of the expanding urban Ireland. He has built a wider coalition of support for the party than ever existed before. He achieved that by modifying his traditional Labour inheritance and bringing it into tune with a new era.

The collapse of communism and hardline socialist economics in recent years proved the correctness of his approach. Spring's lack of a socialist ideology, which was widely regarded as a severe limitation a decade ago, emerged as a positive plus. Both his family Labour tradition and his own liberal impulses could be seen to have much more validity and relevance to the Ireland of the 1990s than the idle dreams of a Red Dawn which informed his opponents within the party.

Of course, the fact that Labour did so well in 1992 doesn't mean that there are not also huge forces in society which reject much of what Spring stands for. Conservative Ireland has been pushed back in recent years but it is not so long since it was able to mobilise a decisive majority to defeat the divorce referendum of 1986. Its strength will be challenged in another divorce referendum which is promised in the next twelve months or so and there will be other tests on issues like control of education.

However, even if conservative Ireland is much stronger than some of its critics now credit, the fact is that Spring has positioned himself as the leader of the liberalising political forces. He has put himself and his party in a very good position to play a pivotal role in the future, whatever happens. He has marked out Labour's territory. Neither of the other two major parties, Fianna Fáil and Fine Gael, are sure who or what they represent any more, while Labour has a clear set of liberal values. It appears to know where it stands and what it wants to do on those issues.

In Government, the party will find things much more difficult than in Opposition and Labour has a big point to prove on that score. The party has always done best while in Opposition where it could be critical of others; Government will provide a much tougher and truer test of the party's mettle. The major issues like unemployment and Northern Ireland are not amenable to easy answers but they represent the really important challenge of political courage.

The deputy leader, Ruairi Quinn, has responsibility for employment and that will be an acid test of whether Labour has any new ideas in the economic field. A frequently-heard criticism of the party is that while it has a clear programme on the liberal agenda issues – contraception, divorce and abortion – and on issues relating to ethics in Government, it has no clear programme on the economy and no answers to the employment problem. It will be up to Ruairi Quinn to demonstrate that the party is capable of original thinking on the issue.

Northern Ireland, the most tragic and intractable problem of all, is the responsibility of Spring himself. He has said on a number of occasions that he wants to make a major contribution to the issue and that is why he chose Foreign Affairs in the first place. He is certainly proud of his role in negotiating the Anglo-Irish Agreement, but devising a new agreement which would bring lasting peace will be a more difficult task still.

At Cabinet level, Labour and Fianna Fáil have begun well and there is a high level of trust between the two sets of Ministers. However, some backbenchers in each party are restive and despite the huge Government majority this could pose a difficulty in time. Spring concedes that problems have arisen on the Labour side.

"One aspect of the whole thing was trying to find a new dynamic in the parliamentary party. It's a new party of forty-two people now and that is obviously very different to sixteen or twenty people who all knew each other very well. There is a whole new scene and people are trying to find their feet. In fairness to them, those of us who would probably be their best assistance are busy from eight o'clock in the morning until eleven o'clock at night. If they had come in to us in an Opposition situation we would be with them on a daily basis, many hours every day and many hours every night. We would have had a chance to develop personal and political relations. But in fairness to the young people they've been excellent. They are not old-style politicians. They are young and want to be part of the changes that are taking place in politics."

Spring hopes he has already achieved one important success for the future by putting an end once and for all to the schizophrenia about power which has dogged the Labour Party for years. Back in the gloomy days of the mid-1980s when a sizable section of the party wanted to withdraw to Opposition and stay there forever, Pat Magner used to joke that his ambition was to make Labour a permanent party of Government like the German Free Democrats. Now after the success of 1992 that is feasible.

"Politics is about Government," says Spring. "We have got to be a party of Government. We have never actually managed to take the full step. We have been half-way there and then back into Opposition. The challenge is to make Labour Party politics and Labour Party politicians a natural part of Government, a party that people will say we want in Government because they are going to do the things we need implemented."

The quality of Spring's own leadership will be vital in determining whether that ambition can be fulfilled. Following the 1992 election and his entry into Government, he was in a stronger position than any previous Labour leader. But in politics nothing stands still and the very fact of being in Government could put him under pressure again. A lot will depend on performance but even more may depend on luck. In the past, Labour have tended to be unlucky in Government. It appeared in the very first weeks of the present Government that this was going to happen again. But things were getting brighter around Easter 1993, with interest rates coming down rapidly, so luck may be on Labour's side this time.

What Spring cannot forget is that his own leadership comes up for review by his party members in October 1996. If the Government runs its course, that will occur in its final year and it will provide an opportunity for any disgruntled elements in the party to have a go, if not at Spring then at his deputy leader, Ruairi Quinn.

On a personal level Spring has always been something of an enigma, even to his closest supporters, and this has been a source of both strength and weakness. When he was under pressure in the 1980s, his aloofness was a major handicap in his bid to win the hearts and minds of those in the party who were opposed to him from the start. Yet that same sense of dignity and reserve contributed to a public image which proved so attractive to the electorate in 1992.

One colleague maintains that Spring is essentially a shy person who hides behind a mask of drollery. Few members of the parliamentary party claim to know him really well. His dry sense of humour forms a barrier which most can't penetrate and it is profoundly irritating to his political opponents.

With almost all of his colleagues in the parliamentary party, Spring's relationship is political rather than personal. For instance, his deputy leader, Ruairi Quinn, has a good political relationship with Spring. This was tested when Quinn was initially passed over for Cabinet promotion when Frank Cluskey resigned. Yet for all that, their relationship is essentially a business one and the two men have had few personal contacts over the years. The same is true of Spring in relation to other senior Labour figures like Barry Desmond, who also loyally supported the leader. With others like Michael D. Higgins, Mervyn Taylor and Emmet Stagg, who have strongly opposed Spring in the past, the relationship is purely political and survives in spite of personal feelings. After the election, Spring put personal views aside when coming to decisions about who should be appointed to office and operated on pragmatic political grounds.

The fact that he has always made important political decisions in consultation with his family and a couple of key advisors like John Rogers and Fergus Finlay has left something of a gulf between the leader and his parliamentary party. As long as things are going well this will not cause serious problems but it could be a source of misunderstanding when the going gets rough, which it inevitably will.

One thing that will stand to Spring, no matter how difficult circumstances become, is that he has been there before. He survived the FitzGerald Coalition; he survived by four votes in North Kerry and he survived a series of vicious assaults on his leadership from his own left wing. Having come through all that he should be well-equipped to deal with whatever the future throws at him.

BIBLIOGRAPHY

I interviewed a number of politicians while preparing this book. I also consulted a range of newspapers, relying most heavily on *The Irish Press*, *The Irish Times*, *The Irish Independent*, *The Sunday Press*, *The Sunday Tribune*, *The Kerryman* and *Magill* magazine. The books that provided me with most assistance were:

Browne, Vincent ed., *The Magill Book of Irish Politics*, (Dublin: Magill Publications, 1981)

Finlay, Fergus, *Mary Robinson, A President with a Purpose*, (Dublin: O'Brien Press, 1990)

FitzGerald, Garret, *All in a Life*, (Dublin: Gill and Macmillan, 1991)

Gallagher, Michael, *The Irish Labour Party in Transition 1957-82*, (Manchester: Manchester University Press, 1982)

Gaughan, J. Anthony, *Thomas Johnson*, (Dublin: Kingdom Books, 1980)

Horgan, John, *Labour The Price of Power*, (Dublin: Gill and Macmillan, 1986)

Hussey, Gemma, *Cabinet Diaries 1982-1987*, (Dublin: Gill and Macmillan, 1990)

Lenihan, Brian, *For the Record*, (Dublin: Blackwater Press, 1991)

Nealon Ted, *Nealon's Guides to Dáil and Seanad elections, 1973 to 1989*, (Dublin: Platform Press)

O'Byrnes, Stephen, *Hiding Behind A Face*, (Dublin: Gill and Macmillan, 1986)

O'Reilly, Emily, *Candidate*, (Dublin: Attic Press, 1991)

INDEX

Ahern, Bertie, 195, 203
Ahern, Kit, 37
Andrews, David, 194
Attley, Bill, 160

Banotti, Mary, 124
Barrett, Sean, 150
Barry, Gerald, 162
Barry, Peter, 103, 104, 140, 199, 201
Bell, Michael, 74 (p), 108, 202
Bermingham, Joe, 56, 83, 88, 103, 119, 141, 147, 158
Bhamjee, Moosajee, 191
Bhreathnach, Niamh, 160, 167, 181, 187, 209, 210
Bird, Charlie, 210
Boland, Kevin, 34
Böll, Heinrich, 28, 29
Bree, Declan, 191, 197
Brennan, Seamus, 194
Broughan, Tommy, 181
Browne, Bernard, 131
Browne, Noel, 26, 29, 30, 32, 34, 35, 38, 39, 40, 42, 44, 87, 176
Browne, Vincent, 46, 60, 83
Bruton, John, 8, 84, 101, 105, 113, 115-9, 136, 137, 138, 139, 144, 148, 180, 188, 189, 197, 198, 199-202, 205, 209
Burke, Dick, 46, 132
Burke, Tim, 163
Burton, Joan, 166, 181, 187, 209
Byrne, Ann, 176
Byrne, Eric, 195, 196

Cahill, Bernie, 212
Carroll, John, 120
Clarke, Sally, 173
Cluskey, Frank, 32, 41, 45, 46, 56, 57, 62, 63, 71 (p), 74 (p), 89, 90-5, 100, 101, 103, 105, 109, 110, 116, 117, 118, 127, 137, 139, 142, 147, 154, 218
Connolly, James, 16
Conway, Timmy, 141
Cooney, John, 167
Cooney, Pat, 45, 114, 117, 139, 145, 146
Cooper, Bryan, 18
Corish, Brendan, 32, 33, 34, 38, 39, 40, 41, 42, 43, 46, 56, 70 (p)
Cosgrave, Liam, 40, 41, 43, 45, 53, 56, 134
Cosgrave, William T., 17, 18

Costello, Joe, 181, 197
Costello, John A., 25
Costello, Michael Joe, 35
Coughlan, Mary, 7
Coughlan, Stevie, 30, 37, 39, 40, 42, 44
Cowen, Brian, 203
Cruise O'Brien, Conor, 27, 34, 36, 38, 41, 43, 44, 45, 47, 56, 96
Currie, Austin, 8, 178, 180

Danaher, Gerry, 205, 206
de Burca, Máirín, 131
de Courcy Ireland, John, 15
De Rossa, Proinsias, 169, 195
de Valera, Eamon, 14, 15, 17, 19, 20, 23, 27, 195
Deasy, Rickard, 35
Deenihan, Jimmy, 155, 156
Dempsey, Noel, 203
Desmond, Barry, 7, 45, 56, 57, 62, 74 (p), 83, 85, 90-5, 101, 103-5, 109, 111, 114, 123, 138, 139, 142-4, 150, 154, 158, 160, 169, 173, 177, 187, 188, 192, 193, 198, 209, 218
Desmond, Eileen, 56, 57, 83, 127, 173
Desmond, Stella, 154
Dillon, James, 32
Doherty, Sean, 84, 89, 183
Dooge, James, 101
Drapier, 212
Duffy, Jim, 178, 179
Duffy, Luke, 193
Dukes, Alan, 100, 101, 103, 105, 106, 107, 108, 109, 113, 115, 118, 119, 124, 132, 137, 142, 144, 156, 158, 169, 170, 172, 180
Duncan, William, 84
Dunphy, Eamonn, 211

Ensor, Tony, 54
Everett, James, 15, 25

Farrell, Brian, 96
Finlay, Fergus, 7, 77(p), 102, 129, 131, 132, 163, 168, 173, 176, 177, 185, 192, 193, 195, 196, 198, 204, 209, 211, 218
Finucane, Pat, 24, 25
Fitzgerald, Brian, 206
Fitzgerald, Eithne, 100, 181, 209
FitzGerald, Garret, 43, 57, 61, 62, 63, 83, 87, 97, 99, 100, 101, 103-110, 113, 114, 118-121, 132-6, 138, 139, 140, 142-6, 148, 149,

150, 153, 170, 172, 178, 189
FitzGerald, Joan, 132
Flanagan, Liam, 144
Flanagan, Oliver, 46
Flynn, Padraig, 183, 194
Foley, John, 156

Gallagher, Michael, 19, 39, 42
Gallagher, Pat, 191
Gaughan, J.Anthony, 17
Geraghty, Des, 196
Gibbons, Jim, 93
Gibson, Mike, 54
Gleeson, Dermot, 97
Glenn, Alice, 147
Gregory, Tony, 88, 93, 145

Hall, Frank, 42
Halligan, Brendan, 33, 37, 122, 123, 193
Hamilton, Mr. Justice Liam, 205
Hardiman, Adrian, 205
Harney, Mary, 141
Harrington, Tadhg, 35
Harris, Eoghan, 184
Haughey, Charles, 57, 60, 61, 87, 88, 93,
97, 99, 102, 121, 134, 135, 139, 140, 142,
158, 168, 170, 171, 172, 173, 174, 178, 179,
181, 182, 183, 186, 189, 204, 205
Higgins, Joe, 120, 164, 165
Higgins, Michael D., 45, 63, 74 (p), 89, 90,
92, 94, 95, 101, 120, 126, 128, 129, 131,
147, 158, 162, 164, 167, 176, 184, 190, 208,
209, 218
Hillery, Patrick, 170, 171, 178
Hogan, Gerard, 205
Hogan, Paddy, 31,
Horgan, John, 33, 34, 37, 44, 46, 56, 62, 94,
96
Houlihan, Con, 12, 165
Howlin, Brendan, 74 (p), 163, 171, 188,
193, 194, 196, 200, 203, 209
Hussey, Gemma, 101, 105, 109, 114, 117,
120, 134, 138, 139, 142, 144, 145, 150
Hutcheson, Kristi, 52, 53, 59, 78 (p), 80
(p), 86, 88, 111, 158

Inglis, Brian, 28

Jennings, Joe, 120
Jinks, John, 18
Johnson, Fred, 19
Johnson, Tom, 16, 17, 19

Joyce, Joe, 159, 160

Kavanagh, Liam, 15, 56, 57, 74 (p), 83, 93,
95, 103, 105, 109, 111, 117, 158, 209, 210
Kavanagh, Ray, 131, 132, 157, 166, 176, 184
Keane, Moss, 20
Keating, Justin, 35, 41, 42, 47, 56, 96, 127,
132
Kelly, J.J., 12, 13
Kelly, John, 45, 46, 100, 102, 103, 106
Kemmy, Jim, 55, 87, 210
Kennedy, Maeve, 90, 125
Kenny, Sean, 181
Kerins, Charlie, 23, 24, 25
Kerrigan, Gene, 129
Kerrigan, Pat, 56
Kinnock, Neil, 164
Kirwan, Christie, 108
Kissinger, Henry, 106, 107

Lacey, Dermot, 93
Laide, Anna (see Spring, Anna)
Larkin, Emmet, 27
Larkin, James, 15, 16, 18, 19
Larkin, James, junior, 15, 19, 24, 31
Lemass, Sean, 34
Lenihan, Brian, 135, 174, 178, 179, 180, 195
Leonard, Tom, 124
Loftus, Sean Dublin Bay, 87
Loughnane, Bill, 93
Lynch, Brendan, 163
Lynch, Ger, 47, 62
Lynch, Jack, 37, 40, 189
Lysaght, Charles, 51

Mac Bride, Sean, 25, 26
Mac Connell, Sean, 97
Mac Menamin, Peter, 176
Mac Sharry, Ray, 158
McArthur, Malcolm, 89
McAuliffe, Helena, 141
McAuliffe, Ita, 176
McAuliffe, Paddy, 28
McCreevy, Charlie, 194
McDowell, Derek, 181
McDowell, Michael, 141, 201
McEllistrim, Tom, 62, 155, 156
McEntee, Sean, 15, 36
McGahon, Brendan, 147
McGuigan, Barry, 197
McGuinness, Diarmaid, 206
McLoughlin, Frank, 153

McStay, Anne, 73 (p)
Magner, Pat, 99, 101, 102, 128, 165, 184, 193, 197, 217
Maher, Mary, 126
Malone, Bernie, 129
Manning, Maurice, 197
Mansergh, Martin, 194, 200
Mara, P.J., 171
Mills, Michael, 173
Mitchell, Jim, 84, 88, 137
Molloy, Bobby, 141, 142
Moran, Michael, 36
Moynihan, Breda, 187
Moynihan, Michael, 95, 111
Mulcahy, Dick, 25
Mulvihill, John, 191
Murphy, Michael Pat, 30, 35, 37, 40, 41, 56, 58
Murphy, Tadhg, 25
Murray, John, 170
Murtagh, Peter, 98
Myers, Bill, 12, 13, 20

Nally, Dermot, 105, 117
Nevin, Donal, 119
Norton, William, 19, 25, 29, 30, 31, 32, 70 (p), 95, 193

O Briain, Colm, 131
O'Brien, William, 15, 16, 19
O'Byrnes, Stephen, 101, 110, 204
O'Connell, Dr. John, 33, 35, 40, 42, 45, 56, 57, 62
O'Connell, Thomas J., 19
O'Donnell, Pa, 27
O'Donoghue, Martin, 89
O'Donovan, John, 35, 44
O'Halloran, Michael, 129
O'Higgins, Kevin, 17
O'Keeffe, Jim, 180
O'Kennedy, Michael, 120
O'Leary, Michael, 32, 34, 41, 45, 56, 57, 62, 63, 71 (p), 83, 87, 89, 90, 91, 93, 94, 96, 97, 98, 99, 102, 117, 124, 125, 131, 145, 160
O'Malley, Des, 45, 89, 138, 141, 142, 158, 169, 172, 174, 185, 190, 204, 205, 206, 209
O'Reilly, Emily, 175, 176
O'Rourke, Sean, 87, 128, 168
O'Sullivan, Gerry, 210
O'Sullivan, Toddy, 63, 74 (p), 95, 137, 162, 209, 210
Owen, Nora, 198

Pattison, Seamus, 56, 74 (p), 111, 202, 209
Penrose, Willie, 191
Power, Brenda, 21
Prendergast, Frank, 108
Prendergast, Peter, 182

Quinn, Ruairi, 7, 56, 62, 74 (p), 92, 93, 95, 117, 118, 131, 150, 158, 160, 177, 181, 182, 185, 188, 193, 194, 195, 200, 201, 203, 207, 209, 216, 217, 218

Rabbitte, Pat, 196, 205
Revington, Joe, 21, 98, 101
Reynolds, Albert, 78 (p), 79 (p), 183, 185, 186, 187, 188, 189, 190, 193, 194, 200, 201, 203, 204, 205, 206, 209, 212
Rice, Rodney, 198
Robinson, Mary, 8, 46, 63, 73 (p), 75 (p), 132, 133, 164, 175, 176, 177, 178, 179, 180, 187
Robinson, Nick, 176
Rogers, John, 26, 30, 50, 51, 97, 98, 99, 101, 132, 133, 134, 135, 136, 150, 156, 163, 170, 171, 173, 176, 189, 193, 198, 206, 218
Rosney, Bride, 176, 177
Ryan, John, 56, 202, 206
Ryan, Richie, 42

Scally, William, 99, 106, 163, 194
Shanley, Peter, 170
Sherlock, Joe, 191
Sherry, Mick, 48
Shortall, Róisín, 181, 187
Skelly, Liam, 145, 147
Smyllie, Robert, 17, 18
Somers, Jimmy, 124
Sparks, Greg, 163, 194
Spring, Aaron, 80 (p), 86, 156
Spring, Adam, 80 (p)
Spring, Anna, 20, 21, 22, 23, 27, 31, 33, 34, 35, 36, 49, 51, 59, 61, 66 (p), 67 (p), 68 (p), 76 (p), 78 (p), 99, 166
Spring, Arthur, 22, 30, 59, 66 (p), 67 (p), 86, 154, 156
Spring, Dan, 39, 40, 51, 53, 60, 62, 65 (p), 66 (p), 67 (p), 68 (p), 98, 99, 165, 166; early career 11-15; family 20-3; Kerins case 24-5; rural politician 25-30; Dan and the left 33-7; Cosgrave Coalition 44-8; end of career 56-8
Spring, Dick, 7, 8, 15, 19, 33, 41, 52-5, 66 (p), 67 (p), 69 (p), 72 (p), 73 (p), 74 (p),

75 (p), 76 (p), 77 (p), 78 (p), 79 (p), 80 (p), 88, 90-1, 97-8, 136, 158, 165, 168, 169, 181-4; family background 21-3, 27, 30, 31; student life 48-51; early days in politics 58-64; junior minister 83-8; elected leader 93-6; Coalition deal ('82) 99-103; 1982-87 Coalition Government 103-121, 132-141, 143-150; Labour in-fighting 122-131; 1987 election 153-7; Cork conference 1987 159-162; gaining control of the party 163-7; in Opposition 170-4, 177-8; presidential campaign 175-180; 1992 election 182-192; Coalition deal ('92) 193-201; in government 209-218

Spring, Donal, 13, 22, 23, 30, 41, 47, 48, 49, 51, 60, 77 (p), 155, 156, 193
Spring, Kay, 30, 66 (p), 67 (p), 155
Spring, Laura, 80 (p)
Spring, Maeve, 30, 67 (p), 211
Spring, Noelle, 30, 67 (p)
Stafford, John, 182
Stagg, Emmet, 74 (p), 142, 147, 158, 159, 160, 161, 162, 163, 164, 165, 166, 167, 176, 184, 192, 208, 209, 210, 212, 218
Sutherland, Peter, 105, 110, 132, 133, 134, 136

Taft, Michael, 163, 184
Taylor, Mervyn, 63, 74 (p), 90, 95, 101, 117, 118, 119, 128, 131, 158, 160, 162, 200, 203, 206, 209, 218
Thatcher, Margaret, 140
Thornley, David, 34, 42, 44, 45, 56, 96
Tierney, Paddy, 35
Treacy, Sean, 41, 42, 44, 138, 147
Tuffy, Eamonn, 73 (p)
Tully, Jim, 31, 41, 44, 47, 56, 83

Upton, Pat, 163, 181, 197, 206, 209

Walsh, Eamonn, 74 (p), 181
Walsh, Joe, 194
Waters, John, 167
Wilson, Harold, 43
Whelehan, Harry, 206
Wrynne, James, 163, 193
Wyse, Pearse, 141, 142